The World Almanac™
5,001
Incredible Facts
for Kids on Nature,
Science, and People

The World Almanac™

5,001

Incredible Facts for Kids on Nature, Science, and People

World Almanac for Kids™

WORLD ALMANAC BOOKS

contents

contents

40 CUTE ANIMAL FACTS

1. Sea otters hold hands while they sleep so they don't float away from each other.

2. Penguins give each other rock gifts when they want to find a mate.

3. Mice and rats are ticklish.

4. Cats say hello by pressing their noses together.

5. Polar bears touch noses to communicate, too.

6. Cows have best friends and like to hang out together.

7. You can hypnotize a frog by placing it on its back and rubbing its stomach.

8. Red pandas and foxes use their tails to keep warm.

9. Elephant friends twist their trunks together.

10. Macaque monkeys like to play with snowballs.

11. Dolphins have names for each other.

12. Seahorse couples hold tails so they stay together while they swim.

13. Crows like to play tricks on each other.

14. A dog's nose print is unique, just like a person's fingerprint.

15. Butterflies taste with their feet.

FACT #7

16. Sea otters have pouches under their arms. They store snacks and favorite pebbles there.

17. Smile at a sheep and it might smile back.

18. Baby elephants suck their trunks to comfort themselves.

19. Unborn chicks "talk" to each other (and their mom!) through their shells.

20. Houseflies always buzz in the key of F.

21. Squirrels will adopt other baby squirrels.

22. If a baby kangaroo is scared, it will jump head-first into its mother's pouch.

23. Wolves babysit young members of their pack.

24. Polar bears are left-handed.

25. Baby chimpanzees like toys and will play with sticks and rocks.

26. Goats have different accents.

27. Ants bow their heads to each other as they pass.

28. Fennec foxes have super-furry feet to protect them from burning-hot desert sand.

29. Male puppies let female puppies win when they play.

30. Prairie dogs say hello by kissing.

31. A wombat's poop is shaped like a cube.

32. Quokkas always look like they're smiling.

33. Nine-banded armadillos always give birth to four identical babies.

34. Ducks like to surf and will ride waves to shore.

35. Female bats give birth upside-down. They catch the baby in their wings.

36. Toucans curl into balls when they sleep.

37. A duck's quack does not echo.

38. Giraffes can clean their ears with their super-long tongues.

39. Kangaroos can't fart.

40. Pigs like to sleep nose to nose.

100 FACTS ABOUT WORLD CITIES

1. There are 456 cities with populations of 1 million or more.

2. Tokyo was once a small fishing village. Today, it has the most populated metropolitan area in the world at more than 37 million people.

3. The city of Shanghai is the most populous city, with more than 24 million people.

4. El Alto, Bolivia, is the highest city in the world. It is 13,615 feet (4,150 meters) above sea level.

5. Bolivia also has the world's highest capital city. La Paz is 11,942 feet (3,640 meters) above sea level.

6. Jericho, in Palestine, is the lowest city in the world. It lies 846 feet (258 meters) below sea level.

7. Baku, Azerbaijan, is the lowest capital city in the world. It lies 92 feet (28 meters) below sea level.

8. Baku is also the largest city in the world located below sea level.

9. Urumqi, China, is the farthest city from the sea. It is 1,600 miles (2,500 km) from the coast.

10. Norilsk, Russia, is the most northern city in the world.

11. Reykjavik, Iceland, is the northernmost capital city.

12. Ushuaia, Argentina, is the southernmost city in the world.

3

13. Punta Arenas, Chile, is the southernmost large city.

14. The southernmost capital city is Wellington, New Zealand.

15. The unofficial slogan of Austin, Texas, is "Keep Austin Weird."

16. New York has the largest population of any city in the United States, at almost 9 million people in 2019.

17. Los Angeles is a distant second with just over four million.

18. Chicago, Houston, Phoenix, Philadelphia, San Antonio, San Diego, Dallas, and San Jose round out the top ten.

19. The northernmost city in the United States is Bellingham, Washington.

20. The southernmost city in the United States is Key West, Florida.

21. Bangkok, Thailand's full name is the longest city name in the world. Its full name is Krung Thep Mahanakhon Amon Rattanakosin Mahinthara Ayuthaya Mahadilok Phop Noppharat Ratchathani Burirom Udomratchaniwet Mahasathan Amon Piman Awatan Sathit Sakkathattiya Witsanukam Prasit.

22. New York has the largest street network in the world. It measures more than 6200 miles (10,000 km).

23. Los Angeles's full name is El Pueblo de Nuestra Senora la Reina de los Angeles de Porciuncula.

24. There are no cemeteries in San Francisco. The city banned burials in 1900 because it was running out of room. More than 150,000 bodies were relocated to the little town of Colma.

25. Vatican City is the smallest city in the world. It covers only 0.17 square mile (0.44 square km).

26. The capital city with the lowest population is Adamstown in the Pitcairn Islands. Only 48 people live there.

27. Hum, Croatia, has the lowest population of any city. Fewer than 30 people live there.

28. London has the oldest subway system in the world. Its Underground opened in 1863.

29. Boston has the oldest subway in the United States. It opened in 1897.

30. Sao Paolo, Brazil, is the largest city in South America.

31. The oldest city in North America is Cholula, Mexico. It was founded in the second century BC, more than 2,000 years ago.

32. The oldest US city founded by Europeans is St. Augustine, Florida. It was settled by the Spanish in 1565.

33. Juneau, Alaska, is the largest state capital in terms of area. It covers 3,255 square miles (8,430 square km). That's larger than the state of Delaware!

34. Sitka, Alaska, is the largest city in the United States in terms of area.

35. Phoenix, Arizona, used to be called Pumpkinville.

36. Little Rock, Arkansas, has the largest pedestrian bridge in North America.

37. Honolulu, Hawaii, is home to the only royal palace in the United States.

38. Many British colonial cities in America were named after cities in England or after English kings and queens.

39. The first drive-through in America opened in Springfield, Illinois, in 1921.

40. Des Moines, Iowa, was almost named Fort Raccoon.

41. Every summer, Annapolis, Maryland, hosts the largest crab feast in the world.

42. America's oldest wooden fort, Old Fort Western, was built in Augusta, Maine, in 1754.

43. Saint Paul, Minnesota, was called Pig's Eye Landing during the 1800s.

44. Santa Fe, New Mexico, is home to the oldest church in America. Mission San Miguel was built in the 1600s.

45. Salem, Oregon, has one of the smallest parks in the world. Waldo Park measures 12 feet by 20 feet (4 by 6 meters) and has just one tree.

46. Yakutsk, Russia, is the coldest city. The lowest temperature recorded there was −88°F (−64°C).

47. Ulaanbaatar, Mongolia, is the coldest capital city.

48. Ahvaz, Iran, and Kuwait City, Kuwait, are the two hottest cities in the world. Both cities often have temperatures above 113°F (45°C) and often hit 122°F (50°C).

49. In 2014, Kuwait City had a high temperature of more than 125°F (52°C).

50. Minneapolis is considered the most literate city in the United States.

51. Cincinnati, Ohio, was the first city to provide ambulance service in 1865.

52. The first gas station opened in Pittsburgh in 1913.

53. Pittsburgh is also home to the world's first baseball stadium, which opened in 1909.

54. Here's another first for Pittsburgh—the first commercial radio station started broadcasting there in 1920.

55. The first electric company opened in New York City in 1878.

56. The nation's first hospital opened in Philadelphia in 1752.

57. Philadelphia also boasts the nation's first daily newspaper, which began in 1784.

58. Boston had the first lighthouse in the United States. It opened in 1716.

59. The first movie theater opened in Los Angeles in 1902.

60. The Ferris Wheel made its first appearance at the Chicago World's Fair in 1893.

61. Chicago is also home to the first skyscraper, which opened in 1885.

62. If you wanted to watch public television in 1953, you had to go to Houston, Texas. It was the first city with a noncommercial TV station.

63. The first traffic light was located in Cleveland, Ohio, in 1914.

64. America's first zoo opened in Philadelphia in 1874. It is still operating today.

65. In 2017, El Paso, Texas, was ranked the safest big city in the United States.

66. What city was ranked the most dangerous? Detroit, Michigan.

67. Asia is home to seven of the top ten most populated cities. They are: Shanghai, Beijing, Istanbul, Karachi, Mumbai, Guangzhou, and Delhi.

68. Shanghai, China, is the world's busiest trading port.

69. Tokyo has the world's busiest train station.

70. Tokyo (including suburbs) has the most populous metropolitan area in the world.

71. Seoul, South Korea, has the second-most-populous metro area (including suburbs).

72. Paris is the most popular tourist city in Europe.

73. More than 300 languages are spoken in London.

74. The world has 33 megacities. These are cities with populations of more than 10 million.

75. In 2016, Vienna, Austria, was named the city with the best quality of life.

46

76. The next-largest South American city is Lima, Peru.

77. People ride boats in the canals for public transit in Venice.

78. All of Australia's major cities lie on or near the coast.

79. Sydney is the largest city in Australia.

80. Sydney is also the oldest Australian city. It was founded in 1788.

81. Perth, Australia, has the largest city park in the world. It covers 10,003 acres (4 square km).

82. Melbourne and Sydney both wanted to be the capital of Australia. In the end, a new capital city, Canberra, was built.

83. Canberra was named Australia's capital in 1913. But the government didn't move there until 1927.

84. Most of Australia's major cities were settled by convicts shipped there from Great Britain.

85. Lagos, Nigeria, is the largest city in Africa. More than 21 million people live there.

86. The second-largest city in Africa is Cairo, Egypt.

87. Cape Town, South Africa, is the southernmost city in Africa.

88. Moscow, Russia, has more billionaires than any other city in the world.

89. The busiest subway systems in the world are in Tokyo, Seoul, and Moscow.

90. More than 6 million people ride Moscow's metro (subway) every day.

91. St. Petersburg, Russia, has more than 1,000 bridges.

92. St. Petersburg is the northernmost city with more than 1 million people.

93. Russia has at least 15 "secret" cities that do not appear on any maps.

77

94. St. Petersburg has had three different names. Its name was changed to Petrograd in 1914. That name honored Russian czar Peter the Great.

95. In 1924, Petrograd became Leningrad to honor Communist leader Vladimir Ilyich Lenin.

96. Finally, in 1991, the city's name was changed back to St. Petersburg.

97. St. Petersburg isn't the only name-changing Russian city. Stalingrad was named after the Russian leader Joseph Stalin. It was the site of a major World War II battle.

98. In 1961, Stalingrad's name was changed to Volgograd, after the Volga River. Stalin was a cruel dictator, and the government wanted to erase his name from the country.

99. In 2013, Russia agreed to call the city "Stalingrad" for a few days in honor of the seventieth anniversary of the Battle of Stalingrad.

100. Even though they are very crowded, many cities have been called lonely places to live.

50 FACTS ABOUT AFRICA

1. Africa is bigger than the United States, India, and Canada put together.

2. There are 54 countries and 9 territories on the continent.

3. It is the second-largest continent.

4. Africa is home to more than 1 billion people.

5. Africa's population comprises 15 percent of the world's population.

6. Algeria is the largest country in Africa.

7. Nigeria has the highest population—more than 185 million people.

8. Seychelles is the smallest country, but it is not on the continent. It's a group of islands in the Indian Ocean.

9. The smallest country on the continent is The Gambia.

10. Africa is surrounded by the Atlantic Ocean and the Indian Ocean.

11. Madagascar is Africa's biggest island. It's also the fourth-largest island in the world.

12. The Nile is the longest river in Africa—and in the world. It is 4,258 miles (6,852 meters) long.

13. The Nile has two sources: the White Nile in Tanzania and the Blue Nile in Ethiopia.

14. Mount Kilimanjaro is the highest mountain in Africa. It is 19,340 feet (5,895 meters) tall.

15. Lake Victoria is the largest lake in Africa. It borders Uganda, Tanzania, and Kenya.

16. Lake Victoria is the second-largest freshwater lake in the world. Only Lake Superior in the United States is bigger.

17. Africa's Sahara Desert is the largest hot desert in the world.

14 . . . .

18. Sixteen countries in Africa are landlocked. That means none of their territory borders an ocean.

19. There are two tiny countries within the nation of South Africa. They are called Eswatini (formerly Swaziland) and Lesotho.

20. Africa is called "the cradle of humankind." Human life started there about 10 million years ago.

21. Africa had many powerful kingdoms.

22. European nations started colonizing Africa in the 1800s.

23. England, France, Spain, Belgium, Germany, and other countries all had African colonies.

24. Zimbabwe was the last nation to win freedom from Europe. It became independent in 1980.

25. Many colonies changed their names once they became independent.

26. More than 3,000 different native groups live in Africa.

27. About 2,000 different languages are spoken in Africa.

28. In addition to African languages, many people speak English, French, Portuguese, or Arabic.

29. Africa is home to the largest land mammal (elephant), the fastest mammal (cheetah), and the tallest (giraffe).

30. The world's largest reptile is the Nile crocodile.

31. The world's largest primate, the gorilla, lives in Africa.

32. Kruger National Park in South Africa is one of the largest national parks in the world.

33. Visitors to Kruger can see lions, rhinos, leopards, buffaloes, and many more animals.

34. Tugela Falls in South Africa are the continent's highest waterfalls.

35. More than half of Africa is covered by grasslands.

36. There are rain forests in Central Africa.

37. South Africa's Cape Floral Region has the most plant varieties in the world.

38. Africa has about 30 percent of the world's mineral resources.

39. Almost half the gold ever mined came from one place in South Africa.

40. Africa is the world's hottest and second-driest continent.

41. China is Africa's biggest trading partner.

42. Africa and Europe are less than 9 miles (14 km) apart at the Strait of Gibraltar.

43. The world's biggest frog lives in Africa. The Goliath frog grows up to 1 foot (0.3 meter) long and weighs up to 8 pounds (14.5 kg).

44. Ethiopia is the only African country with its own alphabet. Ethiopic is the world's oldest alphabet. And it has 345 letters!

45. Twenty-five percent of the Earth's bird species live in Africa.

46. Over half the population of Africa is under 25 years old. That's the youngest population in the world.

47. Egypt is the most popular tourist destination in Africa.

48. The country of Sudan actually has a lot more pyramids than Egypt does.

49. The name "Africa" comes from the Afri tribe that lived in North Africa.

50. Islam is the largest religion in Africa. Christianity is second largest.

20 STRANGE JOBS

1. Cleaning portable toilets has to be one of the grossest jobs. Workers clean them with a vacuum and a big hose.

2. Crime-scene cleaners have to clean up blood and gore and body parts.

3. Some highway department workers have to clean up roadkill.

4. How do you test deodorants? You hire someone to sniff people's sweaty armpits!

5. People also work smelling dirty diapers, cat litter, and stinky shoes.

6. Some workers taste-test dog food and cat food.

7. Here's a fun job: amusement-park workers get to test the rides before the parks open.

8. What happens to golf balls that have been hit into the water? Golf-ball divers go in after them.

9. Gum busters clean gum off city sidewalks, benches, and anywhere else people spit it out.

10. NASA hires professional sleepers. They study their sleep patterns for several months.

SCARY
Sewer Stories

Sewer workers face a lot of nasty things. They have to deal with dirty water, human waste, chemicals, and rats and other animals living in the underwater pipes. But workers in London faced what was possibly the most disgusting job of all. In 2017, they had to get rid of a 130-ton (118 tonne) ball of cooking fat and wet wipes. They called it a fatberg. That fatberg was as hard as a rock and weighed as much as 11 double-decker buses.

It's not easy to get rid of a rock made of disgusting waste. Workers had to spray it with water from high-powered hoses to break off chunks of waste. Things got even worse in Liverpool, England, in 2019. Workers had to use shovels and axes to chop up a monster-sized fatberg there.

11. A hotel in Finland hired someone to sleep in the chain's beds and write reviews.

12. If you don't want to wait in line, you can hire a professional line-stander to do it for you.

13. Tokyo's subways are so crowded, professional pushers are hired to shove as many people as possible onto the trains.

14. Are you good at sewing? You could get a job as a teddy-bear surgeon, repairing stuffed animals and dolls.

15. You can get a job watching paint dry. This tests the quality of new paint mixes.

16. Netflix hires "taggers" to binge-watch all their programs and label what type of show each is.

17. Snake milkers collect venom from poisonous snakes. It's used to make anti-venom drugs.

18. In some Southeast Asian communities, the louder and more crowded a funeral is, the better. People hire professional mourners to attend funerals and weep loudly during the service.

19. An underwater hotel in Florida hired a scuba-diving pizza-delivery person.

20. Some companies hire computer hackers to test their programs' security and look for bugs.

55

FACTS ABOUT ROCKS, MINERALS, AND GEMS

1. Rocks and minerals are not the same thing.

2. A mineral is a naturally occurring inorganic (nonliving) element.

3. A rock is made up of at least two minerals.

4. Rocks can also include fossils.

5. Scientists who study rocks and minerals are called geologists.

6. A rock is bigger than a pebble but smaller than a boulder.

7. There are three types of rocks.

8. Igneous rocks are formed by volcanoes.

9. There are over 700 types of igneous rocks, such as basalt, pumice, granite, and obsidian.

10. There are two kinds of igneous rocks: extrusive and intrusive, depending on whether they formed inside or outside of a volcano.

11. Extrusive igneous rocks form when magma cools and hardens outside a volcano. They often look like shiny glass.

12. Intrusive igneous rocks form inside the Earth. They often look rough.

13. Metamorphic rocks are made by great pressure inside the Earth.

14. Sedimentary rocks are layers of sediment (dirt and mud) pressing together and turning into stone.

15. Rocks can change from one type to another. This is called the rock cycle.

16. Igneous rocks can break down into sediment. Then they can form sedimentary rocks.

17. Sedimentary rocks can move deep into the Earth's crust. Pressure can then turn them into metamorphic rocks.

18. Meteorites are rocks that came here from space. They are mostly made of iron.

19. The word igneous comes from the Latin "ignis," which means "fire."

20. Mohs Scale of Hardness measures how hard or soft a mineral is.

21. A mineral with a higher number can scratch a mineral with a lower number.

22. Talc is #1 on the scale. It is the softest mineral.

23. Diamonds are #10. They are the hardest and can scratch any other mineral.

24. Minerals are judged by seven different properties. They are: crystal form, hardness, fracture, luster, color, streak, and density.

25. There are more than 4,000 different types of minerals.

26. Jade was a royal gem in ancient China.

27. Ancient civilizations believed gems and minerals had magical powers.

28. People have used rocks for millions of years.

29. Rocks can be weapons, tools, or building material.

30. Pumice is an unusual igneous rock. It forms when it is blasted out of a volcano. Pumice is very light because it is full of air holes.

31. Marble is a metamorphic rock formed from the sedimentary rock limestone.

32. Chalk is a soft form of limestone.

33. Limestone is made of seashells and the bodies of tiny sea creatures.

· · · · · · · · · 30

34. The atoms in a mineral are arranged in a specific pattern. This is called crystallization.

35. Fossils are usually found in sedimentary rocks.

36. The layers in a sedimentary rock are called strata.

37. Minerals are found in soap, detergent, toothpaste, and much more.

38. Ninety-five percent of the Earth's crust is made of igneous rock.

39. The biggest nugget of pure gold was found in Australia in 1869. It weighed 156 pounds (71 kg).

40. A gem is a mineral that has been cut and polished.

41. Gemstones are measured in carats.

42. A carat weighs 200 milligrams, or .00643 troy ounce.

43. The minerals in a gem determine its color.

44. Diamonds are the most valuable gems.

45. Amber is the softest gem.

46. The largest diamond found in the United States was the Uncle Sam Diamond.

47. It was found in Arkansas in 1924.

48. The Uncle Sam Diamond weighs more than 40 carats.

49. Quartz comes in more colors than any other gem. Quartz can be purple, yellow, brown, pink, or a mix of colors.

50. Granite makes up a large part of the continents.

51. The sea floor is made of an igneous rock called basalt.

52. Basalt is hardened lava.

53. Some granite rocks in Australia are believed to be more than 4 billion years old.

54. Gemstones were mined in ancient Egypt.

55. Gemstones are graded by the 4 C's: color, clarity, cut, and carat weight.

40
HIGH-FLYING FACTS
ABOUT AIRPLANES

1. Airplanes can fly because air moves faster over the top of the airplane wing than it does underneath. This creates lift.

2. The Wright brothers achieved the first airplane flight in 1903.

3. The first flight lasted just 12 seconds. The plane traveled 120 feet (37 meters). Orville Wright was the pilot.

4. Orville's brother, Wilbur, later flew 852 feet (260 meters) in 59 seconds on the same day.

5. In 1927, Charles Lindbergh became the first person to fly solo across the Atlantic Ocean.

6. The trip took Lindbergh 33½ hours to fly from New York to Paris.

7. Lindbergh might be the most famous person to cross the Atlantic, but he wasn't the first. John Alcock and Arthur Whitten Brown crossed the Atlantic in 16 hours in 1919.

8. Alcock and Brown won a large cash prize for their flight.

9. The Concorde was a supersonic plane that flew between Europe and New York from 1976 to 2003.

10. The Concorde could fly up to 1,354 miles (2,179 km) per hour.

11. The Concorde holds the record for fastest transatlantic flight: 2 hours, 52 minutes, and 59 seconds to fly from London to New York.

· · · · · · 9

12. World War I was the first war to use airplanes in battle.

13. After the war, many military pilots became barnstormers.

14. Barnstormers delighted crowds by performing dives and spins in the air.

15. Barnstorming shows often included performers who walked on the wings of the airplane while in flight.

16. Early airplanes had open cockpits. Pilots were exposed to rain, wind, ice, and freezing temperatures.

17. A Boeing 747 jet has 6 million parts.

18. Each engine on a Boeing 747 weighs almost 9,500 pounds (4,300 kg).

19. A 747's fuel tank holds almost 48,445 gallons.

20. The "black boxes" that contain a flight's data are actually orange. The bright color makes them easy to find.

21. At any moment, 5,000 planes may be flying over the United States.

22. All pilots who fly internationally must know English. That's so they can communicate safely with air-traffic controllers.

23. Pilots and copilots eat different meals on a flight. If one of them gets food poisoning, the other one can still fly the plane.

 24. Pilot Chuck Yeager broke the sound barrier in 1947. He was the first person to fly faster than the speed of sound.

25. The Bede BD-5 microjet is the smallest plane in the world. It weighs only 360 pounds (163 kg) and has a wingspan of 14 ½ feet (4.4 meters).

26. The longest military plane is the United States' C-5 cargo plane. At almost 223 feet (68 meters) long, it can carry large military equipment, such as tanks and trucks.

27. The Wright brothers established the world's first test-flight facility near Dayton, Ohio.

28. That test-flight facility is now called Wright Patterson Air Force Base.

29. The first woman in the United States who was licensed to fly a plane was Harriet Quimby in 1911.

30. Quimby became the first woman to fly across the English Channel.

31. Amelia Earhart was the first woman to fly solo across the Atlantic Ocean.

32. Airplanes usually fly about 35,000 feet (10,668 meters), or 6.5 miles (11 km), above the Earth.

33. A commercial jet flies about 550–580 miles (885–933 km) per hour.

34. The Lockheed SR-71 Blackbird is the fastest plane on Earth. In 1976, this military plane flew 2,193 miles (3,529 km) per hour.

35. The Blackbird is so fast, it can outfly surface-to-air missiles.

36. Most planes use autopilot during flight, but pilots control the plane during takeoffs and landings.

37. In 1985, a plane called Voyager flew around the world without stopping or refueling.

38. Airbus is working on a transparent plane.

39. Fear of flying is called aviophobia.

40. Airplanes that make long flights have secret bedrooms so the crew can nap in flight.

50 TINY FACTS ABOUT THE SMALLEST THINGS

1. The tiniest reptile is the brown leaf chameleon. These little creatures are only 1 inch (2.5 cm) long. They live in Madagascar.

2. A tiny wasp called the fairyfly is the world's smallest insect. It is only 0.005 inch (0.13 mm) long.

3. The tiniest bird is Cuba's bee hummingbird. These birds are about the same size as a large bumblebee.

4. The smallest moth is the Stigmella ridiculosa, which lives in the Canary Islands. It measures just 0.8 inch (2 cm) long and has a wingspan of the same size.

5. Some little creatures have big names. The smallest fish is Paedocypris progenetica. These teeny fish live in Indonesia and have clear bodies that look like glass. They are about a third of an inch (7.9 mm) long.

6. Paedophryne dekot is the big name for a tiny frog that lives in Papua New Guinea. One of these frogs is about the size of an M&M candy.

7. The bumblebee bat is the world's smallest mammal. They are only 1 inch (2.5 cm) long and live in Thailand.

8. The bumblebee bat is also called Kitti's hog-nosed bat because their face looks like a pig's snout.

9. Little creatures called krill swim in all the world's oceans. Even though they are small, they are the main source of food for some big animals, including whales.

10. Krill have to eat, too! They eat tiny phytoplankton.

11. Phytoplankton are microscopic single-celled plants. They drift along the ocean's surface and make food from carbon dioxide and sunlight.

12. The Eh'hausl Hotel in Amberg, Germany, has just 570 square feet (53 square meters) of floor space. It is the smallest hotel in the world.

13. Only two guests at a time can fit into the Eh'hausl Hotel.

14. A German company created the world's smallest pair of glasses. They measured just 0.8 inch (2 cm) wide and could fit on a housefly.

15. A cell phone contains just seven basic parts. All of them are tiny!

16. A cell phone's speaker is about the size of a dime.

17. The Beetle's House is a 43-square-foot (4-square-meter) house on display in London's Victoria and Albert Museum.

18. A house on a New Zealand beach measures just 430 square feet (40 square meters). It's built on two sleds so it can be moved from the beach to a barge.

19. The Keret House in Warsaw, Poland, is just 4 feet (1.2 meters) wide. But it is 30 feet (9 meters) tall.

20. Van Bo Le-Mentzel created a 1-square-meter (11-square-feet) house in Germany. The house is on wheels so it can be turned in any direction.

21. The human body gives off a tiny amount of light, but it's too weak to be seen.

22. The smallest bone in the human body is the stapes bone in the middle ear.

23. The middle ear also has two other tiny bones. They are the malleus and the incus. These bones conduct sound.

24. The smallest muscle is also in the middle ear. It's called the stapedius and measures just 0.04 inch (1 mm) long.

25. The smallest organ is the pineal gland. It's located in the brain. This gland measures just 0.3 inch (0.8 cm) long and weighs less than 1 ounce (gram).

26. The pineal gland gets its name because it looks like a small pinecone.

27. Capillaries are the smallest blood vessels. They are 50 times thinner than a baby's hair.

28. The human body contains about 10 billion tiny capillaries.

29. Scientists have created tiny copies of human organs. They're called "body on a chip." These organs are one-millionth the size of the real thing.

30. They plan to use these organs to test drugs and other medical procedures.

31. "Bonsai" is the art form of growing tiny trees in a container.

32. Bonsai trees grow in small containers called bons. The size of the bon limits how much the tree's roots can grow.

33. Bonsai trees rarely grow taller than 3 feet (1 meter).

34. The world's smallest flowering plant is called watermeal. It is about the size of a grain of rice.

35. Watermeal is part of a family called duckweed. It grows in large patches on lakes and ponds.

36. The dwarf willow is the smallest tree. It grows to only 0.39 to 2.4 inches (1 to 6 cm) in height.

37. Chandra Bahadur Dangi of Nepal was the shortest man who ever lived, according to the Guinness Book of World Records. He was just 21.5 inches (55 cm) tall.

38. The Guinness Book of World Records lists Pauline Masters of the Netherlands as the shortest woman who ever lived. She was 21.5 inches (55 cm) tall and weighed just 3.5 pounds (1.5 kg).

39. BeRobot is the smallest humanoid robot in production. It measures 6 inches (153 mm) high and can walk, kick, and do pushups.

40. The smallest book in the world is *Teeny Ted From Turnip Town*. It was etched onto a microscopic sheet of silicon by scientists in Canada.

41. You need a scanning electron microscope to read *Teeny Ted*.

42. Steven J. Backman built a copy of the Empire State Building out of a toothpick. His "skyscraper" is just 0.78 inch (2 cm) tall.

43. Many people microchip their pets as a form of identity. Microchips are actually tiny radio transmitters. When they are scanned, they transmit a code that links to owner information.

44. A microchip is only the size of a grain of rice.

45. Vets inject microchips into a pet's body through a syringe.

46. Tom Wiberg of Sweden built a motorcycle with a front wheel diameter of 0.62 inch (16 mm) and a rear wheel diameter of 0.86 inch (22 mm). Wiberg actually rode the motorcycle for about 33 feet (10 meters) at a speed of just over 1 mile (2 km) per hour.

47. The smallest electric motor was built in Belgium in 2009. It measured 0.065 inch (1.65 mm) by 0.04 inch (.9 mm).

48. In 1917, Romania issued the smallest paper money. It was about one-tenth the size of a US dollar bill.

49. Claudia Puhlfürst and Andrew Zonenberg created the world's smallest comic strip. "Juana Knits the Planet" fit on one strand of human hair.

50. The smallest commercial movie theater in the world only seats nine people. It is located in Radebeul, Germany.

35
FUN FACTORIES YOU CAN VISIT IN THE UNITED STATES

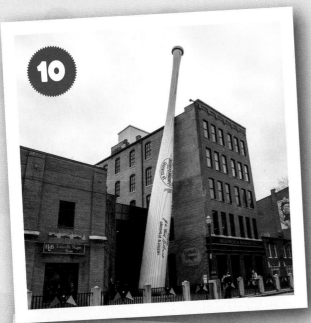

1. Hershey's Chocolate World, Hershey, PA
2. Cabot Cheese Visitors' Center, Cabot, VT
3. Jelly Belly Factory, Fairfield, CA
4. Ben & Jerry's Ice Cream Factory, Waterbury, VT
5. Hammond's Candy Factory, Denver, CO
6. Cape Cod Potato Chip Factory, Hyannis, MA
7. Blue Bell Creameries, Brenham, TX
8. PEZ Visitor Center, Orange, CT
9. Harley-Davidson Factory, York, PA
10. Louisville Slugger Museum and Factory, Louisville, KY
11. Nokona Baseball Gloves, Nocona, TX
12. Crayola Experience, Easton, PA
13. Intel Museum, Santa Clara, CA
14. Mack Truck, Macungie, PA
15. Gibson Guitar Factory, Memphis, TN
16. Fender Guitars, Corona, CA
17. Vermont Teddy Bear Factory, Shelburne, VT
18. World of Coca-Cola, Atlanta, GA
19. Herr's Snack Factory, Nottingham, PA
20. Celestial Seasonings, Boulder, CO
21. Dole Pineapple Plantation, Honolulu, HI
22. The U.S. Mint, Philadelphia, PA
23. John Deere Factory, Waterloo, IA
24. Airstream Factory, Jackson Center, OH
25. Utz Quality Foods, Hanover, PA
26. Boeing, Everett, WA
27. Chevrolet Corvette, Bowling Green, KY
28. Steinway & Sons Piano Factory, Queens, NY
29. Tabasco Factory, Avery Island, LA
30. Bob's Red Mill, Milwaukie, OR
31. Huy Fong Sriracha Factory, Irwindale, CA
32. Hyundai, Montgomery, AL
33. Jiffy Mix, Chelsea, MI
34. Regal Boats, Orlando, FL
35. Pendleton Woolen Mills, Pendleton, OR

40 OUT-OF-THIS-WORLD FACTS ABOUT ALIENS

1. The study of extraterrestrial life is called astrobiology.

2. More than 3,000 planets reside outside our solar system. Scientists believe some of them have the conditions to support life.

3. Life could also exist on planets in other solar systems.

4. Planets have to be a certain distance from their sun(s) in order for life to survive. Scientists call these areas "the Goldilocks zone" because the temperature is not too hot, not too cold, but just right.

5. The earliest recorded UFO sighting occurred in 1440 BC. Ancient Egyptian scribes recorded "fiery disks" hovering in the sky.

6. The ancient Greeks first wrote about extraterrestrial life in 610 BC.

7. Some people believe the Bible's description of the prophet Ezekiel seeing a "wheel in the sky" was a description of a UFO.

8. Alien sightings have been reported at many military bases and nuclear power plants.

9. The first scientific attempt to communicate with aliens was in 1960.

10. Astronomer Frank Drake tried to contact aliens by using radio signals. He didn't get any answers.

11. In 1977, Voyager spacecraft included recordings of whale calls, greetings in different languages, and music, in case any aliens found the craft.

12. The most UFO sightings were recorded between the 1950s and the 1970s.

13. In 1947, the US Army Air Force reported that it had recovered an alien spaceship in Roswell, New Mexico.

14. Later, the government said the "spaceship" was actually a top-secret spy device. However, not everyone believes that story.

15. Nevada's Area 51 is a military site that is closed to the public. Many people believe that alien bodies or spacecraft from Roswell are stored there in secret.

16. Aliens are often reported to be tall, greenish in color, with very large heads and eyes.

17. Astronomers Margaret Turnbull and Jill Tartar created a list of more than 17,000 stars that could have orbiting planets that support alien life.

18. The privately owned SETI Institute in California has been scanning stars for signs of life since 1995. They haven't found anything yet.

19. SETI stands for The Search for Extraterrestrial Intelligence.

20. SETI is building a 350-antenna Alien Telescope Array to search for even more aliens.

21. You can download software from SETI to scan for aliens on your home computer.

22. Scientists believe that the most likely places for alien life have water sources.

23. They list four potential alien spots: underground on Mars, Saturn's moon Enceladus, and two of Jupiter's moons, Callisto and Europa.

24. In 2006, the French Center for National Space Studies broadcast a TV program aimed at extraterrestrials.

25. Cosmic Connexion was beamed to a star named Errai.

26. Errai is 45 light-years from Earth. The video won't reach the star until 2051.

27. In 2007, three US senators created the Advanced Aerospace Threat Identification Program (AATIP). The program is funded by the Department of Defense.

28. AATIP investigates reports of UFO sightings. Many are from members of the military.

29. AATIP reports include evidence that UFOs behave in a way that defies the laws of physics.

30. For example, UFOs travel at extremely high speeds or defy gravity.

31. AATIP scientists also describe finding objects not made of materials found on Earth.

32. Beginning in 2007, scientists began recording FRBs, or fast radio bursts. These bursts only last a few milliseconds but give off more energy than our sun does in 24 hours.

33. Some scientists believe that FRBs, which come from outside the Milky Way, may be signals from an alien civilization on another planet.

34. A group called METI (Messaging Extraterrestrial Intelligence) was founded in 2015.

35. In 2017, METI began broadcasting music to a planet about 12 light-years away from Earth.

36. Barney and Betty Hill claimed that aliens had abducted them in 1961. They described details of the event under hypnosis. But no one knows if their story is true.

37. In 1977, Ohio's Big Ear Telescope picked up a 72-second burst of sound that came from space. Many scientists think it was a communication from another planet.

38. The Big Ear transmission is called the Wow Signal because an astronomer was so surprised that he wrote "Wow!" on the printout.

39. During World War II, many pilots flying over Europe reported very fast, bright lights following their planes.

40. On March 13, 1997, thousands of people in southern Arizona reported seeing a set of lights moving across the sky in a V formation. The Air Force investigated but no explanation was ever given.

45

DARK FACTS ABOUT NOCTURNAL ANIMALS

1. Nocturnal animals have big eyes to help them see in the dark.

2. An owl's eyes are so big, they can't move within their sockets.

3. A cat's eyes have a special layer called a tapetum that reflects light. That's why their eyes glow in the dark.

4. Many nocturnal animals have a slit pupil in their eye. A slit pupil can open and close quickly when light changes.

5. Bioluminescent animals produce their own light.

6. Some fish are bioluminescent.

7. Fireflies are also bioluminescent.

8. Bioluminescent animals create light to communicate with each other.

9. They also use their light to locate food and attract prey.

10. Bioluminescent animals can flash their lights to scare away predators.

11. Bats use sound to find food. They make high-pitched squeaks that bounce off objects.

12. This process is called echolocation.

13. An owl's hearing is so sharp it can hear tiny animals rustling in the grass.

14. Lions hunt at night because it is cooler then.

15. Lions also hunt at night because their prey—zebra and antelopes—have poor night vision.

16. Sea turtles breed in the dark to avoid predators. They come out of the sea to lay their eggs on the beach.

17. Sea birds also breed at night to stay safe.

18. Many fish are active during the night.

19. When it is dark, it is easier for fish to see the tiny zooplankton they eat.

20. Bats and bush babies are only able to see at night.

21. Because scents linger on the night air, it is easier for animals to smell and track prey at night.

22. Owls have special feathers that help them fly very quietly. Their prey never hears them coming!

23. Aardvarks can hear and smell insects as they walk around.

24. Fewer animals hunt at night than during the day, so nocturnal hunters have less competition.

25. Some nocturnal animals, such as foxes, can also be seen during the day.

26. About 80 percent of marsupials and 60 percent of carnivores are nocturnal.

27. About 40 percent of rodents and 20 percent of primates are nocturnal.

14

28. Animals that are active at dawn and dusk are called crepuscular.

29. Both wild cats and pet cats have ears that can move. This helps them locate sounds in the dark.

30. A cat's cupped ear shape helps it take in more sound.

31. Some nocturnal animals can hear separately with each ear. This helps them pinpoint where a sound is coming from.

32. All eyes contain rods and cones. Rods are better at collecting low light.

33. Nocturnal animals' eyes have more rods than animals active during the day.

34. Cones work well in bright light. Nocturnal snakes, lizards, and bats do not have any cones in their eyes.

35. Activity is regulated by a person or animal's circadian rhythm. This rhythm is regulated by light cues.

36. Light signals diurnal (active during the day) animals to wake up and be active.

37. In nocturnal animals, light signals it is time to go to sleep.

38. Zoos often exhibit nocturnal animals in dark rooms so they will be active for daytime visitors to see.

39. Most species of spiders are nocturnal.

40. Many amphibians and reptiles are nocturnal.

41. Nocturnal animals usually hide during the day.

42. Nocturnal salamanders bury themselves in mud.

43. Other nocturnal animals hide under rocks or leaves.

44. Amphibians need to stay wet. Nights are usually more humid than days, so being nocturnal helps these animals survive.

45. Mosquitoes are active at night because it is cooler then. Too much sun can kill them.

35 OLD FACTS ABOUT ANCIENT CIVILIZATIONS

1. Rome was founded around 753 BC by a king named Romulus. Rome is named after him.

2. An old story said that Romulus and his twin brother, Remus, were raised by wolves, but that is not true.

3. Rome had a powerful army.

4. At one time, the Roman Empire covered all of Europe, plus parts of Africa and Asia.

5. Ancient Romans ran water to their cities through a series of pipes called aqueducts.

6. Wealthy Romans used piped water to heat and cool their homes.

7. Rich Romans ate many exotic foods, including parrots and flamingoes.

8. Meanwhile, poor Romans ate mostly bread and other grains.

9. Romans made concrete that is stronger than the concrete we use today.

10. The first supermarket and shopping mall were found in ancient Rome. The Trajan Market, built around 110 BC, housed more than 150 shops and a large food market.

11. The ancient Mayans invented a game that was a lot like basketball. However, players could not use their hands or feet to get the ball into the hoop.

12. The ancient Egyptians invented a form of picture writing called hieroglyphics.

13. Egyptian workers often left graffiti carved into the buildings they constructed.

14. The Mayans also used hieroglyphics.

15. Salt was so valuable in the ancient world that Greeks and Romans used it as money to buy goods and pay wages.

16. In 1259 BC, the Egyptians and the Hittites created one of the earliest peace treaties.

17. Ancient Egyptians loved to play board games.

18. Pharaohs like King Tut even had board games buried with them in their tombs.

19. Ancient Egyptians considered animals to be incarnations of gods.

20. They kept many pets, including cats, dogs, hawks, lions, and baboons.

21. Egyptian pets were often mummified and buried with their owners.

22. Ancient Greeks worshipped many different gods.

23. Greek myths told fantastic stories about gods and mortals.

24. The democratic form of government was invented in ancient Greece.

25. No wars or fighting were allowed in the three months before the ancient Greek Olympic Games so that athletes and spectators could travel safely.

26. Ancient China was ruled by powerful families called dynasties.

27. The dragon is the symbol of Chinese emperors. Some emperors even believed they were descended from dragons.

28. Ancient Ghana sat on an enormous gold mine. The civilization was so rich that even dog collars were made of gold.

29. The ancient city-state of Carthage was one of the most powerful empires. It was located in present-day Tunisia.

30. Carthage craftsmen were extremely skilled at making furniture.

31. Carthage was destroyed by the Roman empire.

32. The solar system was first mentioned in an ancient Indian text called the Rigveda.

33. Chess was invented in ancient India.

34. So was the game Snakes and Ladders.

35. Diamonds were first mined in India around 700 BC.

75 FANTASTIC FOOD FACTS

1. Ketchup was once used as medicine.

2. Crackers have holes in them so air bubbles don't break the crackers while they are baking.

3. White chocolate is not really chocolate. It contains no cacao beans.

4. Bananas are classified as berries.

5. Strawberries, raspberries, and blackberries technically aren't berries.

6. American cheese was actually invented in Switzerland.

7. The Aztecs used cocoa beans as money.

8. The fear of getting peanut butter stuck to the roof of your mouth is called arachibutyrophobia.

9. Americans eat millions of pounds of peanut butter every year.

10. Three Musketeers bars originally had three flavors: vanilla, chocolate, and strawberry.

11. Froot Loops are all the same flavor.

12. Ancient Egyptians paid workers with radishes, onions, and garlic.

13. Pasta comes in 350 different shapes.

14. Margherita pizza is named after Queen Margherita of Italy.

15. Margherita pizza includes the colors of the Italian flag: red (sauce), white (cheese), and green (basil).

16. To test eggs, place them in a glass of cold water. Bad eggs will float, but fresh eggs will sink.

17. Ripe cranberries bounce.

18. Human DNA is 60 percent the same as a banana's.

19. Goat meat is the most popular meat in the world.

20. Food is legally allowed to contain a small portion of insects.

21. Australians eat the most meat of any nation.

22. Indians eat the least amount of meat.

23. One hamburger can contain meat from many different cows.

24. The red dye in Skittles is made from boiled beetles.

25. Pound cake got its name because the original recipe called for one pound each of butter, sugar, and eggs.

26. Cheese is the most stolen food. About 4 percent of cheese in the world ends up being stolen.

27. An ear of corn has an even number of rows, usually 16.

28. An 11-year-old boy invented the Popsicle in 1905. He accidentally left a mixture of soda and water outside overnight, and it froze.

29. Potatoes absorb and reflect wireless signals the same way humans do.

30. Honey never goes bad.

31. In the eighteenth century, Europeans called tomatoes "the poison apple" and were afraid to eat them.

32. Grapes will explode in the microwave.

33. The earliest reference to soup comes from 6,000 BC. It included hippo and sparrow meat.

34. Apples belong to the rose family.

35. So do pears and plums.

36. A cheese called Casu Marzu contains maggots.

37. The twists in pretzels are made to look like arms crossed in prayer.

38. Apples are 25 percent air.

39. Worldwide, there are over 7,500 different varieties of apple.

40. There are more than 3,000 varieties of pear.

41. Cucumbers are 96 percent water.

42. Spam is short for "spiced ham."

43. Tuna eyeballs are a popular snack in Japan.

44. Dry swallowing sugar can cure hiccups.

45. Almonds are not nuts. They are seeds.

46. Peanuts aren't nuts either. They're legumes.

47. Peanuts contain an oil that is used to make dynamite.

48. An American named Thomas Sullivan created the tea bag. He sent small bags of tea to customers as samples.

49. Many food companies use flavorists, scientists whose job is to use chemistry to create and improve food.

50. If you eat way too many carrots, your skin can turn orange.

51. Potatoes were the first vegetables planted in space.

52. Carrots were originally purple.

53. Lollipops have been around for thousands of years.

54. Thomas Jefferson introduced macaroni and cheese to America. He originally had the dish in France.

55. Lobsters were once so common that they were considered a cheap food for the poor and for prisoners.

56. Raw lima beans are poisonous.

57. McDonald's sells 2.5 billion hamburgers a year.

58. That works out to 6.5 million hamburgers a day, or 75 hamburgers every second.

59. Pistachios aren't nuts. They are the seeds of a fruit.

60. Caesar salad was created in Mexico and gets its name from its creator, Caesar Cardini.

61. Americans eat about 20 million hot dogs a year.

62. Ice cream cones were invented at the 1904 World's Fair, when an ice cream vendor ran out of bowls and asked a waffle vendor for help.

63. Astronaut John Young smuggled a corned beef sandwich into space. But when he tried to eat it, the sandwich fell apart because there was no gravity to hold it together.

PIZZA
AROUND THE WORLD

70. Pepperoni is the most popular pizza topping in the United States.

71. People in Brazil like green peas on their pizza.

72. Canned tuna is a popular pizza topping in Germany.

73. A popular type of pizza in Japan is topped with potatoes and spicy mayonnaise.

74. In Russia, you can get a pizza topped with fish.

75. In Costa Rica, you can top your pizza with grated coconut.

64. Lemons float because they have the same density as water.

65. Popcorn was the first food to be microwaved.

66. Garlic is a natural insect repellent.

67. Broccoli contains more protein than steak.

68. A tube of applesauce was the first food eaten in space.

69. The first meal eaten on the moon included a peach, bacon squares, sugar cookie cubes, coffee, and pineapple-grapefruit drinks.

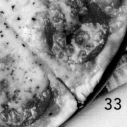

40 COZY FACTS ABOUT HOMES

1. Ancient people were nomadic and moved around a lot. Instead of houses, they lived in tents or caves.

2. Once people started planting crops and raising livestock, they started building permanent homes.

3. Climate has a lot to do with how houses are built.

4. People in Africa and other areas without trees build homes out of dried mud and grass.

5. Some homes in England and Europe have thatched roofs. These roofs are made of dried reeds and grass.

6. Pioneers in the Midwest built houses out of sod because there were no trees to use for wood.

7. Sod houses, or "soddies," were made of strips of sod cut into bricks.

8. Many soddies were built into the sides of hills.

9. Soddies were cool in the summer and warm in the winter.

10. However, the dirt walls and roof were filled with insects, mice, and snakes.

11. In rural parts of Sri Lanka, homes are made of palm fronds and sticks.

12. Concrete and wood are used to build homes in the Dominican Republic. These strong materials keep the houses standing during hurricanes.

13. Homes in the rain forest or other areas that get a lot of rain are often built on stilts to avoid flooding.

14. The Pueblo tribe in the southwestern United States built homes of adobe.

15. Adobe was made from dried mud, straw, and clay.

16. Many of these homes still stand today.

17. The Taos Pueblo is the oldest continuously occupied home in America. It was built between 1000 and 1450.

18. The oldest stone house in New England is the Henry Whitfield House in Connecticut. It was built in 1639. Today, the house is a museum.

19. Ancient cave homes in Tunisia were carved out of sandstone cliffs.

20. Central Asian nomads live in yurts. These tent-like structures are made of animal skins.

21. Ready to live small? Join the tiny house movement. These little homes are less than 500 square feet (45 square meters) in size.

22. Many tiny houses are mounted on wheeled trailers so they can move from place to place.

23. Many residents of the South Australian town Coober Pedy live in underground dugouts. These homes protect them from blistering heat and dust storms.

24. Igloos, or homes made of frozen bricks of snow and ice, were once common in the far north. Today they are still used for temporary structures.

25. Traditional hanok houses in Korea are built of tiled roofs and wooden beams. The roof curves at each end.

26. Hanok houses are often built with a mountain in the back and a river in the front.

27. Victorian homes were built in the late nineteenth and early twentieth century. They feature fancy decorations, gingerbread-style trim, and large windows.

28. Between 1908 and 1940, people could buy a kit from a mail-order catalog to build their own house.

29. These kits cost $6,700 and up.

30. Today, the average American home is just over 2,300 square feet (214 square meters).

31. In 1973, the average home was only 1,660 square feet (154 square meters).

32. Homes in places that get a lot of snow usually have steep roofs. Heavy snow on a flat roof could cause it to collapse.

33. Housewarming parties got their name because guests used to bring firewood to new homes. The practice was thought to ward off evil spirits.

34. A red front door can have many meanings. In Scotland, it means the house is paid for.

35. In the past, a red door in America meant the house was a safe place for travelers.

36. In Asia, some people believe a red door brings positive energy into the home.

37. People in the United States tend to stay in their homes for six to ten years.

38. Row houses were once popular in American and British industrial cities. These houses provided homes for factory workers and other laborers.

39. Each American home contains an average of 300,000 items.

40. Bubble wrap was originally designed to be used as wallpaper.

13

75
HOT AND COLD FACTS

1. Heat happens when energy is burned or used.

2. The hotter an object, the faster its molecules are moving.

3. Heat makes objects expand. Cold makes them contract.

4. Conduction occurs when heat transfers from one object to another until they are the same temperature.

5. Pots and pans are made from metal because metal conducts heat very well.

6. Heat and cold can change states of matter. Objects can melt if they get too hot. They freeze if they get very cold.

7. There are three different temperature scales: Fahrenheit, Celsius, and Kelvin.

8. On the Fahrenheit scale, water freezes at 32° and boils at 212°.

9. On the Celsius scale, water freezes at 0° and boils at 100°.

10. The Kelvin scale is used mostly by scientists because it does not include negative numbers.

11. Water freezes at 273.15°K.

12. It boils at 373.15°K.

13. 0°K is known as absolute zero. At that temperature, all motion stops.

14. The hottest temperature ever recorded on Earth was 134°F (57°C) in Death Valley, California, in 1913.

15. Energy from lightning heats the air up to 60,000°F (33,316°C).

16. Venus is the hottest planet in the solar system.

17. Its surface temperature is a toasty 854°F (457°C).

18. Mercury is the closest planet to the Sun, but it has a thinner atmosphere than Venus. That means the planet doesn't hold in as much heat.

19. Still, Mercury's temperature can rise as high as 801°F (427°C).

20. The temperature at the core of the Sun can be as hot as 27 million °F (15 million °C).

21. The temperature of the surface of the sun is about 10,000°F (5,600°C).

22. The bright light that can be seen during a solar eclipse is called the corona. Its temperature measures between two and 17 million °F (2 to 10 million °C).

23. Scientists think the highest possible temperature is 142 nonillion Kelvins.

24. That's 142 followed by 30 zeroes.

25. The Sahara is the world's largest hot desert.

26. The Ring of Fire is an area in the Pacific Ocean. Three-quarters of the Earth's active volcanoes are found there.

27. A magnifying glass can concentrate the sun's rays enough to start a fire.

28. The hottest sea in the world is the Red Sea. Its warmest spot is 87°F (31°C).

29. A heat wave occurs when temperatures are 9°F (5°C) above average for at least five days in a row.

30. The first use of the term heat wave was in New York City in 1892.

31. The world's hottest pepper is the infinity chili.

32. Fire tornadoes happen when super-hot heat and high winds spin air and debris into a whirling column.

33. Firefighters go into super-hot places. Their protective gear can weigh up to 60 pounds (27 kg).

34. Gold melts at about 1,947°F (1,064°C).

35. Pure silver melts at 1,761°F (961°C).

36. Tungsten is the hardest metal to melt. It has to reach 6,150°F (3,400°C) to melt.

37. Hot coals can reach temperatures of about 1,000°F (537°C).

38. People who walk on hot coals rarely get burned because most of the heat doesn't transfer to their feet.

39. More than half of the homes in the United States are heated by natural gas.

40. Other sources of heat include electricity, propane, oil, and wood.

41. The Chinese were the first to use natural gas for heat, around 500 BC. They built pipes to transport gas coming out of the ground into their homes.

42. During the last Ice Age, one-third of the Earth's surface was covered in ice.

43. Today, ice only covers about one-tenth of the Earth's surface.

44. Water boils at just 10 degrees above freezing on Mars.

45. Early hockey pucks were made of frozen cow poop.

46. Some frogs have special antifreeze-like chemicals in their blood. This allows them to freeze almost solid during the winter.

55

47. A New Zealand insect called the weta freezes solid in the winter and thaws out when the weather warms up.

48. Brain freeze occurs when something really cold touches a nerve in the roof of your mouth.

49. The lowest temperature ever recorded on Earth was –128.6°F (–89.2°C) in Antarctica.

50. Almost all of the world's glacial ice is found in Greenland and Antarctica.

51. Even though they're found in the ocean, icebergs are mostly made of fresh water.

52. In some parts of Antarctica, the ice is 3 miles (5 km) thick.

53. The 30-30-30 rule says that if the temperature is –30°F (–34.4°C) and the wind is blowing at 30 miles (48.3 km) per hour, human skin freezes in 30 seconds.

54. Some animals' fur changes to white during the winter to help them hide in the snow.

55. Some of these animals include the arctic fox, arctic hare, ptarmigan, and ermine.

56. Icebergs are bigger than 16 feet (5 meters) across. Bergy bits are less than 16 feet (5 meters). Growlers are chunks of ice less than 6.6 feet (2 meters) wide.

57. The largest snowflake ever recorded measured 15 inches (38 cm) wide and 8 inches (20 cm) thick. It fell in 1887 in Montana.

58. Snowflakes fall at a speed of about 3 miles (5 km) per hour.

59. One inch (2.54 cm) of snow melts down to just 1/10-inch (0.254 cm) of water.

60. A single snowstorm can drop 39 million tons of snow.

61. Snow is actually ice crystals stuck together.

62. Snow looks white because of light bouncing off the ice crystals.

63. All snowflakes have six sides.

64. The record for the most snow in the United States in a 24-hour period is 76 inches (193 cm) in Silver Lake, Colorado. The big storm occurred in 1921.

65. Mount Baker Ski Area in Washington state received 1,140 inches (2,896 cm) of snow during the 1998–1999 season. That's a world record!

66. Antarctica is the coldest continent.

67. Russia is the coldest country.

68. The next four coldest countries are Canada, Mongolia, Finland, and Iceland.

69. A hotel in Sweden is made from a mix of snow and ice. Everything inside is also made of ice.

70. The hotel melts every spring and is rebuilt every winter.

71. The coldest temperature recorded in the United States was –80°F (–62°C) near Fairbanks, Alaska, in 1971.

72. The coldest US temperature outside of Alaska occurred in Rogers Pass, Montana, in 1954. It was a bone-chilling –70°F (–57°C).

73. Hawaii is the only state to never see a temperature below zero.

74. The coldest temperature ever recorded in Hawaii was 12°F (–11°C) at the Mauna Kea Observatory on May 17, 1979.

75. The coldest temperature in North America occurred in the Yukon territory of Canada on February 3, 1947, when the thermometer plunged to –81.4°F (–63°C).

•••• **69**

60 SCARY STORM FACTS

1. Thunderstorms happen when warm, moist air flows up into the atmosphere. The rising air causes an updraft that creates powerful winds.

2. The friction of raindrops and ice crystals rubbing together in a cloud causes lightning.

3. Thunder happens when lightning heats up the air so fast, it creates a sonic boom.

4. A storm cloud can hold more than 1 million pounds (454,000 kg) of water.

5. Storm clouds look dark because sunlight can't filter through all the rain inside the clouds.

6. Astraphobia is the fear of thunder and lightning.

7. The extra heat around cities can make thunderstorms more intense.

8. Lightning can definitely strike the same place twice.

9. Lightning can travel from one person to another.

15. In the United States, lightning strikes the ground 25 million times a year.

16. Some storms rain frogs or fish. This happens when waterspouts pick up animals and then drop them several miles away.

17. Ice storms occur when the temperature on the ground is lower than the temperature in the air and rain freezes on contact.

18. Ice can increase the weight of tree branches by 30 times.

19. Ice storms often bring down power lines and leave millions of people in the dark.

20. In 1998, an ice storm in New York and New England damaged millions of trees and caused $1.4 billion in damages.

21. The same storm caused $3 billion of damage in Canada.

22. If the center of a storm cloud contains cold air, raindrops can freeze and turn into hail.

23. The largest hailstone in the United States was the size of a volleyball.

24. Baseball-sized hail can hit the ground at 100 miles (161 km) per hour.

25. Hailstones can break windows, damage cars and homes, and flatten crops.

26. In 1995, a hailstorm in Fort Worth, Texas, buried roads under two feet of hail.

27. A hailstorm in India in 1888 killed almost 250 people.

28. Animals can often tell when a storm is coming.

29. A raindrop's top speed is 18 miles (29 km) per hour.

10. Lightning can travel through phone lines.

11. The average bolt of lightning could power a car for up to 910 miles (1,465 km).

12. Tall buildings are often hit by lightning.

13. Lightning kills more people every year than tornadoes do.

14. About 2,000 thunderstorms hit Earth every minute.

30. It takes about an hour for a snowflake to travel from a cloud to the ground.

31. The deadliest blizzard in history struck Iran in 1972. Entire villages were buried under 26 feet (8 meters) of snow during the weeklong storm. At least 4,000 people died.

32. The deadliest winter storm in the United States was the Blizzard of '88. From March 11 through 14, up to 4 feet (1.2 meters) of snow fell in the northeast. More than 400 people died—200 in New York alone.

33. More than 200 ships sank during the Blizzard of '88.

34. On March 12, 1993, the "Storm of the Century" paralyzed the eastern half of the United States. The storm included tornadoes, high winds, floods, ice, and heavy snow.

35. The Storm of the Century caused $5.5 million in damages.

36. The Storm of the Century affected 120 million people over 550,000 square miles (1.4 million square km).

37. The Children's Blizzard hit the Great Plains on January 12, 1888, during a school day—235 people died, and 213 of them were children.

38. The United States experiences more tornadoes than any other country.

39. A waterspout is actually a small tornado over water.

40. In 525 BC, 50,000 Persian soldiers were buried by a sandstorm.

41. Mudslides occur when the ground becomes saturated with heavy rains.

42. Mudslides can carry away buildings, cars, animals, and people.

43. There are three types of floods: flash floods, river floods, and coastal floods.

44. Thunderstorms or heavy downpours can cause flash floods in low-lying areas.

45. Up to 25,000 people died in a flash flood in India in 1979.

46. More than 98 inches (249 cm) of rain fell in Cherrapunji, India, over 48 hours in 2014.

47. Cherrapunji also holds the record for the most rain over 12 months: 86 feet, 10 inches (27 meters), set back in 1860–61.

48. A tropical storm has winds up to 73 miles (117 km) per hour.

49. A hurricane has winds of 74 miles (119 km) per hour or more.

50. These storms are known as hurricanes in the Atlantic and Northeast Pacific Oceans.

51. In the Northwest Pacific, these storms are called typhoons.

52. In the South Pacific and Indian Oceans, they are called cyclones.

53. The World Meteorological Organization names the hurricanes.

54. Names are used on a six-year cycle and alternate between male and female names.

55. If a storm is extremely deadly, that storm's name will not be used again.

56. Hurricane John (also known as Typhoon John) lasted an entire month.

57. Derechos are windstorms combined with thunderstorms.

58. Derecho winds can be more than 58 miles (93 km) per hour.

59. Derecho winds blow in a straight line.

60. Wind damage from a derecho can cover more than 240 miles (400 km).

40 HURRICANE VERSUS TORNADO FACTS

1. A hurricane is a low-pressure storm that spins around a center called the eye.

2. A tornado is a violently spinning funnel cloud that extends down from a thunderstorm to the ground.

3. Hurricanes form over the ocean.

4. Tornadoes form over land.

5. Hurricanes form when warm, wet air rises and leaves an area of lower air pressure underneath.

6. Tornadoes form when a layer of warm, wet air is trapped under a layer of cold, dry air.

7. Hurricanes can range in size between 99 miles (160 km) and 994 miles (1,600 km) wide.

8. Most tornadoes are less than 1 mile (km) wide.

9. A hurricane can last for days or weeks.

10. Most tornadoes only last a few seconds or minutes. The longest last a few hours.

11. Hurricane wind speeds range between 74 miles (119 km) and 200 miles (322 km) per hour.

12. Tornado winds can hit speeds of more than 300 miles (483 km) per hour.

13. Hurricanes usually strike the southern and eastern shores of the United States.

14. The most common area for tornadoes is the Midwest United States. This area is called Tornado Alley.

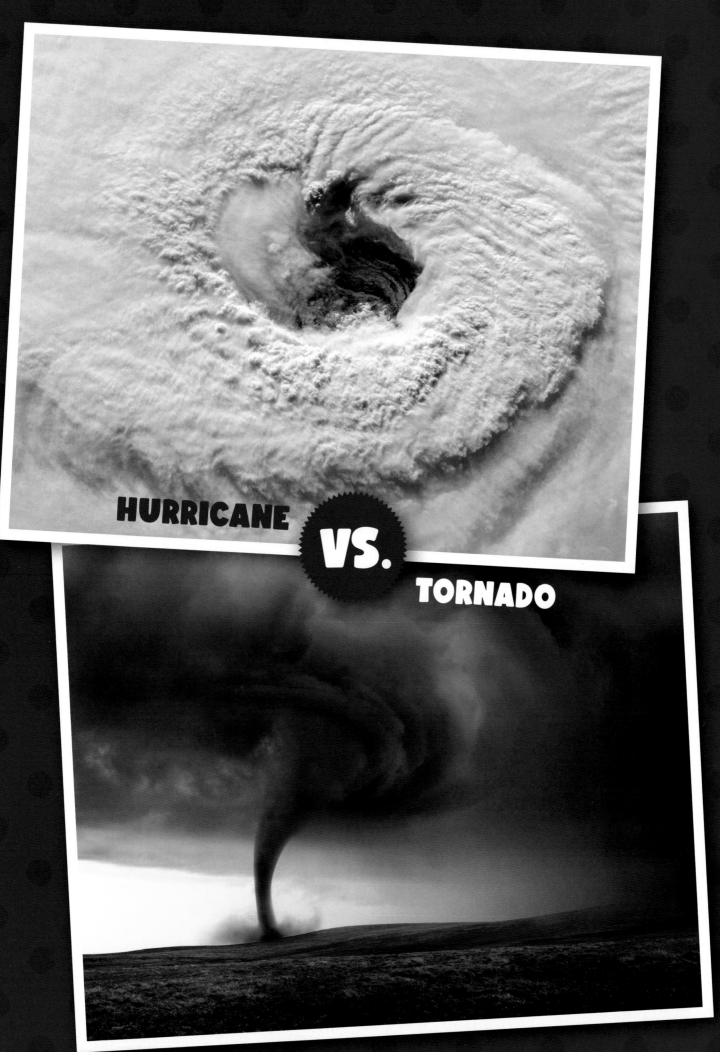

HURRICANE VS. **TORNADO**

HURRICANE DAMAGE

VS.

TORNADO DAMAGE

15. Hurricane season lasts from June to November.

16. Tornadoes can strike anytime, but most occur during the spring and summer.

17. Hurricanes are long-lasting storms that occur during both night and day.

18. Most tornadoes occur between 3 and 9 p.m.

19. Hurricanes are slow-moving storms that can be tracked over long periods of time.

20. Tornadoes are more intense than hurricanes but do not last long.

21. Hurricane/Typhoon John traveled over 8,188 miles (13,177 km) across the Pacific Ocean in 1994.

22. In 1925, a tornado traveled 218 miles (352 km) across three US states.

23. The deadliest US hurricane was the Great Galveston Storm of 1900. It killed between 8,000 and 12,000 people.

24. The deadliest US tornado was the Tri-State Tornado of 1925. It killed 695 people.

25. A typical hurricane season has 6 hurricanes.

26. The US averages 1,274 tornadoes per year. Most do not do any damage.

27. Hurricane winds are measured by the Saffir-Simpson Hurricane Scale. The scale lists five categories.

28. Tornadoes are measured by the EF Scale. It has six categories, from E0 to E5.

29. Specially trained pilots often fly into the eye of a hurricane to collect scientific data.

30. Storm chasers follow tornadoes in cars and trucks and set up equipment to measure the storms.

31. Florida has the most hurricanes per year.

32. Texas has the most tornadoes per year.

33. September is the most active month for hurricanes.

34. May is the most active month for tornadoes.

35. The largest number of hurricanes ever active at once is 6. This has happened several times.

36. The largest number of tornadoes ever active at once was 543, recorded in May 2003.

37. Most hurricane damage is caused by flooding.

38. Most tornado damage is caused by wind.

39. Cape Hatteras has been hit by the most hurricanes.

40. Oklahoma City has been hit by the most tornadoes.

50

FACTS ABOUT DINOSAURS, YA DIG?

1. Dinosaurs first appeared about 230 million years ago.

2. They became extinct about 65 million years ago.

3. Scientists believe a giant meteorite hit the Earth and wiped out the dinosaurs.

4. The word dinosaur means "fearful lizard" in Greek.

5. The word was first used in 1842.

6. Scientists have discovered more than 700 different kinds of dinosaurs.

7. Meat-eating dinosaurs laid long, thin eggs.

8. Plant-eating dinosaurs laid eggs that were round.

9. Big dinosaurs were probably too heavy to sit on their eggs. They might have piled plants on top instead.

10. Spinosaurus had tall, thin spines on its back. They measured up to 7 feet (2 meters) high.

11. Scientists think Spinosaurus's spines created a sail that cooled the dinosaur's body.

12. Some dinosaurs swallowed stones to grind up their food.

13. When large dinosaur bones were first discovered, people thought they were dragon bones.

14. Cryolophosaurus was discovered near the South Pole.

15. It was the first dinosaur discovered in Antarctica.

16. T. Rex had the largest teeth of any dinosaur. They were the size of bananas.

17. A T. Rex named Sue is the largest and most complete T. Rex skeleton ever found.

18. You can visit Sue at Chicago's Field Museum.

19. T. Rex's brain was twice the size of the brains of other giant meat eaters.

20. Diplodocus had a 20-foot-long (6-meter-long) tail.

21. Mamenchisaurus's neck was more than 30 feet (9 meters) long.

22. That's longer than any animal that ever lived.

23. T. Rex could eat up to 500 pounds (230 kg) of meat in one bite.

24. Stegosaurus was 30 feet (9 meters) long but had a tiny brain.

25. Stegosaurus had a second "brain," or nerve center, at the top of its tail.

26. Many dinosaurs had hollow leg and arm bones. This helped them run fast.

27. More dinosaurs have been found in the United States than any other country.

28. The smallest dinosaur found in North America was just 2 feet (0.6 meter) long. It weighed about 2 pounds (0.9 kg).

29. Giganotosaurus was a real giant! This dino was 5 feet (1.5 meters) longer and almost 6,000 pounds (2,700 kg) heavier than T. Rex.

30. Giganotosaurus was discovered in Argentina.

31. Dinosaur fossils have been found on every continent.

32. Argentinosaurus is the world's largest dinosaur. It weighed 100 tons.

33. The world's largest bone belongs to Argentinosaurus. This dino's backbone weighs 2 tons.

34. Deinocheirus's name means "terrible hand." It had three 10-inch (25-cm) claws on each arm.

35. Parasaurolophus had a domed head. It could blow air through a tube to create a trumpeting sound.

36. The smallest adult dinosaur fossil belongs to Lesothosaurus. It was about the size of a chicken.

· · · · · · · · 17

37. The Dinosaur Trail is a series of preserved dinosaur footprints in Colorado.

38. A group of plant-eating dinosaurs called sauropods are the largest land animals that ever lived.

39. They weighed up to 88 tons.

40. Sauroposeidon is the tallest known dinosaur. It was about 61 feet (18.5 meters) tall.

41. Megalosaurus was the first dinosaur to be named, back in 1824. Its name means "great lizard."

42. The first stegosaurus skeleton was found in Colorado.

43. Roy Chapman Andrews was the first person to find a dinosaur nest. He found it in the Gobi Desert in 1923.

44. Some dinosaur eggs were as big as basketballs.

45. Most meat eaters walked on two feet. They could move faster and use their hands to grab prey.

46. Plant-eating dinosaurs walked on four feet to support their heavy bodies.

47. Scientists have found fossilized prints of dinosaur skin.

48. All dinosaurs laid eggs.

49. Scientists make mistakes. Gideon Mantell thought iguanodon's big thumb claw was located on top of its nose. It took 40 years to fix that mistake.

50. Most scientists believe that dinosaurs evolved into birds.

45 FACTS ABOUT SPACE FLIGHT

1. A spacesuit weighs about 280 pounds.

2. It takes 45 minutes to put on a spacesuit.

3. The Soviet Union launched the first satellite, Sputnik I, in 1957.

4. The first US satellite was Explorer 1. It was launched in 1958.

5. It took 115 minutes for Explorer 1 to orbit the Earth.

6. The space shuttles were the world's first reusable spacecraft.

7. Each space shuttle astronaut was allowed 3.8 pounds (1.7 kg) of food per day.

8. All space food is individually packaged and precooked, except for fresh fruit and vegetables.

9. The final space shuttle mission was in 2011.

10. The International Space Station (ISS) launched in 1998. It was a joint venture between the United States and Russia.

11. Some people believe the 1969 moon landing was fake.

12. Astronauts have reported the moon smells like wet ashes or gunpowder.

13. Cartoon dog Snoopy is the safety mascot for NASA.

14. The ISS is the most expensive object ever created. It cost more than $120 billion to build.

15. The ISS has been continually occupied by astronauts from different countries since 2000.

16. Many astronauts get "space sick." Symptoms include nausea, dizziness, headaches, and vomiting.

17. Many animals have been sent into space, including dogs, monkeys, chimpanzees, mice, and frogs.

18. The first human to travel to space was Yuri Gagarin from the Soviet Union in 1961.

19. A 1967 international law prevents any nation from owning planets, stars, or moons.

20. ISS astronauts get weekends off.

21. Space is full of junk, including old satellites, rockets, dropped tools, and gloves.

22. Scientists think there are about 500,000 small pieces of space junk orbiting the Earth.

23. Space junk that is 500 miles (805 km) above Earth will orbit for decades.

24. All space junk is the property of the nation that built it.

25. A spacecraft has to travel 15,000 miles (24,140 km) per hour to break free of Earth's gravity.

26. It took almost 528,000 gallons (2 million liters) of fuel to launch the space shuttle into space.

27. In 1959, an unmanned Soviet spacecraft crash-landed on the moon.

28. Valentina Tereshkova of the Soviet Union was the first woman in space in 1963.

29. On July 20, 1969, Neil Armstrong and Buzz Aldrin became the first people to walk on the moon.

30. Armstrong, Aldrin, and Michael Collins traveled 250,000 miles (402,000 km) to the moon and back.

31. In 2001, a private citizen named Dennis Tito spent $20 million to spend a week on the ISS.

32. Six *Apollo* missions landed on the moon between 1969 and 1972. They were *Apollo* 11, 12, 14, 15, 16, and 17.

33. *Apollo 13* was supposed to land on the moon, but an explosion onboard meant it had to turn back to Earth.

34. In 2012, NASA sent the *Curiosity* robot rover to Mars.

35. *Curiosity* weighed about a ton and was the size of a car.

36. *Curiosity* traveled around the surface of Mars, collected samples, and sent photos back to Earth.

29 ......

37. A complete NASA spacesuit costs $12 million.

38. Most of that cost is for the backpack and control module.

39. The footprints on the moon will be there for millions of years because there is no wind to blow them away.

40. Spacecraft travel so fast when they re-enter Earth's atmosphere that the friction creates intense heat.

41. Spacecraft have special tiles to reflect heat so the ship doesn't burn up on re-entry.

42. There have been three major disasters in the American space program.

43. In 1967, three astronauts were killed in a launch pad fire onboard the *Apollo 1* space capsule.

44. In 1986, the space shuttle *Challenger* exploded after takeoff. All seven astronauts, including school teacher Christa McAuliffe, were killed.

45. Seven astronauts died aboard space shuttle *Columbia* in 2003 when it disintegrated upon re-entering Earth's atmosphere.

100
US PEOPLE AND POPULATION FACTS

HERE ARE THE 50 US STATES IN ORDER OF POPULATION IN 2019:

1.	California	39.51 million	26.	Kentucky	4.47 million
2.	Texas	29.00 million	27.	Oregon	4.22 million
3.	Florida	21.48 million	28.	Oklahoma	3.96 million
4.	New York	19.45 million	29.	Connecticut	3.57 million
5.	Pennsylvania	12.80 million	30.	Utah	3.21 million
6.	Illinois	12.67 million	31.	Iowa	3.16 million
7.	Ohio	11.69 million	32.	Nevada	3.08 million
8.	Georgia	10.62 million	33.	Arkansas	3.02 million
9.	North Carolina	10.49 million	34.	Mississippi	2.98 million
10.	Michigan	9.99 million	35.	Kansas	2.91 million
11.	New Jersey	8.88 million	36.	New Mexico	2.10 million
12.	Virginia	8.54 million	37.	Nebraska	1.93 million
13.	Washington	7.61 million	38.	West Virginia	1.79 million
14.	Arizona	7.28 million	39.	Idaho	1.79 million
15.	Massachusetts	6.89 million	40.	Hawaii	1.42 million
16.	Tennessee	6.83 million	41.	New Hampshire	1.36 million
17.	Indiana	6.73 million	42.	Maine	1.34 million
18.	Missouri	6.14 million	43.	Montana	1.07 million
19.	Maryland	6.05 million	44.	Rhode Island	1.06 million
20.	Wisconsin	5.82 million	45.	Delaware	970,000
21.	Colorado	5.76 million	46.	South Dakota	880,000
22.	Minnesota	5.64 million	47.	North Dakota	760,000
23.	South Carolina	5.15 million	48.	Alaska	730,000
24.	Alabama	4.90 million	49.	Vermont	620,000
25.	Louisiana	4.65 million	50.	Wyoming	580,000

POPULATION DENSITY OF US STATES IN 2019 (NUMBER OF PEOPLE PER SQUARE MILE):

1.	New Jersey	1,208	**26.**	Wisconsin	108
2.	Rhode Island	1,025	**27.**	Alabama	97
3.	Massachusetts	884	**28.**	Missouri	89
4.	Connecticut	737	**29.**	West Virginia	75
5.	Maryland	623	**30.**	Minnesota	71
6.	Delaware	500	**31.**	Vermont	68
7.	New York	413	**32.**	Arizona	64
8.	Florida	401	**33.**	Mississippi	63
9.	Ohio	286	**34.**	Arkansas	58
10.	Pennsylvania	286	**35.**	Oklahoma	58
11.	California	254	**36.**	Iowa	57
12.	Illinois	228	**37.**	Colorado	56
13.	Hawaii	220	**38.**	Oregon	44
14.	Virginia	216	**39.**	Maine	44
15.	North Carolina	216	**40.**	Utah	39
16.	Indiana	189	**41.**	Kansas	36
17.	Georgia	185	**42.**	Nevada	28
18.	Michigan	177	**43.**	Nebraska	25
19.	South Carolina	171	**44.**	Idaho	22
20.	Tennessee	166	**45.**	New Mexico	17
21.	New Hampshire	152	**46.**	South Dakota	12
22.	Washington	115	**47.**	North Dakota	11
23.	Kentucky	113	**48.**	Montana	7
24.	Texas	111	**49.**	Wyoming	6
25.	Louisiana	108	**50.**	Alaska	1

50
UN-BE-LEAF-ABLE PLANT FACTS

1. Dendrochronology is the science of calculating a tree's age by counting its rings.

2. Brazil is named after a tree.

3. Eighty-five percent of plant life is found in the ocean.

4. An average tree provides enough wood to make 170,100 pencils.

5. Without plants, there would be no life on Earth.

6. The first type of aspirin came from the bark of a willow tree.

7. The Amazon rain forest produces half the world's oxygen supply.

8. Washington, DC's famous cherry blossom trees were a gift to the United States from Tokyo, Japan, in 1912.

9. Bamboo is the fastest-growing woody plant in the world.

10. Bamboo can grow 3 feet (1 meter) in a single day.

11. The ginkgo is one of the oldest species of tree, dating back 250 million years.

12. There are more than 300,000 plant species.

13. During the 1600s, tulips were worth more than gold in Holland.

14. The African baobab tree can store thousands of gallons (liters) of water in its trunk.

15. Oak trees don't produce acorns until they are about 50 years old.

16. A sunflower looks like one giant flower, but it is actually made of hundreds of tiny flowers called florets.

17. Sunflowers are the symbol of nuclear disarmament.

18. A sunflower's roots can extract radioactive material through their roots and store them in their stems and leaves.

19. Trees are the longest-lived organisms on Earth.

20. In 2012, Russian scientists resurrected a 32,000-year-old extinct Arctic flowering plant using seeds found in Ice Age squirrel burrows.

21. A cactus can store large amounts of water in its trunk.

22. Cacti have very long roots that can soak up water deep underground.

23. A cactus is covered with a waxy substance to prevent water from evaporating from its surface.

24. Some species of cacti can live for hundreds of years.

25. Almost all species of cacti are native to the Americas.

26. Sundews, pitcher plants, and Venus flytraps all capture insects and eat them.

27. One type of orchid grows underground. It was discovered in Australia in 1928.

28. The largest flower in the world is the Rafflesia.

29. Rafflesia smells like rotting meat.

30. About 70,000 plant species are used for medicine.

31. About 80 percent of the Earth's original forests have been destroyed.

32. Roughly 90 percent of the foods we eat come from just 30 plants.

33. Oak trees are struck by lightning more than any other tree.

34. More than a million trees were planted in Nebraska in 1876 to celebrate the first Arbor Day.

35. The first apple seeds came to America from Europe in 1623.

36. Morning glory flowers open every morning and close every evening.

37. The leaves of poison ivy aren't its only dangerous part; smoke from burning this plant is also toxic.

38. The first plant to grow after the 1980 volcanic eruption of Mount Saint Helens in Washington was a purple prairie lupine.

39. A huge underground vault holds almost a billion seeds for safekeeping.

40. Mosses and ferns produce spores instead of seeds.

41. The gemstone amber is actually fossilized tree resin.

42. Balsa trees only bloom at night.

43. The stem of a sugar cane can grow to be more than 17 feet (5 meters) tall.

44. Corn is the most planted field crop in the United States.

45. Epiphytes are plants that grow on other plants for support.

46. Epiphytes have no roots.

47. Most epiphytes are found in tropical places.

48. Epiphytes do not harm the plants they grow on.

49. Parasitic plants do harm their hosts.

50. Parasitic plants take nutrients from their hosts and can actually kill the host plant.

40 CAVE FACTS TO EXPLORE

1. Caves form when water flows over soft rock.

2. Acid in the water eats away at the rock.

3. Many caves are made of a soft rock called limestone.

4. Caves can also form when hot lava melts rocks and creates holes.

5. Tidal waters on the coast can carve caves out of rocks on the shore.

6. Caves take between 10,000 and 100,000 years to form.

7. The study of caves is called speleology.

8. Caves can also be called caverns.

9. Caves are completely dark inside.

10. Some caves have hanging pieces called stalactites.

11. Stalactites form when water drips from the ceiling. The lime in the water hardens and creates stalactites.

12. Stalagmites are hardened minerals that rise from the floor of a cave.

13. Stalactites and stalagmites can join together to form columns.

14. Sheets of hardened lime on cave walls are called flowstones.

15. Caves can have many long passageways and rooms.

16. Exploring caves is called spelunking.

17. Exploring is also called caving and potholing.

18. Caves provide shelter for many animals.

19. Some species of bats live deep inside caves.

20. Bats are trogloxenes. That means they live in caves part of the time.

21. Troglobites are animals that live deep inside caves and never go outside.

22. Blind cave fish have no eyes. They don't need to see in the dark.

23. Treasures and artifacts from ancient times have been found inside caves.

24. The Kruber-Voronya Cave in the Asian country of Georgia is the world's deepest cave. It is 7,208 feet (2,197 meters) deep.

25. The largest cave in the world is Son Doong in Vietnam.

26. Son Doong covers 1.35 billion cubic feet (38.5 cubic meters).

27. In 2019, divers discovered that Son Doong is connected to another huge cave called Hang Thung.

28. There are about 17,000 caves in the United States.

29. Rhode Island and Louisiana are the only states that do not have caves.

30. The largest cave in the United States is Mammoth Cave in Kentucky.

31. It is also the longest cave in the world.

32. About 365 miles (587 km) of Mammoth Cave have been mapped so far.

33. Most of Mammoth Cave was mapped by enslaved explorers and guides in the 1800s.

34. Many caves are filled with water. Some have rivers running through them.

35. If you discover a new cave, you get to name it.

36. The Great Blue Hole off the coast of Belize is a 400-foot (122-meter)-deep sinkhole.

37. The Great Blue Hole is a favorite spot for scuba diving.

38. It is also home to several species of sharks and tropical fish.

39. New Mexico's Carlsbad Caverns includes more than 100 caves.

40. Missouri is called the Cave State because it contains more than 6,000 caves.

25 LARGEST PUBLIC COMPANIES IN THE WORLD

Here are the largest companies in the world in 2019, according to *Forbes* magazine.

1. Industrial and Commercial Bank of China
2. J.P. Morgan Chase
3. China Construction Bank
4. Agriculture Bank of China
5. Bank of America
6. Apple
7. Ping An Insurance Group
8. Bank of China
9. Royal Dutch Shell
10. Wells Fargo
11. ExxonMobil
12. AT&T
13. Samsung Electronics
14. Citigroup
15. Toyota Motor
16. Microsoft
17. Alphabet
18. Volkswagen Group
19. Chevron
20. Verizon Communications
21. HSBC Holdings
22. PetroChina
23. Allianz
24. British Petroleum
25. Total

50 FACTS ABOUT TECHNOLOGY

1. Email has been around longer than the World Wide Web.

2. To send an email in the 1980s, you had to use a computer and a rotary telephone to connect to a service called Micronet.

3. There were no URLs in those days. Instead, Web pages had numbers.

4. Microsoft, Apple, Google, and HP were all started in garages.

5. Computer programming is one of the fastest-growing occupations.

6. Windows' original name was Interface Manager.

7. The Apple II had a hard drive of just 5 megabytes when it was released in 1977.

8. Technophobia is the fear of technology.

9. Cyberphobia is the fear of computers.

10. Nomophobia is the fear of being without a cell phone.

11. About 51 percent of Internet traffic is non-human.

12. Most of that traffic is made up of hacking, spamming, and phishing.

13. The average computer user blinks 7 times a minute. The normal rate is 20 times a minute.

14. The first computer was almost 8 feet (2.5 meters) tall and weighed more than 66,000 pounds (30,000 kg).

15. About 8 billion devices are connected to the Internet.

16. More than 570 new websites are created every minute.

17. More video content is uploaded to YouTube in a 60-day period than the three major US television networks created in 60 years.

18. An estimated 340,000 tweets are sent per minute.

19. About 500 million tweets are sent per day.

20. Over 4.2 billion data records were stolen in 2016.

21. Approximately 250 million hours of TV shows and movies are watched daily via Netflix.

22. More than 56 million hours of music is streamed daily.

23. The amount of technical information doubles every two years.

24. Domain name registrations were free until 1995.

25. More than 2.3 billion people own an iPhone.

26. In 2013, Amazon had 1,000 robots operating in its warehouses. Now Amazon has 45,000 robots operating across 20 warehouses.

27. About 47 percent of jobs will disappear in the next 25 years as robots replace human workers.

28. Roughly 92 percent of the world's currency is digital.

29. Most large banking transactions are done digitally and not with cash.

30. IBM launched RAMAC in 1956.

31. RAMAC stood for Random Access Method of Accounting and Control.

32. RAMAC was the first computer to save data on randomly accessible hard drives.

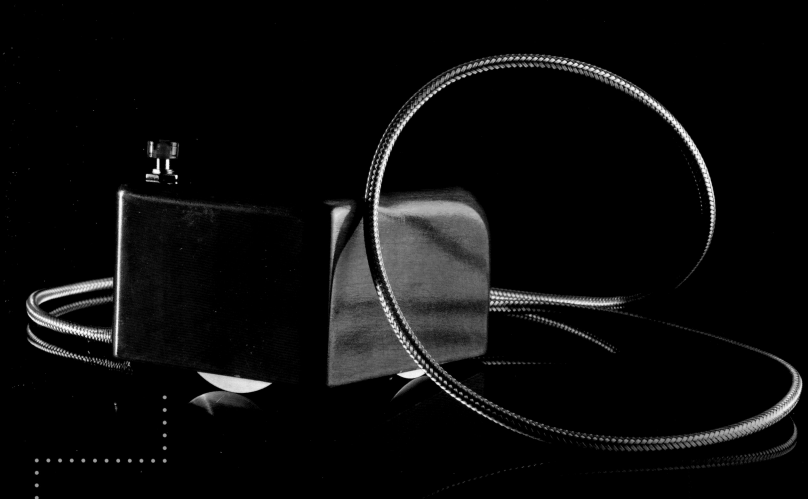

33. On RAMAC, 5 megabytes of data weighed a ton.

34. The first computer mouse was invented by Douglas Engelbart in 1968.

35. The first mouse was made of wood.

36. Engelbart called the device a "mouse" because the cable at the end of the device looked like a mouse's tail.

37. Wikipedia uses anti-vandal bots to make sure people don't edit articles with false information.

38. The word *robot* comes from the Czech word robota, which means "work."

39. Credit card chip technology has been around since 1986.

40. November 30 is Computer Security Day.

41. The barcode was invented in 1952. But it wasn't used to label products until 1974.

42. Nintendo was founded in 1889. Back in those days, the company made playing cards.

43. Amazon started as an online bookstore called Cadabra.com.

44. The first cell phone call was made in New York City in 1973.

45. The first text message was sent in 1992.

46. The text message read, "Merry Christmas."

47. More people have cell phones than have indoor toilets.

48. The first Web page has been running since 1991.

49. The top three most-used passwords are 123456, password, and 12345.

50. About 220 million tons of old computers and other devices are thrown away in the United States every year.

50 BRAIN-BUSTING BRAIN FACTS

1. The human brain weighs about 3 pounds.

2. About 60 percent of the brain is made up of fat.

3. Your brain isn't fully formed until age 25.

4. Brain development occurs from back to front.

5. The first successful brain surgeries were performed during the Stone Age.

6. Some brain surgeries are done with the patient still awake.

7. The brain has three parts: the medulla, cerebrum, and cerebellum.

8. The medulla is the lower part of your brain. It controls breathing, swallowing, and other automatic functions.

9. The cerebellum is above the medulla. It is in charge of sensory functions and movement.

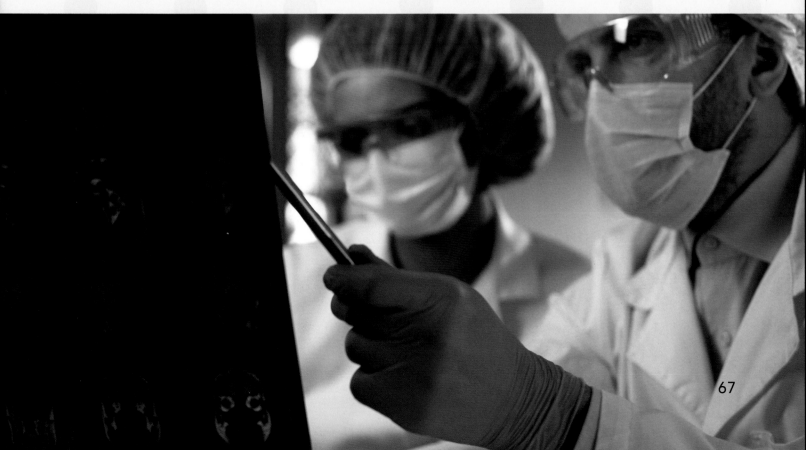

10. The cerebrum is the largest part of the brain. It interprets speech, reasoning, and emotion.

11. The cerebrum has two parts, the right hemisphere and the left hemisphere.

12. Each hemisphere controls the opposite side of the body.

13. The brain generates about 23 watts of electricity. That's enough to power a light bulb.

14. There are about 100,000 miles (160,934 km) of blood vessels in the brain.

15. There are about 100 billion neurons, or nerve cells, in the brain.

16. Neurons generate electrical impulses that send information from one cell to another.

17. Information can move at a speedy 268 miles (431 km) per hour along neurons.

18. Your brain is always active, even when you are sleeping.

19. The sperm whale has the largest brain of any animal. It weighs up to 20 pounds (9 kg). But that's really small compared to the whale's huge size.

20. Most of a sperm whale's huge head is filled with fat.

21. The human brain grows about three times in size during the first year of life.

22. The brain interprets pain signals from other parts of the body, but the brain itself cannot feel pain.

23. The brain gets smaller as we get older.

24. Brains lose some of their ability to think and remember things by the late twenties.

25. Your brain uses about 20 percent of the oxygen in your body.

26. If brain cells are deprived of oxygen, they will die.

27. Synesthesia occurs when a person mixes up sensory signals. People with this condition can hear colors or see sounds.

28. Telephone numbers in the United States are seven digits long because that's how many numbers our short-term memory can hold on to.

29. Our brains prefer images over text.

30. The attention span of the human brain is getting shorter.

31. The average attention span is now just 8 seconds.

32. Reading promotes brain development in children.

33. The human brain is about three times larger than the brains of animals the same size.

34. Human brains float in cerebrospinal fluid. This fluid cushions and protects the brain from injuries and infections.

35. Scientists used to think people only used about 10 percent of their brain. Today, we know that we use almost all of the brain.

36. Your brain is very active while you are dreaming.

37. A person's brain activity is as unique as their fingerprints.

38. The brain has more different kinds of cells than any other part of the body.

39. Dolphin brains are bigger than human brains.

40. A spider's brain is too big to fit inside its head. It also extends down the creature's legs.

41. More than half of an octopus's neurons are in its tentacles and suckers. This allows an octopus to solve puzzles with their tentacles.

42. Leeches have 32 small brains.

43. A nematode's tiny brain has just 302 neurons.

44. A woodpecker's skull is made of thick bones with air pockets inside to protect the bird's brain as it bangs against tree trunks.

45. Crows, ravens, and jays are the smartest birds.

46. An ostrich's eyeballs are so big that there isn't much room for the bird's brain inside its skull. So this bird's brain is smaller than its eyes.

47. Whales use half their brain for sleeping and half for breathing. The breathing part of the brain stays awake while the whale sleeps.

48. A whale keeps one eye open on the side of its brain that is awake while the other eye is closed when it's sleeping.

49. Dolphins and sea lions do the same thing.

50. A cockroach can live for a short time without its head or brain.

30
CHILLY FACTS
ABOUT ANTARCTICA

1. The South Pole is located in Antarctica.

2. Between 60 and 90 percent of the world's fresh water is locked in Antarctica's ice sheet.

3. If all that ice melted, sea levels would rise about 200 feet (60 meters).

4. In some places, the ice in Antarctica is 2.7 miles (4.5 km) thick.

5. Almost 99 percent of the continent is covered with ice.

6. Antarctica is a desert.

7. The average yearly rainfall at the South Pole is just 0.4 inch (10 mm).

8. If you stand at the South Pole, every direction is north.

9. Antarctica has two active volcanoes.

10. Antarctica is the fifth-largest continent.

11. Blood Falls is a waterfall that stains the ice blood-red.

12. The red color occurs because the water has a high iron contact. When the iron comes in contact with oxygen, it turns red.

13. In 1959, 12 countries signed the Antarctic Treaty. The treaty states that the nations would govern the continent together and it would be reserved for "peace and science."

14. Since 1959, 48 countries have signed the Antarctic Treaty.

15. Antarctica is the only continent that does not have an indigenous, or native, population.

16. No one lives permanently in Antarctica. However, scientists live and work there for part of the year.

17. Penguins and seals are among the animals that live in Antarctica.

18. The name Antarctica comes from a Greek word meaning "opposite of the north."

19. Antarctica isn't just the coldest continent; it is also the windiest.

20. Wind speeds can reach up to 200 miles (320 km) per hour.

21. Antarctica's Gamburtsev Mountains rise up to 9,000 feet (3,000 meters) and are completely covered by more than 15,000 feet (4,572 meters) of ice.

22. Antarctica's Ross Ice Shelf measures 197,000 square miles (510,680 square km).

23. Antarctica wasn't discovered until 1820.

24. Norwegian explorer Roald Amundsen was the first person to reach the South Pole, on December 14, 1911.

25. British explorer Robert Falcon Scott was also trying to be the first person to the South Pole. He arrived just over a month after Amundsen.

26. Scott and his team died on the journey back.

27. Antarctica has only two seasons: winter and summer.

28. The continent has six months of sunlight and six months of darkness.

29. The continent also has about 200 lakes buried under the ice.

30. The largest of these lakes is Lake Vostok. It is covered by 2.5 miles (3.7 km) of solid ice.

50

FANTASTIC FACTS ABOUT THE FIVE SENSES

1. Sound waves travel into our ears. These vibrations are picked up by tiny hairs that turn them into electrical signals.

2. The brain figures out what sounds you are hearing.

3. If the tiny hairs in your ears are damaged or lost, you will lose your hearing.

4. Our outer ears are curved to help gather sounds.

5. Your inner ears are responsible for both hearing and balance.

6. Your ears keep working even while you are asleep.

7. The inner ear is found inside the temporal bone, which is the hardest bone in the body.

8. Some animals do not have outer ears.

9. Snakes hear through their jawbones.

10. Fish "hear" by sensing changes in pressure.

11. There are five different tastes: sweet, sour, salty, bitter, and umami (savory).

12. Each person has between 2,000 and 10,000 taste buds on their tongue.

13. Taste buds are also found on the inside of your mouth and throat.

14. The senses of taste and smell work together. You can't taste something you can't smell.

15. Taste buds only live for five to ten days.

16. Your body is constantly producing new taste buds.

17. Taste buds are the only sensory organs that can regenerate.

18. Taste buds can protect you from eating spoiled or dangerous foods.

19. Each taste bud has tiny nerve hairs. These nerves send signals about the taste to the brain.

20. You don't sense different flavors on different parts of your tongue.

21. Your eyes can focus on 50 different objects a second.

22. The brain is the only organ more complicated than the eye.

23. Your eyes have special cells called rods and cones.

24. Rods see shapes. Cones detect colors.

25. The optic nerve has more than a million nerve cells.

26. Your pupil can contract faster than any other part of your body. It can close in just 1/100th of a second.

27. Babies can only see black, white, and red until they are about two months old.

28. Your eyeballs grow as you age.

29. If your eyeball is too long, you will be nearsighted. If it's too short, you're farsighted.

30. Parts of your eye can get sunburned.

31. People can detect at least one trillion scents.

32. When odors enter the nose, they travel up to receptors at the top of the nose. These receptors send signals to the brain.

33. Your body produces new scent cells every 30 to 60 days.

34. Women usually have a better sense of smell than men.

35. Dogs have about 44 times more scent receptors than humans do.

36. Each human has their own distinct smell, except identical twins. They smell the same.

37. The sense of smell has a stronger link to the emotional parts of the brain than any other sense.

38. Our sense of smell is better later in the day than it is in the morning.

39. Our sense of smell is stronger in the spring and summer because of added moisture in the air.

40. About 5 percent of the population is anosmic. They lack the sense of smell.

41. Touch is the only sense that is found all over the body.

42. Tiny receptors under our skin send nerve signals to the brain when we touch something.

43. Some parts of the body have more receptors than others, such as the back.

44. Your lips, tongue, face, and fingers have the most receptors.

45. Your back, chest, and thighs have the fewest.

46. Women usually have a better sense of touch than men.

47. The skin is the largest organ in the human body.

48. Scientists think fingerprints amplify the sense of touch.

49. Scratching an itch feels good because the scratching sends a different signal to our brain that helps it ignore the itch—until you stop scratching, of course!

50. Touch is the first sense we develop in the womb.

50 WET FACTS

1. Rain forests cover about 6 percent of Earth's land.

2. The largest rain forests are in South America, Southeast Asia, and western Africa.

3. Tropical rain forests are located near the equator.

4. Tropical rain forests are very warm, with temperatures around 86°F (30°C).

5. Temperate rain forests are cooler than tropical rain forests.

6. They are located in the northwestern parts of North America, New Zealand, and a few other countries.

7. Rain forests are found on every continent except Antarctica.

8. Brazil and Indonesia have the largest amount of rain forest.

9. Rain forests have four layers: the emergent layer, the canopy, the understory, and the forest floor.

ABOUT RAIN FORESTS

10. The emergent layer is the top layer. The trees here can be between 230 feet (70 meters) and 328 feet (100 meters) tall.

11. The leaves of these tall trees are coated with wax to protect them from the intense heat, heavy rain, and high winds.

12. Because branches at the tops of these trees are thin, only small animals live in the emergent layer.

13. These animals include birds, bats, and small monkeys.

14. Most rain forest trees are in the canopy layer.

15. These trees are about 100 feet (30 meters) tall.

16. About 90 percent of rain forest animals live in the canopy.

17. The understory is very humid and hot.

18. The understory is home to vines, bushes, ferns, climbing plants, and small trees.

19. Many insects live in the understory.

20. The forest floor only receives about 2 percent of the sunlight.

21. Fallen fruit and leaves decay on the forest floor and provide many nutrients.

22. The forest floor is home to large animals, such as tigers, jaguars, and tapirs.

23. Animals that live in the top layers of the rain forest rarely or never come down to the ground.

24. It can take up to 10 minutes for a raindrop to travel from the canopy to the floor.

25. If the Amazon rain forest were a country, it would be the ninth-largest country in the world.

26. A forest has to get between 98 and 177 inches (250 to 450 cm) of rain a year to be called a rain forest.

27. Many ingredients used in modern medicine come from rain forest plants.

28. A 4-square-mile (10-square-km) area of rain forest contains as many as 1,500 flowering plants, 750 species of trees, 400 species of birds, and 150 species of butterflies.

29. Rain forests are home to 50 percent of the world's plants and animals.

30. About 70 percent of the plants identified by the US National Cancer Institute as useful in the treatment of cancer are found only in rain forests.

31. Scientists have identified more than 2,000 tropical forest plants as having anti-cancer properties.

32. Less than 1 percent of tropical rain forest species have been analyzed for their medicinal value.

33. Between 2000 and 2012, more than 720,000 square miles (2 million square km) of forests around the world were cut down.

34. Rain forests are cut down for ranching, mining, logging, and agriculture.

35. About 80 percent of the natural foods we eat originally came from rain forests.

36. These foods include rice, bananas, potatoes, mangoes, coffee, and cacao.

37. Roughly 20 percent of the world's fresh water supply is located in the Amazon basin.

38. Rain forests are Earth's oldest living ecosystem.

39. They have been around for tens of millions of years.

40. There are 225 species of amphibians in the Amazon rain forest.

41. Rain forests help regulate Earth's weather patterns and temperature.

42. About 50 million indigenous people live in rain forests.

43. There are more freshwater fish in rain forest waterways than anywhere else.

44. Although rain forests are often cleared for agriculture, the land there is not good for farming because the soil has few nutrients.

45. The rain forest is home to many scary and dangerous animals.

46. The green anaconda is the largest snake in the world. It measures up to 30 feet (9 meters) long and weighs more than 500 pounds (227 kg).

47. The Amazon is home to the dangerous bull shark, which can weigh up to 700 pounds (318 kg). This shark eats many different animals and has been known to attack humans.

48. The Amazon's electric eel can still give a nasty shock 8 hours after its death.

49. Poison dart frogs are small, colorful, and deadly. Indigenous people once dipped their blow darts into their poison.

50. The golden poison frog has enough poison to kill 10 men.

50 AMAZING FACTS ABOUT ASIA

1. Asia is the largest continent.

2. It covers more than 17 million square miles (44 million square km).

3. That's about one-third of all the land on Earth.

4. Asia has both the highest and lowest points on Earth.

5. It also has the longest coastline.

6. Asia is surrounded by three oceans.

7. About 4.6 billion of the 7.7 billion people in the world live in Asia.

8. China and India both have populations of more than 1 billion people.

9. China has the largest population in the world.

10. Hundreds of different languages are spoken in Asia.

11. The most common are English, Arabic, and Mandarin Chinese.

12. The Caspian Sea is Asia's largest lake.

13. The Caspian Sea's coast touches five different countries.

14. They are Russia, Turkmenistan, Kazakhstan, Azerbaijan, and Iran.

15. The Caspian Sea is one of the deepest lakes in the world at 3,300 feet (1,000 meters).

16. The word Asia may come from the ancient Assyrian word asu, which means "east."

17. Islands make up about 7 percent of Asia's land.

18. Asia's Mount Everest is the tallest mountain in the world. It is 29,035 feet (8,850 meters) high.

19. Mount Everest is part of the Himalayas, which is the highest mountain range in the world.

20. The lowest point on Earth is the Dead Sea, which is 1,410 feet (430 meters) below sea level.

21. Asia's coastline covers about 39,000 miles (62,800 km).

22. All the world's major religions started in Asia.

23. Borneo is the largest island in Asia and the third-largest island in the world.

24. Borneo belongs to three countries: Malaysia, Brunei, and Indonesia.

25. Other large Asian islands include Sumatra, Honshu, and Celebes.

26. Asia includes 48 countries.

27. Russia is the largest country in Asia.

28. Maldives is the smallest.

29. Maldives is a chain of islands. They cover just 116 square miles (300 square km).

30. Asia's longest river is the Yangtze in China.

31. The Yangtze is also called Chang Jiang.

32. It is 3,964 miles (6,380 km) long.

33. Tokyo, Japan, is Asia's largest city.

34. Mongolia's Gobi Desert is the driest place in Asia.

35. Asia has 12 countries with no coastline.

36. They are Uzbekistan, Armenia, Turkmenistan, Kyrgyzstan, Afghanistan, Tajikistan, Laos, Mongolia, Kazakhstan, Nepal, Bhutan, and Azerbaijan.

37. Asia is home to many endangered animals.

38. Many venomous snakes live in Asia.

39. These snakes include the king cobra and the Malayan pit viper.

40. Asia's main natural resources are minerals, oil, and natural gas.

41. Saudi Arabia produces more oil than any other nation.

42. Indonesia is the only Asian country located entirely in the Southern Hemisphere.

43. Some of Earth's oldest civilizations began in Asia.

44. Even though China is one of the world's largest countries, it has only one time zone.

45. Russia has 11 time zones.

46. About 90 percent of the world's rice is eaten in Asia.

47. The highest number of billionaires in the world live in Asia.

48. Nine of the top ten tallest buildings are found in Asia.

 49. The ten largest shopping malls in the world are all in Asia.

50. Asia is the only continent that borders two other continents: Europe and Africa.

40 SUPER SOCCER FACTS

1. The earliest versions of soccer can be traced back 3,000 years.

2. The British established the rules for modern soccer in 1863.

3. In most parts of the world, soccer is called football.

4. Soccer is the most popular game in the world.

5. More than 250 million people in 200 countries play soccer.

6. At any point during a soccer game, 11 players should be on the field for each team.

7. Only the goalie can touch the ball with their hands.

8. Other players use their feet, bodies, and heads to move the ball.

9. Soccer is the only major sport where players can't use their hands to move the ball.

10. In Europe during the Middle Ages, soccer balls were made from inflated pig bladders.

11. In ancient China, soccer balls were made of clothes filled with rubble.

12. A traditional soccer ball has 32 panels.

13. Each panel represents a nation in Europe.

14. Soccer balls are actually slightly oval in shape. The pattern on the ball makes it look round.

15. An international soccer game is 90 minutes long.

16. The game is divided into two 45-minute halves.

17. A regulation soccer field must be between 100 to 130 yards (91 to 119 meters) long and 50 to 100 yards (46 to 91 meters) wide.

18. The Fédération Internationale de Football Association (FIFA) governs international soccer.

19. FIFA sponsors the World Cup championships.

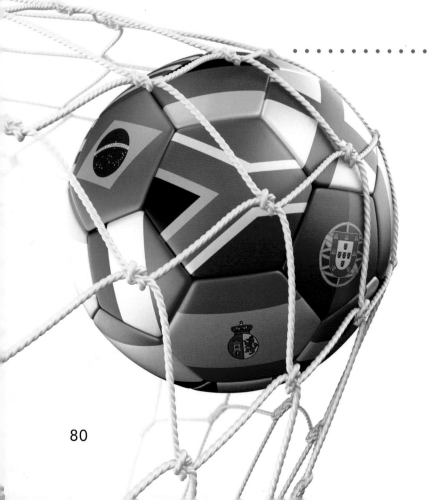

20. The World Cup is the most-watched sporting event in the world.

21. The first World Cup was held in Uruguay in 1930. Uruguay won.

22. Brazilian star Pelé is considered to be the best soccer player of all time.

23. Pelé played in his first World Cup in 1958 when he was 17. He was the youngest to ever play in a World Cup game.

24. He scored six goals and led Brazil to victory.

25. After the 1958 World Cup, Brazil declared Pelé a national treasure to prevent him from playing for any other country.

26. Pelé scored 1,280 goals in 1,360 games during his career.

27. The Women's World Cup was created in 1991.

28. The United States has won more Women's World Cups than any other country.

29. The 1999 Women's World Cup final was the most-watched soccer game in US television history.

30. Soccer matches in England did not have referees until 1881. Instead, they relied on good sportsmanship.

31. FIFA uses a microchip in the ball and sensors in the goal to track the ball to make sure a goal is actually scored.

32. As of 2018, the World Cup has only been held outside of South America or Europe three times in its history.

33. Those three events were held in the United States, South Africa, and jointly between Japan and South Korea.

34. Only seven countries have won the men's World Cup.

35. Those countries are Uruguay, Italy, Brazil, Germany, Argentina, England, and Spain.

36. Approximately 1.1 billion people watched the 2006 World Cup final.

37. More than 3 million young people play soccer in the United States.

38. The biggest blowout in soccer history was a 149-0 score between two teams in Madagascar.

39. Soccer players can run up to 9.5 miles (15 km) in a single match.

40. The first soccer goals were wicker baskets.

50 DEADLY FACTS ABOUT DISEASES

10 REALLY STRANGE AND RARE DISEASES

1. **Fatal Familiar Insomnia:** a hereditary disease that causes permanent insomnia

2. **Aquagenic Urticaria:** an allergy to water

3. **Electromagnetic Hypersensitivity:** a severe reaction to electromagnetic radiation

4. **Cotard's Delusion:** a condition where sufferers think they're dead

5. **Exploding Head Syndrome:** causes extremely loud noises in your head

6. **Fibrodysplasia:** a genetic disease that causes body tissue to turn into bone

7. **Xeroderma:** a severe reaction to sunlight

8. **Argyria:** a build-up of silver in the body that turns the skin blue

9. **Progeria:** a disease that causes people to age seven times faster

10. **Pica:** a disease that causes patients to crave eating paint, dirt, and other nonfoods

TOP 10 DEADLIEST PANDEMICS IN HISTORY

1.	Bubonic Plague	1347–1351	200 million deaths
2.	Smallpox	1520	56 million deaths
3.	Spanish Flu	1918–1919	40–50 million deaths
4.	Plague of Justinian	541–542	30–50 million deaths
5.	HIV/AIDS	1981–present	25–35 million deaths
6.	Third Plague	1855	12 million deaths
7.	Antonine Plague	165–180	5 million deaths
8.	17th Century Plague	1600	3 million deaths
9.	Asian Flu	1958–1959	1.1 million deaths
10.	Russian Flu	1889–1890	1 million deaths

10 Myths and Facts About the Common Cold

10 FLU FACTS

1. *Flu* is short for *influenza*.

2. Flu is caused by a virus. There are different strains of flu viruses.

3. Between 5 and 20 percent of Americans contract the flu each year.

4. Between 3 and 5 million catch the flu worldwide each year.

5. Between 290,000 and 650,000 people die of the flu each year.

6. The flu virus can survive on surfaces for 2 to 8 hours.

7. Flu season usually lasts between October and April.

8. Flu season peaks in December and February.

9. The first flu vaccine was developed in 1938.

10. The Centers for Disease Control recommend that everyone 6 months or older get the flu vaccine each year.

MYTHS	FACTS
1. You can catch a cold by going outside with wet hair.	2. Colds are caused by viruses, not temperature.
3. Antibiotics can cure a cold.	4. Colds are caused by viruses. Antibiotics treat bacterial infections.
5. Chicken soup can cure a cold.	6. Chicken soup can help you feel better, but there is no cure for the common cold.
7. An upper respiratory infection is more serious than a cold.	8. Upper respiratory infection is just a fancy name for the common cold.
9. All colds are the same.	10. Colds can be caused by many different viruses.

Top 10 Deadliest Diseases in the World

1. Coronary Artery Disease
2. Stroke
3. Lower Respiratory Infections
4. Chronic Obstructive Pulmonary Disease
5. Respiratory Cancers
6. Diabetes
7. Alzheimer's Disease and Dementia
8. Dehydration from Diarrheal Diseases
9. Tuberculosis
10. Cirrhosis of the Liver

15 UNUSUAL ANIMAL FRIENDSHIPS

Sometimes animals can pair up in unusual and surprising ways. Animals that would usually be predator and prey become friends instead. Or animals from two completely different species are thrown together and discover they really like each other. Animals can become friends if they are raised together. Other animals just find each other and form a friendship that's meant to be!

1. **Cassie and Moses:** A couple in Massachusetts noticed a crow bringing food to an orphaned kitten and protecting the tiny animal from predators. After Cassie the kitten was taken inside, Moses the crow pecked at the door every morning, and the two, who should have been enemies, spent the days hanging outside together.

2. **Sahara and Alexa:** This cheetah and dog were raised together by a worker at the Cincinnati Zoo. The two lived together at the zoo and went on tours to promote cheetah conservation.

3. **Themba and Albert:** Orphaned baby elephant Themba went to live in a sanctuary in South Africa. He spent the first day chasing Albert, a sheep, around their enclosure. By the next day, the two were buddies.

4. **Leo, Baloo, and Shere Khan:** Police found the young, abused lion, bear, and tiger in the basement of a house. The three were moved to an animal sanctuary. When Baloo needed surgery, his two feline buddies cried and paced until Baloo returned.

5. **Simon Cow-Ell and Leonardo:** Simon the cow lost part of his hind leg and was sent to a sanctuary in Thailand to recover. He became close to Leonardo the tortoise. Simon follows Leonardo around and often lays with his head on the tortoise's shell.

6. **Anthony and Riley:** This lion and coyote duo lived together at an animal sanctuary in Arizona. The two were so close that when Anthony needed surgery, Riley had to go to the hospital with him or else he wouldn't eat.

7. **Owen and Mzee:** Owen the hippo was rescued after a tsunami struck Kenya. He met Mzee the tortoise at an animal sanctuary and the two became inseparable.

8. **J'aime and Joey:** Orphaned baby rhino J'aime was too small to be placed with the adult rhinos at a South African sanctuary, so she hung out with Joey, an orphaned lamb, instead. The two enjoyed taking walks and eating meals together. Later, they were joined by another lamb, Penny.

9. **Strong Impact and Charlie:** Like many racehorses, Strong Impact was high-strung and needed a buddy. Charlie the pig walked through the stable one day and chose Strong Impact as his friend.

10. **Suryia and Roscoe:** Roscoe was a stray dog who followed Suryia, an orangutan, and her handlers home to an American sanctuary one day. The handlers adopted Roscoe, and he and Suryia spend time cuddling, playing, and even swimming together.

11. **Kate and Pippin:** What do a baby deer and a Great Dane have in common? Not much, but that didn't stop this pair from becoming best friends. The two were featured in a National Geographic TV series.

12. **Bea and Wilma:** Bea the giraffe and Wilma the ostrich share a huge enclosure at Busch Gardens, but the two stay close together and can often be seen sitting together and touching heads.

13. **Tinni and Sniffer:** This dog and wild fox spend a lot of time together exploring the forests in Norway.

14. **Bonedigger and Milo:** Who says a 500-pound (227-kg) lion can't be friends with a tiny dachshund? Don't tell this amazing animal pair, who live together in an American sanctuary.

15. **Anjana and the tiger cubs:** Anjana is a chimpanzee who lives at a sanctuary in the United States. She often "adopts" orphaned tiger cubs and helps her human caretaker raise them.

40 EXPLOSIVE FACTS ABOUT VOLCANIC ERUPTIONS

1. The deadliest eruption in recent history was Mt. Tambora in Indonesia.

2. Mt. Tambora erupted in 1815 and killed as many as 120,000 people.

3. The eruption sent volcanic ash 25 miles (40 km) into the sky.

4. Tambora's eruption caused the global temperature to drop and led to crop failures around the world.

5. When Krakatoa erupted in Indonesia in 1883, it completely destroyed the island it sat on.

6. Krakatoa's eruption has been called the loudest sound in history.

7. The eruption could be heard thousands of miles (km) away.

8. Krakatoa's eruption and the following tsunamis killed more than 36,000 people.

9. When a volcano named Laki erupted in Iceland in 1783, toxic gases poisoned crops and killed more than half of Iceland's livestock.

10. It also killed more than 10,000 people in Iceland.

11. Toxic gases traveled to Great Britain and killed another 23,000 people.

12. The Laki eruption lasted for eight months.

13. People thought the Mt. Pele volcano on the island of Martinique was dormant. They were wrong.

14. Mt. Pele erupted in 1902, burying the city of Saint Pierre and killing more than 28,000 people.

15. Only two people in Saint Pierre survived. One was a prisoner locked in an underground cell.

16. The eruption also capsized 15 ships in the harbor.

17. It was the most powerful eruption in the twentieth century.

18. Japan's deadliest volcanic eruption was Mt. Unzen in 1792.

19. The eruption caused a landslide that buried the city of Shimabara.

20. When the landslide flowed into the ocean, it created tsunami waves 187 feet (57 meters) high.

21. The Mt. Unzen eruption killed about 15,000 people.

22. Colombia's Nevada del Ruiz eruption caused a mudslide that killed 20,000 people.

23. Nevada del Ruiz caused $1 billion in damages, making it the most expensive volcano eruption.

24. The second-largest eruption in the twentieth century was Mt. Pinatubo in the Philippines.

25. The 1991 eruption left 200,000 people homeless.

26. When Mt. Vesuvius erupted in Italy in the year 79, it buried the cities of Pompeii and Herculaneum.

27. The hot, toxic gases of the eruption killed 2,000 people in an instant.

28. Pompeii and Herculaneum were buried and preserved under layers of volcanic ash.

29. The most destructive volcanic eruption in the United States was Mt. Saint Helens in Washington on May 18, 1980.

30. The Mt. St. Helens eruption killed 57 people and thousands of animals.

31. About 200 square miles (518 square km) of trees were blown down by the eruption and the mudflows that followed.

32. In 1982, the area around Mt. St. Helens was named a National Volcanic Monument. Visitors can tour the area and see how nature has reclaimed the land.

33. Mauna Loa in Hawaii is the largest active volcano on Earth.

34. Its last eruption was in 1984.

35. In 2010, the Eyjafjallajökull volcano erupted in Iceland and sent huge clouds of ash into the air. European air travel was disrupted for a week.

36. Planes could not fly after the eruption because the ash would cover the windows and damage the engines.

37. In 1943, a farmer in Mexico was working in the fields when the ground suddenly cracked open in front of him and ash and rocks burst from the ground. It was the birth of a volcano named Paricutin.

38. Paricutin erupted from 1943 until 1952.

39. Scientists rushed to Paricutin. Until then, they had never been able to watch a volcano form.

40. The eruption buried two villages in tons of lava and rocks.

51 WONDERFUL WOMEN IN SPORTS

1. **Babe Didrikson Zaharias:** Considered by many to be the best female athlete of all time, Zaharias excelled at track and field, golf, and baseball.

2. **Jackie Joyner-Kersee:** Possibly America's greatest track-and-field athlete, Joyner-Kersee won 6 Olympic medals in the heptathlon and long jump.

3. **Ronda Rousey:** Considered one of the greatest female athletes ever, Rousey is the only woman to win both a UFC and WWE championship.

4. **Billie Jean King:** One of the greatest women's tennis players of all time and winner of 39 Grand Slam titles.

5. **Lindsey Vonn:** One of the greatest skiers of all time, Vonn won 4 skiing World Cups as well as a gold medal in the 2010 Winter Olympics.

6. **Sonja Henie:** Considered one of the top figure skaters of all time, this Norwegian won multiple Olympic, World, and European championships between 1928 and 1936.

7. **Katie Ledecky:** This swimmer won her first Olympic medal when she was 15 and went on to win a record 5 Olympic gold medals and 14 world championship gold medals.

8. **Simone Biles:** The most decorated American gymnast, Biles has achieved moves that no one else has even attempted.

9. **Missy Franklin:** This swimmer was the first American woman to win 4 gold medals in a single Olympics.

10. **Megan Rapinoe:** This outspoken soccer star helped lead the US women's team to victory in the 2019 World Cup.

11. **Martina Navratilova:** This top tennis player won the Wimbledon title a record 9 times and is the only player ranked #1 in singles and #1 in doubles for more than 200 weeks.

12. **Annika Sörenstam:** Considered one of the best female golfers of all time, this Swedish American athlete won 90 international tournaments.

13. **Bonnie Blair:** An American speed skater who dominated the sport and won 6 Olympic medals between 1988 and 1994.

14. **Wilma Rudolph:** This track-and-field star was the first American woman to win 3 gold medals in a single Olympics.

15. **Nadia Comaneci:** This Romanian gymnast stunned the world when she scored 7 perfect 10s at the 1976 Olympics.

16. **Serena Williams:** One of the greatest women's tennis players, she dominated the courts in the twenty-first century.

17. **Venus Williams:** Serena's older sister and another dominant tennis player.

18. **Florence Griffith Joyner:** This American track-and-field star has been called the fastest woman in the world.

19. **Mia Hamm:** This soccer star led the US team to victory in the 1999 World Cup.

20. **Mary Lou Retton:** In 1984, Retton became the first American woman to win the all-around gold medal in gymnastics.

21. **Steffi Graf:** The only tennis player to win each Grand Slam tournament at least 4 times and win all 4 Grand Slams plus an Olympic gold medal in the same calendar year.

22. **Michelle Kwan:** Kwan is the most decorated American figure skater in history.

23. **Larisa Latynina:** This Russian athlete holds the record for the most Olympic gold medals by any gymnast with 9. She won a total of 18 medals for the Soviet Union between 1956 and 1964.

24. **Marta Vieira da Silva:** This Brazilian soccer player is one of the best of all time, and the first to score at five FIFA Women's World Cups.

25. **Olga Korbut:** This teenage Soviet gymnast won 3 gold medals at the 1972 Olympics and has several moves named after her.

26. **Danica Patrick:** The most successful woman to drive race cars, she finished third in the Indy 500 and had a great impact on the sport.

27. **Joan Benoit Samuelson:** American distance runner who won the first Olympic women's marathon in 1984.

28. **Julie Krone:** American jockey who was the first female to win a leg of the Triple Crown at the Belmont Stakes in 1993.

29. **Ann Meyers:** American basketball player and the only woman to sign with an NBA team.

30. **Suzanne Lenglen:** This French player was one of tennis's biggest stars in the 1920s, winning Wimbledon 6 times and changing women's tennis with her athletic style of play.

31. **Jean Driscoll:** American wheelchair racer who won the Boston Marathon's wheelchair division 7 consecutive times in the 1990s.

32. **Grete Waitz:** This Norwegian distance runner was the first to complete a marathon in under two-and-a-half hours.

33. **Susan Butcher:** This American sled-dog racer dominated the sport in the 1980s and became the first woman to win 3 consecutive Iditarod races.

34. **Gertrude Ederle:** An American distance swimmer and Olympic medalist, Ederle became the first woman to swim across the English Channel in 1926.

35. **Diana Nyad:** American swimmer who holds many distance records, including swims between Cuba and Florida, the Bahamas to Florida, and around the island of Manhattan.

36. **Misty May-Treanor and Kerri Walsh**
37. **Jennings:** The greatest beach volleyball team of all time, May-Treanor and Jennings won 3 consecutive Olympic gold medals between 2004 and 2012.

38. **Diana Taurasi:** The all-time leading scorer in the WNBA, Taurasi is one of the few women to win an Olympic gold medal, a WNBA championship, and an NCAA championship.

39. **Astrid Benöhr:** Called the toughest woman in the world, this German holds world records in the Triple Ultra Triathlon, which she won every year between 1992 and 2006.

40. **Yu Chui Lee:** This Chinese athlete has won 7 gold medals in wheelchair fencing at the Paralympics.

41. **Terezinha Guilhermina:** This blind Brazilian runner is one of the fastest women alive, with numerous Paralympic and World Championship medals.

42. **Bethany Hamilton:** This American surfer lost her left arm in a shark attack when she was 13 but went on to win many competitions and championships.

43. **Lisa Leslie:** This WNBA star once scored 101 points in a high-school game. She led the US team to 4 Olympic gold medals between 1996 and 2008.

44. **Nancy Lopez:** An American golfer who won 48 LPGA Tour events and the youngest woman to qualify for the LPGA Hall of Fame.

45. **Tracy Caulkins:** Called one of the best competitive swimmers of all time, this American won 48 national championships and set records in all four swimming strokes.

46. **Chris Evert:** One of the most dominant women in tennis during the 1970s, Evert achieved records that have yet to be broken.

47. **Abby Wambach:** This American soccer star has scored more goals than any other player—184 goals in international competition.

48. **Toni Stone:** Stone became the first woman to play professional baseball when she joined the Negro League team the Indianapolis Clowns.

49. **Flo Hyman:** A groundbreaking volleyball player, Hyman was a star at the Olympics and the World Championships in the 1970s and 1980s.

50. **Shannon Miller:** American gymnast who won 7 Olympic medals and was a member of the "Magnificent Seven," the first US team to win gold in the women's all-around.

51. **Jennie Finch:** American softball pitcher who led the US team to a gold medal at the 2004 Olympics and a silver at the 2008 Games.

75 PRESIDENTIAL FACTS

1. John Adams was the first president to live in the White House.

2. James Madison was the shortest president, at just 5 feet, 4 inches (1.63 meters) tall.

3. Abraham Lincoln was the tallest. He was 6 feet, 4 inches (1.9 meters) tall.

4. John Tyler had 15 children.

5. Two of Tyler's grandchildren were still alive in the twentieth century.

6. George Washington's false teeth were made of ivory, gold, and elephant and walrus tusks.

7. James Buchanan was the only president who never married.

8. Abraham Lincoln is honored in the Wrestling Hall of Fame.

9. Ulysses S. Grant once got a ticket for speeding—on a horse!

10. Rutherford B. Hayes was the first president to have a telephone.

11. Hayes's phone number was 1.

12. Benjamin Harrison had electricity installed in the White House.

13. However, he was too afraid of it to touch the light switches.

14. James Garfield could write Latin with one hand and Greek with the other at the same time.

15. Abraham Lincoln was the first president to be assassinated.

16. Grover Cleveland was the only president to be married in the White House.

17. Cleveland is also the only president to serve two non-consecutive terms.

18. William Taft later served as a Supreme Court Justice.

19. Taft swore in Presidents Calvin Coolidge and Herbert Hoover.

20. There have been four presidential assassinations: Lincoln, Garfield, McKinley, and Kennedy.

21. Theodore Roosevelt and Franklin D. Roosevelt were cousins.

William McKinley

Theodore Roosevelt

22. There have been two father-and-son presidential pairs: John and John Quincy Adams and George H.W. and George W. Bush.

23. Calvin Coolidge's nickname was Silent Cal.

24. Bill Clinton was the first president to hold an internet chat, in 1999.

25. George H.W. Bush loved to wear colorful socks.

26. James Madison was Princeton University's first graduate student.

27. Monrovia, the capital of Liberia, is named after James Monroe.

28. John Quincy Adams enjoyed skinny-dipping in the Potomac River.

29. Andrew Jackson fought in more than 100 duels.

30. James Buchanan regularly bought slaves in the South and brought them to Pennsylvania, where he set them free.

31. Three presidents—Andrew Johnson, Bill Clinton, and Donald Trump—have been impeached by the House of Representatives.

32. Nixon is the only president to resign from office.

33. Gerald Ford, who replaced Nixon, was never actually elected to the presidency.

34. Ronald Reagan was a successful movie actor before becoming president.

35. While he was president, Grover Cleveland had a secret surgery to remove a cancerous tumor from his mouth.

36. Theodore Roosevelt was shot while giving a speech. He continued speaking for 90 minutes.

37. William Taft, the heaviest president, weighed 340 pounds (154 kg).

38. James Madison was the lightest. He weighed 100 pounds (45 kg).

39. Woodrow Wilson's face is on the $100,000 bill.

40. Herbert Hoover's son had two pet alligators that lived in the White House.

41. He also had an opossum.

42. Theodore Roosevelt had many unusual pets while he was president, including a pig, several bears, a badger, a snake named Emily Spinach, and a one-legged rooster.

43. Calvin Coolidge had a pet raccoon named Rebecca that walked on a leash.

44. Franklin Roosevelt was the only president to serve four terms.

45. Gerald Ford worked as a fashion model during college.

46. Several pro football teams wanted to draft Ford after he graduated from college.

47. Jimmy Carter once reported seeing a UFO.

48. Martin Van Buren was the first president born in the United States.

49. William Henry Harrison was only president for a month before dying of pneumonia.

50. Millard Fillmore and his wife established the first White House library.

51. Andrew Johnson came from a very poor family and never went to school.

52. His wife taught him to read and write.

53. The middle initial "S" in Ulysses S. Grant's and Harry S. Truman's names doesn't stand for anything.

54. Rutherford B. Hayes started the traditional Easter Egg Roll on the White House lawn.

55. Woodrow Wilson was the first president to give a speech over the radio.

56. Franklin Roosevelt's radio broadcasts were called "Fireside Chats."

57. Calvin Coolidge was born on the Fourth of July.

58. Herbert Hoover was the first president born west of the Mississippi River.

59. Lyndon Johnson is the only president to be sworn in on an airplane.

60. He is also the only president sworn in by a woman.

61. Ronald Reagan was the first divorced president.

62. Bill Clinton won two Grammy awards for spoken word recordings.

63. Jimmy Carter and Barack Obama have also won Grammys.

64. Theodore Roosevelt, Woodrow Wilson, Jimmy Carter, and Barack Obama have all won the Nobel Peace Prize.

65. Donald Trump is the first president who did not have a background in politics or the military.

66. Trump appeared in several movies and TV shows and starred in the reality show *The Apprentice*.

67. Eight presidents were left-handed.

68. They were James Garfield, Herbert Hoover, Harry Truman, Gerald Ford, Ronald Reagan, George H.W. Bush, Bill Clinton, and Barack Obama.

69. Only five presidents have had beards.

70. All were president during the nineteenth century.

71. Five presidents did not have biological children.

72. They were George Washington, James Madison, Andrew Jackson, James Polk, and James Buchanan.

73. Washington adopted his wife's two children from a previous marriage.

74. Five men became president without winning the popular vote: John Quincy Adams, Rutherford B. Hayes, Benjamin Harrison, George H.W. Bush, and Donald Trump.

75. Jimmy Carter became the longest living president in March 2019, at age 94 years, 172 days.

TOP SECRET

30 SUPER SPY FACTS

1. During the 1960s, the CIA, a US spy agency, spent $15 million trying to use cats to spy on the Soviet Union.

2. Shocker: It didn't work.

3. During World War II, tiny cameras were attached to homing pigeons to film German military positions.

4. In 1917, the Germans replaced a real tree with a fake one so a spy could hide inside.

5. It took seven months for anyone to notice the tree was fake.

6. Ian Fleming, the author of the James Bond novels, was himself a spy.

7. James Bond was based on a real person who was a friend of Ian Fleming's.

8. In 1963, Kim Philby, the head of British intelligence's anti-Soviet unit, was revealed as a Soviet spy.

9. Philby escaped to the Soviet Union before he could be arrested.

10. The cameras in spy satellites can photograph license plates from 50 miles (80 km) up in space.

11. Paul Revere formed a spy ring called the Mechanics. The spies reported British troop movements.

12. Confederate leader Jefferson Davis thought his dinner was being served by his slave, Little Mary. Little Mary was actually a spy who passed information back to the Union.

13. The Culper Spy Ring was one of the largest spy operations in the American Revolution.

14. One of the members of the Culper Spy Ring was a woman known only as 355.

15. 355's identity remains unknown to this day.

16. Spies often hide secret papers or radio transmitters in ordinary objects.

17. These objects can include pipes, eyeglasses, and baseballs.

18. In 1953, a boy delivering newspapers was paid with a hollow coin. Inside was a coded message. The coin turned out to be from a Russian spy.

19. Spies often hide their true identity from their own family members.

20. The US Navy has trained dolphins to locate and report underwater mines.

21. It is against international law for governments to force anyone under age eighteen to be a spy.

22. Ex-Russian spy Alexander Litvenenko fled to Great Britain in 2000. Six years later, he died of radiation poisoning after drinking poisoned tea with two Russian agents.

23. Juan Pujol Garcia was a British double agent during World War II. He told Hitler D-Day would be at a different location than it really was. Hitler awarded Garcia a medal.

24. Garcia also received a medal from Great Britain for deceiving Hitler!

25. During World War II, fake charity groups gave special *Monopoly* games to prisoners of war.

26. These games included tools and real money to help the prisoners escape.

27. A British spy named Frederick Bailey created elaborate drawings of butterflies. He hid information about the Russians inside the drawings.

28. Gevork Vartanian was a nineteen-year-old spy when he uncovered and stopped a plot to kill Franklin Roosevelt, Winston Churchill, and Joseph Stalin during a World War II meeting.

29. Hercules Mulligan was a tailor in New York City during the American Revolution. He passed along plans he overheard while measuring British officers for new clothes.

30. One of these plans was the capture of General George Washington.

25 RADICAL RACE CAR FACTS

1. Formula One race cars are the fastest. They travel up to 220 miles (360 km) per hour.

2. A Formula One car's exhaust is hot enough to melt aluminum.

3. The tailpipes of a Formula One car alone cost more than an average "regular" car.

4. The Monaco Grand Prix is raced on city streets.

5. The manholes along the Grand Prix's route need to be welded shut so the race cars don't suck them out of the road.

6. The average Formula One pit stop lasts just 3 seconds.

7. A top drag-race car can hit 300 miles (483 km) per hour in just over 3 seconds.

8. Dragsters deploy parachutes to slow down.

9. Dragsters can be heard up to 8 miles (13 km) away.

10. The first road race was held in France in 1895.

11. NASCAR stands for the National Association for Stock Car Auto Racing.

12. Stock cars are large sedans built especially for racing.

13. Stock cars have oversized engines that let the car travel more than 200 miles (322 km) per hour.

14. A Formula One race car's steering wheel can cost $50,000.

15. A Formula One car has no dashboard.

16. All the controls and indicators are mounted on the steering wheel.

17. The "500" in Indy 500 stands for 500 miles, the length of the race.

18. It takes 200 laps to complete the Indy 500.

19. The first Indy 500 took place in 1911.

20. The winner, Ray Harroun, drove at an average speed under 75 miles (121 km) per hour.

21. Today's Indy 500 winners average between 140 miles (225 km) and 186 miles (299 km) per hour.

22. The temperature inside a Formula One car can reach 122°F (50°C).

23. A Formula One cockpit is so small, the driver has to remove the steering wheel to get out.

24. The 24 Hours of Le Mans race has happened almost every year in Le Mans, France, since 1923.

25. The deadliest auto racing accident occurred at Le Mans in 1955. A car flew into the crowd, killing the driver and 83 spectators.

100 WILD AND WEIRD WEATHER FACTS

1. All weather is caused by heat from the sun and movement of the air.

2. Weather happens in the lowest level of the Earth's atmosphere.

3. As the sun warms the air, that warm air rises.

4. Cold air rushes in underneath the warm air.

5. This movement creates wind.

6. Water evaporates on Earth and then rises as water vapor to form clouds.

7. There are six main components of weather.

8. They are temperature, atmospheric pressure, wind, humidity, precipitation, and cloudiness.

9. Scientists who study the weather are called meteorologists.

10. The coldest weather is usually found at the North and South Poles.

11. The warmest weather is usually found at the Equator.

12. A high-pressure weather system usually brings clear skies.

13. A low-pressure system usually brings storms.

14. Wind tends to blow from areas of high pressure to areas of low pressure.

15. Strong winds called the jet stream occur in the upper atmosphere, about 5 to 9 miles (8 to 15 km) above the Earth.

16. These winds push weather systems around the Earth.

17. Jet-stream winds usually blow at 80 to 140 miles (129 to 225 km) per hour.

18. Jet-stream winds can reach top speeds of more than 275 miles (443 km) per hour.

19. Because of the jet stream, weather systems usually move from east to west.

20. However, weather systems can move in any direction.

21. Humidity is the amount of moisture in the air.

22. When there is 100 percent humidity, it will rain. That's because the atmosphere cannot hold any more water.

23. Clouds come in a variety of forms. Not all of them produce precipitation.

24. Cirrus clouds are thin, wispy clouds. They usually signal mild weather.

25. Nimbostratus clouds produce steady precipitation over a period of time.

26. Enormous cumulonimbus clouds, or thunderheads, release heavy downpours.

27. Cumulonimbus clouds can also produce thunderstorms and tornadoes.

28. Because clouds affect the amount of sunlight reaching the Earth's surface, cloudy days are cooler than clear ones.

29. The opposite is true at night, when clouds act as a blanket, keeping the Earth warm.

30. Heat waves can bend train tracks.

31. Heat waves can also ground planes.

32. Hot air is less dense than cold air, so planes can have trouble taking off and landing in extreme heat.

33. You can figure out the temperature by counting a cricket's chirps and using a number of different formulas.

34. Sandstorms can swallow up entire cities.

35. A 2003 heat wave turned grapes into raisins.

36. Lightning often occurs after a volcanic eruption.

37. It sometimes rains frogs or fish.

38. This happens when a waterspout picks up animals from one place and drops them in another.

39. In July 2001, a blood-red rain fell in India.

40. The red color might have been caused by bits from a meteorite, or sand from the desert.

41. In 2015, a milky rain fell on parts of Washington, Oregon, and Idaho. The strange rain was caused by chemicals in a dust storm.

42. In England in 1894, jellyfish rained from the sky.

43. Eight alligators fell from the sky over South Carolina in 1887.

44. Rain contains vitamin B12.

45. Windstorms include tornadoes, dust devils, squalls, and gales.

46. Storms with a lot of precipitation include hailstorms, ice storms, snowstorms, blizzards, ocean storms, thunderstorms, and hurricanes.

47. Christopher Columbus encountered a tropical cyclone in 1494.

48. Columbus's notes were the first written account of this type of storm by a European.

49. Robert Fitzroy was the first weather forecaster.

50. Fitzroy was appointed to the position in England in 1860.

51. Fitzroy also started the practice of printing the weather forecast in daily newspapers.

52. In some mountains in Colorado and California, algae mixes with snow and turns it pink.

53. Sometimes lightning forms a ball. Scientists don't know what causes ball lightning.

54. Ball lightning was first captured on film in 2012.

55. Arica, Chile, went for 14 years without any rain.

56. Wind doesn't make a sound unless it blows against an object.

57. Fire whirls are tornadoes caused by wildfires.

58. It was so cold in 1684 that the Thames River in England froze solid for two months.

59. In 1932, it was so cold that Niagara Falls froze solid.

60. A cubic mile (4 cubic km) of fog contains less than a gallon of water.

61. In 1899, the Mississippi River froze down its entire length.

62. Chunks of ice were seen in the Gulf of Mexico.

63. The 1899 cold spell has been called the greatest cold snap in American history.

64. Snowflakes can take up to an hour to reach the ground.

65. The windiest city in the United States is Mt. Washington, New Hampshire, with an average wind speed of 35 miles (56 km) per hour.

66. The least windy city is Oak Ridge, Tennessee, with an average wind speed of 4 miles (6 km) per hour.

67. Weather balloons have been used to observe the atmosphere since the late 1930s.

68. Weather balloons are also called radiosondes.

69. Radiosondes are released two times a day from about a thousand locations around the world.

70. The US National Weather Service sends up radiosondes from more than 90 weather stations across the country.

71. In the United States, the Citizen Weather Observer Program depends on amateur meteorologists with homemade weather stations and Internet connections to provide forecasts.

72. The first weather satellite was launched on April 1, 1960.

73. Geostationary satellites track the weather over one region.

74. Other satellites orbit the Earth every 12 hours. They trace weather patterns over the entire part of the globe they orbit.

75. Conventional radar shows clouds and precipitation.

76. Doppler radar measures changes in wind speed and direction.

77. Doppler radar provides information within a range of about 143 miles (230 km).

78. Doppler radar allows meteorologists to forecast when and where severe thunderstorms and tornadoes develop.

79. Microbursts are powerful winds that originate in thunderstorms.

80. Microbursts are among the most dangerous weather a pilot can encounter.

81. If an aircraft attempts to land or take off through a microburst, the suddenly changing wind conditions can cause the craft to lose lift and crash.

82. In the United States alone, airline crashes because of microbursts have caused more than 600 deaths since 1964.

83. "Red sky in morning, sailors take warning/Red sky at night, sailors delight" is actually a weather prediction.

84. A red sky in the morning shows that the sun is reflecting off rain clouds.

85. A red sky at night indicates clear, calm weather.

86. In 1938, a hurricane formed in the Atlantic Ocean on January 1, making it the earliest-ever hurricane in the calendar year.

87. The heaviest snowfall recorded in Los Angeles occurred on January 10 to 11, 1949.

88. That total snowfall was just 0.3 inch (0.8 cm).

89. The world's biggest snowflake was reportedly observed in Montana in January 1887. A rancher described seeing a 15-inch (38-cm)-wide flake.

90. However, no one knows if the snowflake was actually that big.

91. Scientists used to think no two snowflakes were alike.

92. However, in 1988, a research center identified a set of twin crystals from a Wisconsin storm.

93. The Grand Banks of Newfoundland, Canada, see fog more than 200 days a year.

94. An estimated 1.23 inches (3 cm) of rain fell in a single minute on July 4, 1956, in Unionville, Maryland.

95. In 1925, the "Tri-State Tornado" traveled 219 miles (352 km) from Ellington, Missouri, to Princeton, Indiana, over 3.5 hours.

96. In April 1991, a tornado carried a cancelled personal check for 223 miles (359 km) from Stockton, Kansas, to Winnetoon, Nebraska.

97. A 253-mile (407-km)-per-hour wind gust blew through Barrow Island, Australia, in 1996.

98. Miami, Florida, is the rainiest city in the United States, with an average total of 62 inches (158 cm) per year.

99. The winds that create a tornado form on the ground and work their way up to the clouds.

100. Phoenix, Arizona, receives 211 days of sunshine a year.

45
SUPER SEA CREATURE FACTS

1. Jellyfish have been around for more than 650 million years.

2. A jellyfish's body is 95 percent water.

3. The box jellyfish kills more people each year than any other marine creature.

4. The box jellyfish's sting can kill in 3 minutes.

5. A box jellyfish has enough venom to kill 60 people.

6. The world's largest known jellyfish is the lion's mane jellyfish.

7. A specimen caught in 1870 measured 8 feet (2.5 meters) in diameter.

8. Its tentacles were half the length of a football field.

9. Sponges are older than dinosaurs.

10. An electric eel produces enough electricity to power 10 light bulbs.

11. An octopus has 3 hearts and blue blood.

12. An adult octopus can squeeze through a hole the size of a coin.

13. Octopuses are some of the smartest animals on Earth.

14. The blue whale makes the loudest animal sound on the planet. Their calls measure 188 decibels.

15. The sound of a whale's whistle can travel up to 500 miles (805 km).

16. Oysters can change from male to female and back again.

17. A shrimp's heart is in its head.

18. A sea star pushes its stomach out of its mouth to feed.

19. Sea sponges are alive, yet they have no brain, heart, lungs, head, mouth, or eyes.

29. Seahorses are the only animal where the male gives birth and cares for the babies.

30. Seahorses mate for life.

31. The largest animal in the ocean (the blue whale) eats tiny creatures called krill.

32. A blue whale's heart is the size of a Volkswagen Beetle.

33. The blue whale's heart pumps 100 tons of blood through its body.

34. There are more than 230,000 known species living in the world's oceans.

35. Since only a small part of the world's oceans have been explored, there are likely millions of ocean animal species still undiscovered.

36. We know of about 500 species of sharks.

37. Most are less than 5 feet (1.6 meters) long or are harmless to humans.

38. The three deadliest species of sharks are the great white, the tiger, and the bull shark.

39. The Great Barrier Reef covers an area larger than Great Britain.

40. It is the largest living structure on Earth and can be seen from space.

41. The Great Barrier Reef comprises 400 species of coral.

42. More than 2,000 different fish, 4,000 species of mollusk, and many other invertebrates live there.

43. The sailfish is the fastest fish in the ocean, leaping out of the water at up to 68 miles (109 km) per hour.

44. Bluefin tuna can reach sustained speeds of up to 56 miles (90 km) per hour.

45. A mouthful of seawater can contain millions of bacterial cells, hundreds of thousands of phytoplankton, and tens of thousands of zooplankton.

20. Sharks are covered with tiny little teeth called denticles.

21. Damselfish farm little algae gardens.

22. Moray eels open and close their mouths to breathe.

23. Parrotfish encase themselves in a bubble of mucus to stay safe while they sleep.

24. A boxfish's body is a bony cage with the eyes, mouth, and fins sticking out.

25. Many fish are born female and turn into males later on.

26. In a school of clownfish, all are male except the largest fish, which is female.

27. A mimic octopus can imitate a flounder, jellyfish, stingray, sea snake, lionfish, or even a piece of coral.

28. Frogfish do not have teeth. They swallow their prey whole.

10 SCARY SURVIVAL STORIES

Sometimes people are thrown into amazing situations. They have to fight for their lives to survive. Survival stories can happen on land or sea. Here are a few of the most dramatic.

1. **The Wild Boars Soccer Team:** In June 2018, 12 members of a Thai soccer team and their coach made what they thought was a quick visit to a cave. A flash flood trapped them there for 17 days until a team of divers finally saved everyone during a dangerous 3-day rescue.

2. **The Chilean Miners:** In August 2010, a rockslide trapped 33 miners deep inside a mine in Chile. The men huddled in a dark, tiny cave with no fresh air, and little food or water. It took weeks before a new shaft was drilled through the thick rock. Sixty-nine days later, all 33 miners were lifted to safety.

3. **Steven Callahan:** After sailing across the Atlantic Ocean in his small boat in 1981, Callahan was headed back home when a whale or shark punched a hole in his boat. Callahan jumped into a tiny raft and floated helplessly on the vast ocean. Seventy-six days later, sick and starving, Callahan was finally rescued by some fishermen.

4. **Harrison Okene:** When the cargo ship *Jacson-4* capsized off the coast of Nigeria, rescuers assumed no one survived. They were wrong. They found Okene, the ship's cook, alive in a small air bubble so deep within the ship that the pressure of the water should have killed him.

5. **Aldi Novel Adilang:** The 18-year-old Indonesian boy worked alone on a floating fishing hut in the Indian Ocean. In 2018, a terrible storm broke the hut's anchor, and Adilang and the hut were swept out to sea. He had to use his cleverness to find fresh water, food, and fuel for a fire. Forty-eight days later, a passing cargo ship finally spotted Adilang and rescued him.

6. **The Stolpa Family:** In December 1992, James and Jennifer Stolpa and their 5-month-old son got stranded on a back road during a blizzard. They spent 5 days in their truck, then moved to a small cave. Leaving Jennifer and the baby behind, James hiked for 30 hours and more than 50 miles (80 km) through waist-deep snow to find help and save his family.

7. **Ann Rodgers:** Rodgers got lost in the Arizona desert in 2016. The elderly woman built a fire, ate plants, and even killed a turtle for food. Rodgers also made a giant "Help" sign out of rocks and sticks. Nine days later, a pilot spotted her sign and rescued Rodgers.

8. **Juliane Koepcke:** Koepcke was lucky enough to survive two terrible ordeals between 1971 and 1972. First, the teenager fell out of a plane that had been struck by lightning. Koepcke landed deep in the Peruvian rain forest with broken bones. She spent the next 9 days walking through the forest, where she was nearly eaten alive by insects. Koepcke finally stumbled across a logging camp and was airlifted to a hospital.

9. **Hugh Glass:** In 1823, fur trapper Glass was attacked by a grizzly bear and left for dead by his companions. Badly injured, Glass spent 6 weeks crawling to the Cheyenne River, then made a raft and floated to a friendly Native American settlement. Glass finally reached Fort Kiowa, 200 miles (322 km) away, where he was nursed back to health.

10. **The Shackleton Expedition:** In 1914, Sir Ernest Shackleton set out with his crew in an attempt to cross Antarctica on foot. When their ship, the *Endurance*, became stuck in an ice floe, the 28 men were stranded for almost 2 years. For the first year, the men stayed deep inside the ship to stay warm. Then ice crushed the ship, and the men spent the next few months on the frozen sea. Finally, Shackleton took one of the open lifeboats and crossed 800 miles (1,287 km) of icy water to South Georgia Island, where he found a small whaling station and arranged a rescue for his entire crew, all of whom survived.

50 TOP TOURIST SITES

Here are the top sites in the world according to *Travel & Leisure* magazine.

1. Grand Bazaar, Istanbul, Turkey
2. The Zócalo, Mexico City, Mexico
3. Times Square, New York City, USA
4. Central Park, New York City, USA
5. Union Station, Washington, DC, USA
6. Las Vegas Strip, Las Vegas, USA
7. Meiji Jingu Shrine, Tokyo, Japan
8. Sensoji Temple, Tokyo, Japan
9. Niagara Falls, New York, USA, and Ontario, Canada
10. Grand Central Terminal, New York City, USA

11. Basilica of Our Lady of Guadalupe, Mexico City, Mexico
12. Disney World, Magic Kingdom, Orlando, USA
13. Faneuil Hall Marketplace, Boston, USA
14. Tokyo Disneyland, Tokyo, Japan
15. Disneyland, Anaheim, California, USA
16. Forbidden City, Beijing, China
17. Golden Gate National Recreation Area, San Francisco, USA
18. Tokyo DisneySea, Tokyo, Japan
19. Notre Dame Cathedral, Paris, France

106

35 ENGINEERING MARVELS

1. **Venice Tide Barrier Project, Italy:** The world's largest flood prevention project.

2. **Three Gorges Dam, China:** The world's largest concrete structure and largest hydroelectric power plant.

3. **National Stadium, China:** Site of the 2008 Summer Olympics and the world's largest steel structure.

4. **Palm Islands, Dubai:** The world's largest man-made island.

5. **Large Hadron Collider, Switzerland:** The largest particle accelerator in the world.

6. **Channel Tunnel, England and France:** The world's longest underwater tunnel.

7. **Chandra X-Ray Observatory, Outer Space:** The most powerful X-ray telescope and the largest satellite in space.

8. **New Valley Project, Egypt:** This massive irrigation system will reclaim half a million acres (202,342 hectares) of desert.

9. **Hoover Dam, United States:** This giant dam revolutionized dam construction.

10. **Bailong Elevator, China:** The highest and heaviest outdoor elevator in the world.

11. **Burj Khalifa, Dubai:** The world's tallest building at more than half a mile (0.8 km) high.

12. **Panama Canal, Panama:** This canal shortened the trip around North America from weeks to hours.

13. **Hong Kong-Zhuhai-Macau Bridge, China:** The world's longest sea bridge and tunnel at more than 34 miles (55 km) long.

14. **The International Space Station, Outer Space:** The largest human-made object orbiting the Earth, the ISS has been home to astronauts continuously since 2000.

15. **The Great Pyramid, Egypt:** This pyramid was the tallest structure in the world until the nineteenth century and was built with simple tools.

16. **Great Wall of China, China:** This defensive wall stretches over 2,500 miles (4,023 km).

17. **Forbidden City, China:** Once home to emperors, the Forbidden City is the largest palace complex in the world.

18. **Machu Picchu, Peru:** The "Lost City of the Inca" was hidden in the rain forest.

19. **Hagia Sophia, Turkey:** Built in the sixth century, this holy place had a great influence on architecture.

20. **Chichen Itza, Mexico:** This marvel was built by the Maya as an administrative and religious center.

21. **Capital Gate, United Arab Emirates:** This building leans on purpose! It was built on a crooked foundation.

22. **Laerdal Tunnel, Norway:** This tunnel penetrates 15 miles (24 km) of solid rock, making it the longest road tunnel in the world.

23. **Large Zenith Telescope, Canada:** This telescope's huge mirror is made of liquid mercury.

24. **China Central TV Headquarters, China:** This structure is made of two leaning towers connected by a loop.

25. **Rolling Bridge, England:** This ordinary-looking bridge rolls up into a sculpture when a boat needs to pass through London's Grand Union Canal.

26. **Gateshead Millennium Bridge, England:** The arches of this bridge twist and tilt to allow ships to pass underneath.

27. **Tarbela Dam, Pakistan:** The largest earth-and-rock dam in the world.

28. **Ericsson Dome, Sweden:** A sports stadium that is the world's largest spherical structure.

29. **Melbourne Rectangular Stadium, Australia:** The roof of this stadium is made of several metal spheres called geodesic domes.

30. **Stoosbahn Railway, Switzerland:** Called a funicular railway, a cable pulls two cars on train tracks; as one car goes up, the other comes down.

31. **Raurimu Spiral Railway, New Zealand:** To solve the problem of traveling up a steep hill, this railway uses big loops and curves.

32. **Crooked House, Poland:** This twisted building houses a restaurant, radio station, and stores.

33. **Cubic Houses, Netherlands:** These houses on top of a bridge are designed to look like a forest of cubes.

34. **Dancing House, Czech Republic:** Architect Frank Gehry created this building, which looks like it is twisting in on itself.

35. **Millay Viaduct, France:** The world's tallest cable-stayed road bridge.

50 FACTS ABOUT AUSTRALIA

1. Australia is the only continent covered by a single country.

2. Three times as many sheep as people live there.

3. There are more kangaroos in Australia than people.

4. Two native Australian animals are the only mammals that lay eggs.

5. Those animals are the platypus and the echidna.

6. Australia is home to four different species of kangaroo.

7. Nearly 90 percent of Australia's population lives on the coast.

8. Australia was the second country in the world to grant women the right to vote.

9. That right was granted in 1902.

10. A desert area called the outback covers most of the middle of the continent.

11. The name Australia comes from the Latin word australis, which means "southern."

12. Australia has one of the world's lowest population densities.

13. Only about 24 million people live in Australia.

14. Before it was colonized, Australia was widely populated by people known today as Aboriginal Australians.

15. They are estimated to have lived in Australia for 50,000 years.

16. Uluru, or Ayers Rock, is the largest monolith in the world.

17. It is over 5 miles (8 km) wide.

18. Australia is the second-driest continent. Only Antarctica is drier.

19. The Great Barrier Reef is the world's largest living organism.

20. It is also the world's largest ecosystem.

21. The Daintree Rain Forest is the country's largest rain forest.

22. It covers around 463 square miles (1,200 square km).

23. Australia has the world's largest cattle ranch.

24. The ranch is larger than Belgium.

25. Australia is the second-smallest continent in terms of land area.

26. Only Europe is smaller.

27. The world's longest straight road stretches across the Nullarbor Plain.

28. It is 91 miles (146 km) long.

29. Australia is the only continent without an active volcano.

30. Canberra was built specifically to be the nation's capital.

31. Australia has more than 750 reptile species.

32. That's more than anywhere else in the world.

33. All the marsupial species in the world except one are found only in Australia.

34. Australia has hosted two Summer Olympics.

35. These were held in Melbourne in 1956 and Sydney in 2000.

36. Because Australia is in the Southern Hemisphere, its seasons are opposite the seasons in North America.

37. Tasmania, Australia, has the cleanest air in the world.

38. Fraser Island is the largest sand island in the world.

39. The Indian Pacific train track is the longest straight track in the world.

40. About 80 percent of the animal species in Australia are not found anywhere else.

41. Australia has more than 10,000 beaches.

42. Australia's Highway 1 is the longest highway in the world.

43. Highway 1 covers about 9,000 miles (14,484 km).

44. Australia is one of the most multicultural nations in the world.

45. More than 200 different races and cultures live there.

46. Australia is the flattest continent on Earth.

47. The Dingo Fence is the longest fence in the world.

48. It was built to keep away wild dogs called dingoes.

49. New South Wales, a state in southeast Australia, was founded by the British as a penal colony in 1788.

50. Between 1788 and 1868, more than 160,000 convicts were sent to Australia from England, Ireland, Scotland, and Wales.

50 FESTIVE HOLIDAY FACTS

1. The first candy cane was made in Germany in the 1600s.

2. Almost 2 billion candy canes are produced for the holidays.

3. About 33 million real Christmas trees are sold each year.

4. Santa Claus was named after Saint Nicholas, a generous man who lived in Turkey during the fourth century.

5. The Rockefeller Center Christmas tree has more than 250,000 lights.

6. Norway sends a Christmas tree to Great Britain every year as a thank-you for Britain's help during World War II.

7. The number of gifts in the song "The 12 Days of Christmas" adds up to 364.

8. Roughly 17.5 million doughnuts, called sufganiyot, are eaten in Israel during Hanukkah.

9. Hanukkah candles are added to the menorah right to left, but they are lit from left to right.

10. The largest menorah in the world weighs 4,000 pounds.

11. Turkey was not on the menu at the first Thanksgiving.

12. Instead, the Pilgrims and Native Americans probably ate venison, duck, goose, oysters, lobster, eel, fish, pumpkins, and cranberries.

13. The first Thanksgiving celebration lasted for 3 days.

14. Abraham Lincoln proclaimed Thanksgiving a national holiday in 1863.

15. Sarah Josepha Hale, who wrote "Mary Had a Little Lamb," wrote letters to Lincoln for 17 years to persuade him to make Thanksgiving a national holiday.

16. The tradition of football on Thanksgiving began with a college game in 1876.

17. The first NFL game on Thanksgiving was played in 1920.

18. The first Macy's Thanksgiving Day Parade did not feature any balloons.

19. In 1924, the Macy's parade featured live animals from the Central Park Zoo.

20. About 46 million turkeys are cooked for Thanksgiving every year.

21. In the United States, Thanksgiving is celebrated on the fourth Thursday in November. In Canada, it is celebrated on the second Monday in October.

22. Easter was named after an old Anglo-Saxon goddess named Eostre.

23. Eostre celebrated new life and the coming of spring.

24. An old superstition says that wearing new clothes on Easter will bring good luck for the rest of the year.

25. The idea of the Easter Bunny giving out candy started in Germany during the Middle Ages.

26. Immigrants brought the Easter Bunny tradition to the United States.

27. Americans eat more than 16 million jellybeans during the holiday.

28. Around 90 million chocolate bunnies are sold for Easter.

29. The White House Easter Egg Roll has been celebrated since 1878.

30. The tradition started when some children asked President Rutherford B. Hayes to let them roll eggs on the White House lawn.

31. The jack-o'-lantern is based on an Irish folk character named Stingy Jack.

32. Halloween began as a day to scare off evil spirits during ancient Celtic times.

33. Trick-or-treating began in Scotland in medieval times.

34. In those days, trick-or-treaters used to sing or recite poetry in exchange for food or money.

35. Halloween is the second-largest commercial holiday in the United States.

36. Christmas is the first.

37. In 2018, Americans spent more than $9 billion on Halloween candy, costumes, and decorations.

38. Jack-o'-lanterns used to be carved out of turnips, potatoes, and beets.

39. When the tradition came to America, people began using pumpkins instead.

40. New York City throws the biggest Halloween parade every year.

41. Princesses and superheroes are the most popular Halloween costumes.

42. Irish immigrants began observing St. Patrick's Day in Boston in 1737.

43. The first St. Patrick's Day parade in America was held in New York City in 1766.

44. Chicago dyes the Chicago River green every St. Patrick's Day.

45. The date for Lunar New Year (also called Chinese New Year) changes every year.

46. It is celebrated during the second new moon after the Winter Solstice and can fall any time between January 21 and February 20.

47. Lunar New Year lasts for 15 days, and each day has its own traditions.

48. Tradition includes giving cash in a red envelope, called a hongbao, to children and single adults.

49. Chinese legend says that Buddha asked all of the animals to meet him on New Year's Day and named a year after each of the twelve animals that showed up.

50. The animals in the Chinese calendar are the dog, boar, rat, ox, tiger, rabbit, dragon, snake, horse, sheep, monkey, and rooster.

50 AMAZING INVENTIONS

(In no particular order)

1. Wheel
2. Nail
3. Paper
4. Compass
5. Sextant
6. Gunpowder
7. Printing Press
8. Optical Lenses
9. Penicillin
10. Vaccines
11. Semiconductors
12. Steam Engine
13. Internal Combustion Engine
14. Light Bulb
15. Radio
16. Television

17. Automobile
18. Airplane
19. Personal Computer
20. Clock
21. Refrigeration
22. Telephone
23. Internet
24. Mass-Produced Steel
25. Nuclear Power
26. Camera
27. Plow
28. Telegraph
29. Archimedes' screw
30. Cotton Gin
31. Pasteurization
32. Gregorian Calendar
33. Cement

34. Telescope
35. Microscope
36. Rockets
37. Money
38. Abacus
39. Lever
40. Anesthesia
41. Air Conditioning
42. Microwave Oven
43. Computer Hard Drive
44. Integrated Circuit
45. Pacemaker
46. Satellites
47. Fiber Optics
48. GPS
49. 3-D Printing
50. Smart Phone

70 AWESOME OLYMPICS FACTS

1. Olympic gold medals are mostly made of silver.

2. The Olympic torch relay started in the 1936 Olympics.

3. Only three Olympic Games have been canceled.

4. The Games in 1916, 1940, and 1944 were canceled because of war.

5. The Tokyo 2020 Games were postponed until 2021 because of the COVID-19 virus.

6. Only five nations have competed in every Summer Games.

7. They are Great Britain, Greece, France, Switzerland, and Australia.

8. Eddie Eagen is the only person to win gold medals in both Summer and Winter Olympics.

9. He won a gold in boxing in 1920 and a gold in bobsledding in 1932.

10. Athletes from the former Soviet Union competed as the Unified Team in the 1992 Summer Games.

11. Two athletes have won gold medals competing for two different nations.

12. Daniel Carrol won gold in rugby for Australia in 1908. He won gold again in 1920 for the United States.

13. Kakhi Kakhiashvili won gold in weightlifting as part of the Unified Team in 1992. He won again as a Greek citizen in 1996 and 2000.

14. The youngest Olympian was Greek gymnast Dimitrios Loundras. He competed at the 1896 Games when he was just 10 years old.

15. The youngest to win a gold medal is Marjorie Gestring, who won a diving title at the 1936 Games when she was 13.

16. Greece won the most medals—47—at the first modern Olympic Games in 1896.

17. The first Winter Olympics were held in Chamonix, France, in 1924.

18. Norway has won the most medals at the Winter Games.

19. The United States has won the most medals at the Summer Games.

20. From 1924 until 1992, the Summer and Winter Games were held in the same year, every four years. Starting in 1994, the Winter and Summer Games have alternated every two years.

21. The first Olympics covered by US television was the 1960 Summer Games in Rome, Italy.

22. No country in the Southern Hemisphere has ever hosted a Winter Olympics.

23. Australia and Brazil are the only countries in the Southern Hemisphere to host the Olympics.

24. Africa has never hosted an Olympics.

25. In the Opening Ceremonies, Greece leads the athletes' procession.

26. The last team in the procession is the host country's.

27. Other teams march in alphabetical order in the host country's language.

28. At the Opening Ceremonies, athletes march in representing their countries. At the Closing Ceremonies, the athletes march in as one big group.

29. The ancient Olympic Games were held in Greece from 776 BC until 393 AD.

30. The ancient Games were also a religious festival to honor Zeus.

60
PURR-FECT PET FACTS

1. People have kept pets since prehistoric times.

2. Dogs have been domesticated for about 10,000 years.

3. There are more than 350 dog breeds.

4. Americans own more than 20 million pet birds.

5. Large members of the parrot family can live more than 75 years.

6. Fish are the most popular pet in America.

7. There are more than 142 million fish in American homes.

8. Cats are the second-most-popular pet, at more than 88 million.

9. Dogs are number 3 at almost 75 million.

10. About 60 percent of American households have at least one pet.

11. There are between 8 and 10 million pet ferrets in the United States.

12. The word pet comes from the Middle English word petty, which means "small."

13. Cats were first domesticated in Egypt around the sixteenth century BC.

14. Archeologists discovered a grave dug in 10,000 BC where a person was buried with a puppy.

15. Egyptian art shows cats being used to catch mice.

16. Egyptians also kept hyenas, cheetahs, lions, and monkeys as pets.

17. They often mummified their pets and buried them with their owners.

18. Horses were domesticated by 2000 BC.

19. The first dog shows in America took place in the 1860s.

20. About 2.3 million pets are adopted from American animal shelters every year.

21. Christopher Columbus brought back two parrots for Queen Isabella when he returned from his trip to America in 1492.

22. Interacting with pets can lower blood pressure, slow heart rate, regulate breathing, and relax tense muscles.

23. Playing with pets increases hormones in the brain that make us happy and relaxed.

24. Owning a dog may decrease the risk of heart disease–related death by 36 percent.

25. Around 10 percent of pet owners are allergic to their pets.

26. Between 5,000 and 7,000 tigers are kept as pets in the United States.

27. This is not a good idea.

28. The United States has more dogs, cats, and fish as pets than any other nation.

29. Brazil has the most birds.

30. Americans spent about $72 billion on their pets in 2018.

31. Most dog and cat owners buy presents for their pets.

32. A pet chameleon can live up to 10 years.

33. Chameleons only live about 3 years in the wild.

34. Calico cats are almost always female.

35. Goldfish will keep growing if you place them in a larger aquarium.

36. The oldest known koi fish lived to be 226 years old.

37. The wealthiest cat in history inherited $13 million when its owner died.

38. The Saluki is the world's oldest breed of dog.

39. Labradors are the most popular dog pet in the United States.

40. A rabbit's teeth never stop growing.

41. Neither do the teeth of hamsters, gerbils, and guinea pigs.

42. Pigs are hypoallergenic pets.

43. Pigs are one of the smartest pets.

44. They can learn tricks and recognize their names.

45. Rats are also smart pets and easy to train.

46. The ancient Egyptians and Mayans worshipped rats.

47. Chocolate is toxic to dogs and birds.

48. Goldfish can live up to 43 years.

49. Rabbits are social creatures and like to be kept in pairs.

50. When rabbits are happy, they jump, twist, and kick in the air.

51. This behavior is called binkying.

52. Lizards are territorial and see other lizards as competition.

53. For this reason, it can be dangerous to put more than one lizard in a tank.

54. Reptiles need heat lamps or basking rocks in their tanks to stay warm.

55. Guinea pigs are not related to pigs at all.

56. Guinea pigs prefer short naps over a long sleep.

57. The gerbil's scientific name means "little clawed warrior."

58. Despite their name, gerbils make great pets.

59. Gerbils often make a thumping noise with their back feet.

60. Gerbils like to tunnel and dig.

50 GRAND GEOGRAPHY FACTS

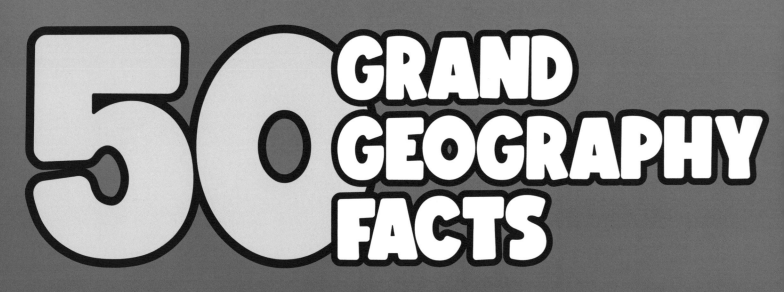

1. Timor-Leste was the first new country of the twentieth century. It declared independence from Indonesia in 2002.

2. The highest point in Australia is only about one-quarter the size of Mount Everest.

3. The Andes Mountains make up the entire west coast of South America.

4. The Mississippi River drains 40 percent of the continental United States.

5. Almost half of the Netherlands is below sea level.

6. Africa has more countries than any other continent.

7. People in Belgium don't speak Belgian.

8. They speak Flemish and French.

9. Switzerland has four official languages.

10. They are French, Italian, German, and Romansh.

11. A forest more than 11 times the size of Texas stretches across Russia and Norway.

12. Russia produces more natural gas than the next six top-producing countries combined.

13. About 900,000 square miles (2.3 million square km) of farmland in northern China are blown away each year.

14. Oregon's D River is only 120 feet (37 meters) long.

15. Lake Eyre, Australia's largest lake, is less than 20 feet (6 meters) deep.

16. Almost half of South America's land is in Brazil.

17. The country of Bahrain comprises 35 islands.

18. The five smallest countries in the world by area are Vatican City, Monaco, Nauru, Tuvalu, and San Marino.

19. Vatican City, Monaco, and San Marino are in Europe.

20. Nauru and Tuvalu are islands in the Pacific Ocean.

21. Indonesia has more square miles (km) of coral reefs than any other country.

22. Continents shift at about the same rate your fingernails grow.

23. Australia is wider than the Moon.

24. The deepest lake in the United States is Oregon's Crater Lake. It is 1,932 feet (589 meters) deep and lies inside the collapsed crater of an ancient volcano.

25. Crater Lake has no streams feeding into it and is filled solely by precipitation and snowmelt.

26. The world's tallest mountain, Mount Everest, could fit inside the Marianas Trench, the deepest part of the Pacific Ocean.

27. During the winter, you could walk from the United States to Russia.

28. The islands of Big Diomedes (part of Russia) and Little Diomedes (part of the United States) are only 2.4 miles (3.9 km) apart.

29. Despite that short distance, Big and Little Diomedes lie on opposite sides of the International Date Line.

30. That means there is a twenty-one-hour time difference between them.

31. Africa is the only continent that covers all four hemispheres.

32. Alaska is both the westernmost and easternmost state in the United States.

33. That's because an island called Semisopochnoi stretches so far west that it actually enters the Eastern Hemisphere.

34. About 90 percent of the world's population lives in the Northern Hemisphere.

35. Parts of Canada are south of Detroit.

36. Istanbul, Turkey, is the only city in the world located on two continents.

37. Reno, Nevada, is farther west than Los Angeles, California.

38. Because tectonic plates under the surface keep pushing up, the Himalayas grow taller every year.

39. Mount Thor in Canada has the greatest vertical drop in the world at 4,101 feet (1,250 meters).

40. Three countries are completely surrounded by other countries.

41. They are Lesotho (surrounded by South Africa) and San Marino and Vatican City (both surrounded by Italy).

42. Canada has more than half of all the natural lakes in the world.

43. There are more than two million lakes in Canada.

44. Canada also has the world's longest coastline, at 152,100 miles (244,781 km).

45. China and Russia are both bordered by fourteen countries.

46. Due to the bulge of the earth at the Equator, the peak of Ecuador's Mount Chimborazo is farthest from the center of the Earth.

47. That peak is 20,700 feet (6,310 meters), making Chimborazo the highest point on Earth.

48. However, Mount Everest is still the highest point above sea level.

49. Mount Chimborazo is an extinct volcano.

50. For every 500-foot (152-meter) change in elevation, the boiling point of water drops by one degree.

50 FACTS ABOUT MOVIES

1. The motion picture camera was invented in 1892.

2. It was invented by Thomas Edison.

3. The first movies were a single scene and only lasted about a minute.

4. The first feature-length film was *The Story of the Kelly Gang*.

5. It was released in 1906.

6. The first movie theaters opened in 1907.

7. Fort Lee, New Jersey, was once the movie capital of the world.

8. Most movie-making had moved to Hollywood by 1918.

9. The first movie shot in Hollywood was D.W. Griffith's *In Old California* in 1910.

10. Dorothy's slippers in *The Wizard of Oz* were originally silver.

11. The studio changed them to ruby so they would show up better in the film.

12. The dog who played Toto made twice as much money as the actors who played the Munchkins.

13. The most filmed author is William Shakespeare.

14. The smallest set for the entire action of a movie was the lifeboat used in Alfred Hitchcock's 1944 film *Lifeboat*.

15. John Wayne played the most leading roles of any actor.

16. John Carradine has the most screen credits. He appeared in more than 230 movies.

17. *Jaws* (1975) was the first movie to gross more than $100 million.

18. The original title for 1984's *Ghostbusters* was *Ghost Smashers*.

19. The first picture to sweep all five major Academy Awards—Best Picture, Best Actor, Best Actress, Best Director, and Best Screenplay (adaptation)—was Frank Capra's *It Happened One Night* (1934).

20. The largest cast of living creatures in a movie were 22 million bees in *The Swarm* (1978).

21. *Avatar* made $2.8 billion at the box office, the most of any movie.

22. *Avatar* was also one of the most expensive movies ever made, at a cost of $280 million.

23. The first sound cartoon was *Steamboat Willie*, a Mickey Mouse cartoon released in 1928.

24. The world's biggest IMAX theater screen is in Sydney, Australia.

25. The screen is 96 feet (29 meters) high by 117 feet (36 meters) wide.

26. Jim Carrey spent a total of 230 hours getting his makeup done during the filming of *How the Grinch Stole Christmas* (2000).

 27. Count Dracula is the most-portrayed character in horror movies.

28. *Snow White and the Seven Dwarfs* was the first full-length animated movie in color and with sound.

29. *The Lion King* was the first Disney animated movie to use an original storyline, not one adapted from another source.

30. Every scene in *Pocahontas* was rewritten at least thirty-five times.

31. It took more than 300 million hours to complete *Frozen*.

32. Six hundred people worked on *Frozen* for two-and-a-half years.

33. *The Lion King* is the bestselling home video of all time.

34. Tiana in 2009's *The Princess and the Frog* is the first African American Disney princess.

35. Over one million bubbles were hand-painted and inked for *The Little Mermaid*.

36. The original *Dumbo* is the shortest Disney film, at just sixty-four minutes long.

37. The wildebeest stampede in *The Lion King* took three years to animate.

38. *Toy Story* (1995) was the first movie created entirely by computer-generated imagery (CGI).

39. *Toy Story*'s Woody was originally a ventriloquist's dummy.

40. The number of balloons lifting the house in *Up* was 10,297.

10 STAR WARS FACTS

1. The lightsabers in *Star Wars* were actually rods coated with reflective material. The color was added later by animation.

2. The same actor who voiced Yoda voiced Miss Piggy.

3. Originally Yoda was supposed to be played by a monkey wearing a mask.

4. Chewbacca's voice is a mixture of lion, seal, walrus, and badger.

5. George Lucas's original script was more than two hundred pages long, twice as long as average.

6. Some of the asteroids in the scene where the Millennium Falcon escapes were actually spray-painted potatoes.

7. It took seven puppeteers and other crew members to control Jabba the Hut.

8. All the Clone Troopers in the Star Wars prequels were created by CGI.

9. The sound of a TIE fighter's engine is a combination of an elephant bellow and a car driving on wet pavement.

10. C-3PO and R2-D2 are the only characters to appear in all nine Star Wars movies.

50 MAGNIFICENT MUSEUM FACTS

1. The United States is home to more than 35,000 museums.

2. That's more than all the US McDonald's and Starbucks combined.

3. The word *museum* comes from the Muses, who were goddesses in Greek mythology.

4. To encourage crowds to keep moving through Barnum's American Museum, Barnum put up signs saying THIS WAY TO THE EGRESS. Not knowing egress was another word for exit, people followed the signs and ended up outside.

5. The largest art heist in history occurred at the Isabella Stewart Gardner Museum in Boston in 1990. Thirteen paintings worth $500 million were stolen. The art was never recovered.

6. All the empty frames are still hanging at the Gardner.

7. You can see old presidential limousines at the Henry Ford Museum in Dearborn, Michigan.

8. The Smithsonian has about 154 million objects.

9. The American Museum of Natural History is the largest natural history museum in the world.

10. There are more than 33 million objects in the American Museum of Natural History's collection.

11. A 94-foot (29-meter)-long replica of a blue whale hangs in the American Museum of Natural History.

12. It takes three days to clean that whale. Workers use long-handled brushes and vacuum cleaners.

13. The largest art museum in the world is the Louvre in Paris. It covers 782,910 square feet (238,631 square meters).

14. The Louvre includes about 38,000 pieces.

15. It is also the most visited museum, with 7.4 million guests each year.

16. The Vasa Museum in Sweden has the only seventeenth-century warship still in existence.

17. The National WWII Museum in New Orleans has more than 100,000 artifacts donated by WWII veterans.

18. Rome's Capitoline Museums are the oldest in the world.

19. They were founded by Pope Sixtus IV in 1471.

20. The oldest museum ever discovered is Ennigaldi-Nanna in Iraq.

21. It was built by a Babylonian princess 2500 years ago.

22. Archaeologists discovered Ennigaldi-Nanna in 1925.

23. Washington, DC's International Spy Museum features the world's largest collection of espionage artifacts.

24. The Mütter Museum in Philadelphia houses many unusual medical artifacts, including slides of Einstein's brain.

25. New York City's Metropolitan Museum of Art showcases 15 period rooms from the completely intact Temple of Dendur (dating to 10 BC) to the Frank Lloyd Wright room (1912-14).

TOP 10 MOST VISITED MUSEUMS

1. Louvre Museum (France)
2. National Museum of Natural History (USA)
3. National Museum of China (China)
4. National Air and Space Museum (USA)
5. British Museum (England)
6. Metropolitan Museum of Art (USA)
7. National Gallery (England)
8. Vatican Museums (Italy)
9. Natural History Museum (England)
10. American Museum of Natural History (USA)

15 REALLY ODD MUSEUMS

1. Momofuku Ando Instant Ramen Museum (Japan)
2. Food Additives Museum (Germany)
3. Museum of Failed Products (USA)
4. Museum of Questionable Medical Devices (USA)
5. Toilet Seat Art Museum (USA)
6. World Brick Museum (Japan)
7. The Dog Collar Museum (Great Britain)
8. Kansas Barbed Wire Museum (USA)
9. Sulabh International Museum of Toilets (India)
10. Beijing Tap Water Museum (China)
11. British Tap Water Museum (Great Britain)
12. Museum of Really Bad Art (USA)
13. Avanos Hair Museum (Turkey)
14. The Bread Museum (Germany)
15. Kazoo Museum (USA)

30
HISTORIC WOMEN YOU NEED TO KNOW

1. **Maya Angelou**, writer and civil-rights activist

2. **Susan B. Anthony**, fought for women's right to vote

3. **Ruth Bader Ginsburg**, Supreme Court justice

4. **Josephine Baker**, entertainer and spy

5. **Clara Barton**, battlefield nurse who founded the American Red Cross

6. **Nellie Bly**, investigative journalist

7. **Sarah "Madam Walker" Breedlove**, African American entrepreneur

8. **Rachel Carson**, environmentalist

9. **Shirley Chisholm**, politician and civil-rights activist

10. **Eugenie Clark**, marine biologist known as The Shark Lady

11. **Marie Curie**, scientist, first to win Nobel Prizes in two different sciences

12. **Cixi**, empress of China

13. **D.C. Fontana**, pioneering science-fiction scriptwriter

14. **Elizabeth Friedman**, code breaker

15. **Indira Gandhi**, India's first and (so far) only female prime minister

16. **Martha Gellhorn**, journalist

17. **Jane Goodall**, scientist and animal-conservation activist

18. **Caroline Herschel**, astronomer

19. **Grace Hopper**, computer scientist and Navy admiral

20. **Dolores Huerta**, civil-rights activist

21. **Katherine Johnson**, mathematician who helped Americans land on the Moon

22. **Frida Kahlo**, artist

23. **Hedy Lamarr**, actress and inventor

24. **Dorothea Lange**, photographer

25. **Ada Lovelace**, mathematician and inventor of the first computer

26. **Zora Neale Hurston**, writer

27. **Marie Severin**, comic-book artist

28. **Junko Tabei**, mountaineer

29. **Harriet Tubman**, activist

30. **Malala Yousafzai**, activist

3

22

29

131

40 TERRIFYING DISASTERS

1.	1865	**Sultana Explosion:** A ship's boiler exploded, killing 1,547, most of them prisoners returning home after the Civil War.
2.	1889	**Johnstown Flood:** Faulty construction and heavy rains led to a dam break and a flood that killed more than 2,200 people.
3.	1903	**Iroquois Theatre Fire:** A fire in a Chicago theater killed 602 people.
4.	1904	**General Slocum Fire:** A ship carrying people to a church picnic caught fire and sank in New York City's East River, killing 1,021 people.
5.	1911	**Triangle Shirtwaist Factory Fire:** A fire in a factory killed 146 young women and led to improved working conditions.
6.	1912	**Titanic Sinking:** A collision with an iceberg sank this ocean liner, killing 1,522 passengers and crew.
7.	1917	**Halifax Explosion:** Two ships collided in the harbor of Halifax, Canada, creating an explosion that destroyed much of the city and killed about 2,000 people.
8.	1919	**Boston Molasses Flood:** A storage tank burst and flooded the city with a 40-foot (12-meter) wave of sticky molasses. Twenty-one people died.
9.	1928	**St. Francis Dam Collapse:** A poorly built dam in California collapsed, killing between 400 and 600 people.
10.	1934	**Morro Castle Fire:** This ship caught fire at sea and ran aground near Asbury Park, New Jersey. The crew abandoned ship, leaving 135 passengers to die.

11. 1937 **Hindenburg Explosion:** The German airship caught fire while landing at Lakehurst, New Jersey, killing 36 people and ending the age of airship travel.

12. 1937 **New London, TX, School Explosion:** A gas explosion at a school killed more than 295 people.

13. 1942 **Coconut Grove Fire:** A fire at a crowded Boston nightclub killed 492 people who were trapped inside.

14. 1944 **Hartford Circus Fire:** During a performance in Hartford, Connecticut, a circus tent caught fire, killing 167 people.

15. 1944 **Balvano, Italy, Train Disaster:** 520 people died of carbon monoxide poisoning when a train stalled inside a tunnel.

16. 1947 **Texas City Disaster:** A fire onboard a ship carrying chemicals set off a chain reaction of fires and explosions that killed at least 581 people in America's worst industrial accident.

17. 1963 **Thresher Submarine Sinking:** A US nuclear submarine sank off the coast of Massachusetts during diving tests, killing all 129 sailors onboard.

18. 1966 **Aberfan Disaster:** Rain caused the collapse of a huge pile of coal waste in a small Welsh town, killing 116 children and 28 adults.

19. 1974 **Turkish Airlines Flight 981 Crash:** The plane crashed into a forest shortly after taking off from Orly Airport in Paris, killing all 346 people onboard.

20. 1975 **Banqiao Dam Collapse:** A dam collapse in China may have killed up to 240,000 people. The incident was kept secret for many years.

21. 1977 **Tenerife Airport Disaster:** Two airplanes collided on the runway in the world's worst air disaster, killing 583 people.

22. 1979 **American Airlines Flight 191 Crash:** The worst air crash in the United States occurred when this plane crashed on takeoff, killing 273 people.

23. 1981 **Hyatt Regency Walkway Collapse:** Two walkways collapsed and crashed into the hotel's lobby, where a dance was being held, killing 114 people.

24. 1984 **Bhopal Chemical Leak:** An overnight gas leak at a chemical plant killed more than 3,800 people and injured thousands more.

25. 1985 **Japan Airlines Flight 123 Crash:** Mechanical problems caused this plane to crash into a mountain, killing 520 people. Only 4 passengers survived.

26.	1986	**Challenger Explosion:** The space shuttle exploded 73 seconds after takeoff, killing all seven astronauts onboard, including teacher Christa McAuliffe.
27.	1986	**Chernobyl Nuclear Accident:** An accident at the Soviet Union's nuclear reactor released radiation, creating a long-term death toll of thousands.
28.	1987	**Herald of Free Enterprise Ferry Sinking:** This ferry left its Belgian port with a loading door open, causing the sea to rush in and sink the ferry. All 193 passengers and crew were killed.
29.	1989	**Exxon Valdez Oil Spill:** A massive oil spill in Alaska's Prince William Sound killed hundreds of thousands of birds and other animals and contaminated 1,300 miles (2,100 km) of coastline.
30.	1989	**Ufa Train Disaster:** A train set off an explosion when it passed near a leaking gas pipeline, killing more than 575 people onboard the train.
31.	1989	**Hillsborough Stadium Crush:** In England, 96 people were killed during a crush during a soccer match.
32.	1994	**Estonia Ferry Disaster:** The ferry rolled and sank during an overnight crossing from Estonia to Sweden, killing 852 people.
33.	2002	**Ayyat, Egypt, Train Fire:** A cooking gas cylinder exploded onboard the train, causing a fire that killed hundreds of passengers as the train continued to roll.
34.	2003	**Columbia Destruction:** The space shuttle broke apart during re-entry because of damaged heat tiles, killing all seven crew members.
35.	2005	**Amagasaki Train Derailment:** A speeding train in Japan derailed and crashed into an apartment building, killing 107 people.
36.	2008	**Princess of the Stars Ferry Sinking:** A crowded ferry sank during a typhoon in the Philippines, killing 814 of the 870 people onboard.
37.	2010	**Deepwater Horizon Oil Spill:** The largest marine oil spill occurred in the Gulf of Mexico when a rig exploded, releasing almost 210 million gallons (795 million liters) of oil into the water.
38.	2011	**Fukushima Nuclear Disaster:** A tsunami flooded the nuclear reactor, causing several meltdowns, explosions, and the release of deadly radiation.
39.	2013	**Rana Plaza Factory Collapse:** 1,134 workers were killed when a poorly designed garment factory collapsed in Bangladesh.
40.	2013	**Runaway Train Explosion Lac-Mégantic, Canada:** An unattended runaway freight train exploded in a Quebec town, killing 47 people and destroying most of the downtown.

50 BASEBALL FACTS

1. Each baseball has 108 double stitches.

2. All the stitching is done by hand.

3. A baseball is retired after just six pitches.

4. Up to six dozen baseballs are used in a game.

5. Many people believe that Abner Doubleday (1819–1893) invented baseball in 1839 in Cooperstown, New York.

6. However, baseball actually developed from bat-and-ball games played in Europe in the eighteenth and nineteenth centuries.

7. The major-league game with the most innings took place between the Brooklyn Robins and the Boston Braves in 1920.

8. The game ended in a 1-1 tie after 26 innings when the game was called because of darkness.

9. The longest baseball game in terms of time was an 8-hour, 6-minute game that lasted 25 innings between the Chicago White Sox and the Milwaukee Brewers in 1984.

10. The shortest game was a 51-minute contest between the New York Giants and the Philadelphia Phillies in 1919.

11. Boston's Fenway Park is the oldest MLB stadium. It was built in 1912.

12. The first World Series was played between Pittsburgh and Boston in 1903.

13. The New York Yankees have won the most World Series titles with 27.

14. The first All-Star Game was played in 1933.

15. Baltimore Orioles shortstop Cal Ripken, Jr., played a record 2,632 consecutive games between 1982 and 1998.

16. In 2001, Barry Bonds broke the all-time single-season home run record with 73 homers for the San Francisco Giants.

17. Fourteen players have hit four home runs in one game.

18. Pitcher Nolan Ryan played twenty-seven seasons in major-league baseball.

19. He holds the MLB strikeout record, with 5,714.

20. Ryan is also the only pitcher to throw a 108-mile (174-km)-an-hour fastball.

21. Pitcher Jim Abbott was born without a right hand and had a ten-season baseball career.

22. In 1993, Abbott threw a no-hitter for the New York Yankees.

23. Hoyt Wilhelm hit a home run in his very first at-bat as a 28-year-old rookie pitcher. Despite a 21-year career and 493 plate appearances, he never hit another home run.

24. Joe Sewell only struck out 3 times during 353 at-bats during the 1930 season.

25. Two of those strikeouts came in the same game.

26. The most stolen base in a game is second base.

27. "Take Me Out to the Ballgame" was written in 1908 by two men who had never been to a baseball game.

28. Mo'ne Davis is the first female pitcher to win a Little League World Series game.

29. The New York Yankees were the first team to wear numbers on the backs of their uniforms.

30. The numbers were based on batting order.

31. William Taft was the first president to throw out the opening-day first pitch.

32. The tradition started in 1910.

33. Ken Griffey Sr. and Ken Griffey Jr. became the first father and son to play in the major leagues as teammates for the Seattle Mariners in 1990.

34. On September 14, 1990, the Griffeys hit back-to-back home runs, another father-son baseball first.

35. The New York Yankees have the most members in the Baseball Hall of Fame.

36. Boston Red Sox player Jimmy Piersall celebrated his one-hundredth home run by running the bases backward.

37. The most valuable baseball card is a 1909 Honus Wagner card worth about $2.8 million.

Babe Ruth 49 **17B**

38. In 1919, the Chicago White Sox earned the nickname the Black Sox when eight players were accused of intentionally losing the World Series.

39. Those players were banned from baseball for life.

40. The National Baseball Hall of Fame was founded in Cooperstown, New York, in 1935.

41. The Hall of Fame includes more than 40,000 artifacts.

42. Only one major league player has been killed by a pitched ball.

43. That player was Ray Chapman of the Cleveland Indians, who was fatally hit in the head on August 16, 1920, by a ball thrown by Yankee pitcher Carl May.

44. The shortest player to ever bat in a major league baseball game was Eddie Gaedel, who was 3 feet, 7 inches (1.09 meters) tall.

45. Gaedel's strike zone was just 1.5 inches (3.8 cm).

46. The first professional baseball team was the Cincinnati Red Stockings, organized in 1869.

47. Evar Swanson holds the record for the fastest time around the bases. On September 15, 1929, he ran the bases in 13.3 seconds.

48. The 1927 New York Yankees lineup was called Murderer's Row because it had so many powerful hitters.

49. In 1927, Babe Ruth hit sixty home runs. That was more than the totals of any other team.

50. Joe Nuxhall is the youngest pitcher in major league baseball history. Nuxhall was just fifteen when he pitched for the Cincinnati Reds in 1944.

137

100 MIND-BLOWING FACTS ABOUT THE UNIVERSE

1. Space doesn't have a temperature. Only items in space have a temperature.

2. Distances in the solar system are calculated using astronomical units, or AUs.

3. One AU equals the distance from the Earth to the sun, about 93 million miles (about 150 million km).

4. The universe is so big, scientists measure it in light-years.

5. A light-year is the distance light travels in one year. That's about 5.88 trillion miles (9.46 trillion km).

6. Venus is the brightest planet in the sky because the thick clouds covering it reflect a lot of sunlight.

7. Venus has the densest atmosphere of any planet.

8. The pressure is so great, it could crush you like a soda can.

9. The three brightest objects in our sky are the sun, the Moon, and Venus.

10. Our sun is more than four billion years old.

11. Jupiter, Saturn, Uranus, and Neptune do not have solid surfaces.

12. These planets are called gas giants.

13. Their surface is made of gases with just a small, rocky core.

14. Jupiter has at least fifty moons.

15. Uranus tilts so much that it looks like it is lying on its side.

16. Because of its tilt, Uranus has forty-two years of darkness followed by forty-two years of sunshine.

17. The wind on Neptune blows more than 1,200 miles (2,000 km) per hour.

18. A supernova is the explosive death of a very large star.

19. Supernova explosions can cause black holes.

20. Black holes condense all of a star's matter in a very small space.

21. The force of gravity in a black hole is so strong that it sucks in everything around it.

22. Not even light can escape a black hole.

23. Scientists think there could be up to 100 million black holes in our galaxy alone.

24. Black holes can grow billions of times bigger than the sun.

25. The universe is always expanding.

26. A comet's tail can be hundreds of millions of miles (km) long.

27. Comets are made of ice, sand, and carbon dioxide.

28. The Kuiper Belt lies beyond Neptune and has many comets.

29. The planet Pluto was discovered in 1930.

30. In 2006, Pluto was demoted to a dwarf planet.

31. The dwarf planet Eris is the coldest object in our solar system.

32. Eris orbits the sun once every 557 years.

33. There are anywhere between 200 and 400 billion stars in the Milky Way.

34. There are an estimated 100 billion planets in the Milky Way.

35. Scientists estimate that some planets in the Milky Way could contain liquid water.

36. That means there could be 8.8 billion planets within the galaxy capable of supporting life.

37. Since 1991, astronomers have discovered more than 550 planets outside our solar system.

38. Most galaxies are spiral-shaped.

39. NASA monitors more than 1,200 potentially hazardous asteroids.

40. Meteors are space materials that heat up and burn once they enter Earth's atmosphere.

41. Meteors are also called shooting stars.

42. Meteorites are meteors that don't burn up completely and make impact on Earth's surface.

43. The largest meteorite ever found landed in Africa and weighed 119,000 pounds (54,000 kg).

44. The word planet comes from the Greek *planets*, which means "wanderer."

45. A plane ride to Pluto would take more than 800 years.

46. It's estimated that the universe is 13.7 billion years old.

47. Only 4 percent of the universe is made up of things we can see, such as stars and planets.

48. Most of the universe is made of invisible matter, called dark energy and dark matter.

49. It takes so long for light from some stars to travel to Earth that looking at the night sky is actually a glimpse into the past.

50. There is no sound in space.

51. A day on Venus is longer than a year on Venus.

52. Venus is the only planet that rotates backward.

53. You could fit 1.3 million Earths inside the sun.

54. There are more stars in the universe than there are grains of sand on Earth.

55. Neutron stars are the fastest spinning objects in the universe.

56. These stars can spin up to six hundred times a second.

57. A spoonful of matter from a neutron star weighs about a billion tons.

58. Almost every element found on Earth was created in the burning core of a star.

59. That means our bodies are made of stardust!

60. Astronomers estimate that 275 million stars are born and die throughout the observable universe each day.

61. That adds up to more than 100 billion over the course of a year.

62. Mercury is super-hot, but it has ice on its surface.

63. The ice is located in craters that don't receive any sunlight.

64. Mars's Olympus Mons volcano is the largest in the solar system.

65. Olympus Mons is 374 miles (602 km) wide. That's the size of Arizona.

66. The volcano is 16 miles (25 km) high, or triple the height of Mount Everest.

67. Mars also has the longest valley. Valles Marineris is 2,500 miles (4,000 km) long. That's ten times as long as the Grand Canyon.

68. Jupiter's Great Red Spot is actually a violent storm.

69. That storm has been raging for more than three hundred years.

70. The Great Red Spot is about three times as wide as Earth.

71. Huge dust storms on Mars can last for months and bury the entire surface.

72. The winds on Neptune move at more than 1,500 miles (2,414 km) per hour.

73. Mercury has the most extreme temperature swings of any planet.

74. The surface of Mercury can reach a scorching 840°F (450°C).

75. Since Mercury doesn't have enough atmosphere to trap any heat, night-time temperatures can plunge to −275°F (−170°C).

76. That's more than a 1,100°F (593°C) temperature change.

77. Pluto is smaller in diameter than the United States.

78. There are Mars rocks on Earth.

79. These meteorites might have been blasted from Mars to Earth by a large asteroid strike or a volcanic eruption.

80. Jupiter has the biggest ocean of any planet.

81. But it's made of metallic hydrogen.

82. This ocean is about 25,000 miles (40,000 km) deep.

83. Mercury is only about as wide as the Atlantic Ocean.

84. Eighteen Mercurys could fit inside our Earth.

85. Earth is the only planet not named after a Roman or Greek god or goddess.

86. Saturn's rings are made of billions of pieces of ice, dust, and rocks.

87. Jupiter, Uranus, and Neptune also have rings, but only Saturn's are visible to us.

88. The dwarf planet Haumea, which orbits in the Kuiper Belt, has two moons.

89. A day on Haumea only lasts four hours.

90. Some astronomers think it's possible for moons to have moons.

91. They call these objects moonmoons, moonitos, submoons, grandmoons, moonettes, or moooons.

92. Saturn's Hyperion moon gives off static electricity.

93. Saturn's moon Pan is disc-shaped because it absorbs some of the particles given off by Saturn's rings.

94. In September 2018, astronomers found a long stream of infrared light coming from a neutron star eight hundred light-years away from Earth.

95. Ceres is the largest asteroid in our solar system.

96. Ceres is 600 miles (966 km) in diameter.

97. That's as big as India or Argentina.

98. The sun makes up more than 99 percent of our solar system's mass.

99. A small asteroid called Chariklo has two icy rings around it.

100. All the planets in the solar system could fit between the Earth and the Moon.

40 BOUNCING BASKETBALL FACTS

1. James Naismith, a gym teacher at a YMCA in Springfield, Massachusetts, invented basketball in 1891.

2. The first basketball hoops were peach baskets with the bottoms still in. An official had to climb a ladder to remove the ball after each basket.

3. String nets were first used in the early 1900s.

4. Basketball was originally played with a soccer ball.

5. The 24-second shot clock was introduced in 1954 to keep players from hogging the ball.

6. Basketball became an Olympic sport in 1936.

7. The National Basketball League (NBL) and the Basketball Association of America (BAA) merged after the 1948-49 season to become today's National Basketball Association (NBA).

8. The American Basketball Association (ABA) was a ten-team rival league to the NBA that existed between 1967 and 1976.

9. Four current NBA teams—Indiana Pacers, Denver Nuggets, Brooklyn Nets, and San Antonio Spurs—originated in the ABA.

10. NBA introduced the three-point shot in 1979. They got the idea from the ABA.

11. The Chicago Bulls have won all six NBA Finals in which they appeared.

12. The Boston Celtics have won the most championships with seventeen wins.

13. They won seven straight titles between 1960 and 1966.

14. Michael Jordan holds the record for most points scored in a playoff game with 63 against the Boston Celtics in 1986.

15. LeBron James scored 6,911 points in playoff games between 2006 and 2018.

16. Muggsy Bogues is the shortest NBA player at just 5 feet, 3 inches (1.6 meters) tall.

17. The tallest NBA players are Manute Bol and Gheorghe Muresan. They are each 7 feet, 7 inches (2.3 meters) tall.

18. Kobe Bryant was only seventeen when he entered the NBA.

19. Bryant was the youngest to ever play in an All-Star Game, at nineteen years old.

20. Women's basketball was added to the Olympics in 1976.

21. The Denver Nuggets and the Detroit Pistons played the highest-scoring regular-season NBA game on December 13, 1983.

22. The game had three overtimes, and the final score was 186-184.

23. The average NBA player can jump 28 inches (0.7 meter) off the ground.

24. The basket is 10 feet (3 meters) high and has a diameter of 18 inches (.46 meter).

25. Originally, two teams of nine players made up a basketball game. The number was copied from baseball.

26. The 2010–2011 season was a rough one for the Cleveland Cavaliers. They lost a record twenty-six games in a row.

27. In 1991, the Cavaliers beat the Miami Heat 148-80, the record for the largest win margin in NBA history.

28. The Sacramento Kings are the oldest franchise in the NBA, founded in 1923.

29. Despite being around for so long, the Kings have only won a single championship.

30. Kareem Abdul-Jabbar scored the most career points with 38,387.

31. Wilt Chamberlain scored 100 points in a game in 1962.

32. The closest anyone has come to beating that record was when Kobe Bryant scored 81 points in a 2006 game.

33. Karl Malone holds the record for most career free throws with 9,787.

34. Before 1923, basketball teams could choose which player would shoot a free throw after a foul.

35. Basketball has the most injuries of any sport. The most common injury is a sprained ankle.

36. NBA players run about 4 miles (6.4 km) during a game.

37. John Stockton is the NBA's all-time leader in total assists with 15,806.

38. He also has the most total steals with 3,265.

39. The Women's National Basketball Association (WNBA) was founded in 1996.

40. The first woman to dunk in a professional basketball game was all-star center Lisa Leslie of the Los Angeles Sparks in 2002.

25. The Rungrado 1st of May Stadium in North Korea holds 114,000 people, making it the largest sports stadium in the world.

26. American Robert Wadlow was the tallest man who ever lived.

27. Wadlow was 8 feet, 11 inches (2.7 meters) tall.

28. Wadlow also had the largest feet ever, size 37AAA.

29. The heaviest person ever was American Jon Brower Minnoch. At one point, his weight was 1,400 pounds (635 kg).

30. The skin is the largest organ in the human body. Stretched out, an adult's skin would cover 22 square feet (2 square meters).

31. The largest internal organ in the human body is the liver. It weighs just over 3 pounds (1.5 kg).

32. A person's lungs contain 1,500 miles (2,400 km) of airways.

33. The total internal surface area of the lungs equals one side of a tennis court.

34. The aorta is the largest blood vessel in the human body.

35. The aorta carries blood from the heart to the rest of the body.

36. In 2016, a man in Germany grew a 2,624.6-pound (1,190-kg) pumpkin.

37. The largest pumpkin grown in the United States weighed 2,528 pounds (1,147 kg).

38. In 2012, chefs in Italy created the Ottavia, the largest pizza ever created.

39. Ottavia measured 131 feet (40 meters) in diameter.

40. The dough for the pizza had to be baked in 5,000 separate batches.

41. China's Winsun printer is the largest 3-D printer in the world.

42. Winsun can create an entire house in one day.

43. The world's largest banknote is a 100,000 peso note created by the Philippines in 1998.

44. The 100,000-peso note was the size of a sheet of legal paper and was only offered to collectors.

45. In 2011, the Perth Mint in Australia made a gold coin weighing 2,231 pounds (1,012 kg).

46. The coin measured 31 inches (80 cm) across.

47. The largest book in the world is a 2012 text on the Prophet Muhammad that measures 16.4 feet (5 meters) by 26.44 feet (8 meters).

48. The heaviest newspaper was the September 14, 1987, issue of the *New York Times*. It weighed more than 12 pounds (5.4 kg) and had 1,612 pages.

49. The heaviest rock brought back from the Moon was nicknamed Big Muley. It weighs 25.79 pounds (11.7 kg).

50. The heaviest rideable bicycle was built by Antanas Kontrimas of Lithuania in 2016. It weighed 3,053 pounds (1,385 kg).

40 AMAZING AIRPORT FACTS

1. Atlanta's Hartsfield-Jackson International Airport is the busiest airport in the world.

2. In 2018, more than 107 million passengers traveled through Hartsfield-Jackson.

3. Almost all of those passengers were traveling on domestic flights.

4. More than 60,000 people work at Hartsfield-Jackson.

5. Dubai International is the world's busiest airport in terms of international flights, with more than 89 million passengers in 2018.

6. Los Angeles International Airport has a special private club. Members pay $4,500 a year to join, plus $2,700 per flight to use a separate VIP terminal.

7. London's Heathrow Airport has a terminal that is only used by heads of state, royals, and some celebrities. It is not open to the public.

8. Hong Kong International Airport handles more than 5 million tons of cargo each year.

9. The highest commercial airport in the United States is Telluride Regional Airport in Colorado. At 9,070 feet (2,765 meters) above sea level, the runway is often covered in snow.

10. Nashville International Airport in Tennessee features 6 concert stages.

11. Miami International Airport has trained therapy dogs that are available for hugs and snuggles.

12. San Francisco International Airport has a therapy pig who wears costumes and performs tricks.

13. Mitchell International Airport in Milwaukee, Wisconsin, installed ping-pong tables for people to play while they wait for their flights to board.

14. The world's tallest air traffic control tower is at Thailand's New Bangkok International Airport. At 434 feet (132 meters) tall, it's the height of a 40-story skyscraper.

15. Juancho E. Yrausquin Airport on the Caribbean island of Saba has the shortest commercial runway on Earth. At 1,299 feet (396 meters) long, it is much too short for jets to use.

16. Hong Kong International Airport boasts a golf course next to one of its terminals.

17. Sao Paulo/Guarulhos International Airport in Brazil has an in-house dentist to treat passengers.

18. Singapore's Changi Airport advertises a nature trail and a butterfly garden with over 1,000 butterflies.

19. Airport runway numbers indicate direction on a compass.

20. When three-letter airport codes became standards, airports that had been using two letters added an X to the end of their codes.

21. Tijuana International Airport, on the border between Mexico and the United States, is the only airport to have terminals in two countries.

22. Los Angeles International's Theme Building was built in 1961. It looks like a giant steel and concrete spider.

23. The Theme Building once housed a restaurant and an observation deck.

24. Items seized by security are often sold at auctions.

25. Planes landing at Princess Juliana Airport on the island of St. Maarten fly just 100 feet (30.5 meters) above the beach.

26. The world's oldest continuously operated airport is College Park Airport in Maryland.

27. College Park was established in 1909 by Wilbur Wright, one of the Wright brothers.

28. At Ben Gurion Airport in Israel, staff collect lost balloons from people greeting travelers and distribute them to children's hospitals.

29. In 2017, more than $869,000 in loose change was left at security checkpoints in the United States.

30. Unclaimed money is deposited in a special account to fund security at airports.

31. JFK International Airport in New York has an ARK Pet Oasis. It is the only facility of its kind in North America.

32. The Pet Oasis includes kennels, medical personnel, exercise areas, and more.

33. JFK also has virtual reality stations with games to entertain passengers.

34. Airports make about 41 percent of their revenue from parking fees.

35. One-third of the world's airports are in the United States.

36. Denver International Airport covers 53 square miles (137 square km).

37. Denver International Airport is bigger than the cities of New York City, Miami, or San Francisco.

38. Paro Airport in Bhutan is said to be the most difficult airport to land in.

39. Only eight pilots are authorized to land at Paro because of the level of difficulty.

40. The runway at Gibraltar International Airport crosses a busy highway.

50
TOP GOOGLE TRENDS

Here are the top-trending terms in the United States in 2019:

SEARCHES

1. Disney+
2. Cameron Boyce
3. Nipsey Hussle
4. Hurricane Dorian
5. Antonio Brown
6. Luke Perry
7. Avengers: Endgame
8. Game of Thrones
9. iPhone 11
10. Jussie Smollett

PEOPLE

1. Antonio Brown
2. Jussie Smollett
3. James Charles
4. Kevin Hart
5. R. Kelly
6. 21 Savage
7. Lori Loughlin
8. Jordyn Woods
9. Bryce Harper
10. Robert Kraft

ATHLETES

1. Antonio Brown
2. Bryce Harper
3. David Ortiz
4. Andrew Luck
5. Myles Garrett
6. Megan Rapinoe
7. Russell Westbrook
8. Zion Williamson
9. Melvin Gordon
10. Alex Morgan

MOVIES

1. Avengers: Endgame
2. Captain Marvel
3. Joker
4. Toy Story 4
5. The Lion King
6. IT Chapter Two
7. Frozen 2
8. Once Upon a Time in Hollywood
9. Midsommar
10. Scary Stories to Tell in the Dark

NEWS

1. Hurricane Dorian
2. Notre Dame Cathedral
3. Women's World Cup
4. Area 51 Raid
5. Copa America
6. El Paso Shooting
7. Sri Lanka
8. Government Shutdown
9. Equifax Data Breach Settlement
10. California Earthquake

40 GHASTLY GHOST FACTS

People who believe in ghosts think a person's spirit can exist separately from their body.

Ghosts have been important figures in folklore since ancient times.

Ghosts often haunt their former homes or places where they died.

More than half of people do not believe in ghosts and say ghost sightings can be explained by psychology, misperceptions, and hoaxes.

Ghosts don't just come out at night; people have reported seeing them at all times of day.

Ghosts don't only show up in haunted houses.

There have been reports of ghosts in hospitals, prisons, museums, forests, and ships.

8. Specific people, rather than places, can be the focus of a ghost.

9. Ghosts can take several different forms.

10. Some people report seeing a person who has died, or smell an odor associated with that person, such as perfume.

11. Ghosts that appear as swirling mist are called ectoplasm.

12. A funnel ghost can be a swirling shaft of light.

13. Funnel ghosts are often associated with cold spots in houses.

14. Orbs are pale balls of light that hover over the ground.

15. Some people believe orbs are ghosts traveling from one place to another.

16. The word *poltergeist* means "noisy ghost."

17. Poltergeists are known for throwing things, slamming doors, and turning lights on and off.

18. Animals often act strangely in the presence of ghosts.

19. Ghost hunters travel to haunted places looking for evidence of ghosts.

20. Ghost hunters use equipment such as cameras, night-vision photography, and audio recording equipment to capture evidence of ghosts' existence.

21. Ghost hunters use an EMF meter to detect changes in electromagnetic fields.

22. More than one-third of Americans believe in ghosts.

23. About 23 percent of Americans say they have personally seen or felt a ghost.

24. The first documented haunting in the United States occurred in 1799 in Sullivan, Maine.

25. Residents of Sullivan reported seeing the ghost of a young woman named Nelly Butler.

26. Many photographs appear to show ghosts.

27. Some of these images are the result of double-exposing the negative, though.

28. However, some photographs cannot be explained.

29. One of the most famous ghost photos ever taken was the "Brown Lady" of Raynham Hall in England.

30. The photo reportedly shows a veiled woman gliding down the staircase.

10 FAMOUS HAUNTED PLACES

1. Winchester Mystery House, San Jose, California

2. Tower of London, London, England

3. The White House, Washington, DC

4. Stanley Hotel, Estes Park, Colorado

5. Villisca Axe Murder House, Villisca, Iowa

6. Hoia Baciu Forest, Cluj-Napoca, Romania

7. Castle of Good Hope, Cape Town, South Africa

8. *Queen Mary* Ocean Liner, Long Beach, California

9. Eastern State Penitentiary, Philadelphia, Pennsylvania

10. Catacombs, Paris, France

33. Throughout history, people have used many different items for money, including cocoa beans, elephant-tail hair, seashells, feathers, and bird claws.

34. The eagle pictured on the American silver dollar was a real bird named Peter who lived at the US Mint in Philadelphia from 1830 to 1836.

35. After he died, Peter was stuffed and can still be seen at the Mint today.

36. In 1946, Hungary printed the highest denomination ever created: bank note worth 100 quintillion pengoes.

37. The oldest "money" ever found are small pieces of obsidian used in Turkey as far back as 12,000 BC.

38. The oldest surviving bank in the world is the Banca Monte dei Paschi di Siena, also known as BMPS. It was founded in 1472.

39. The first chartered bank in the United States was the First Bank of the United States.

40. The First Bank was founded by the US Congress in Philadelphia in 1791.

41. The first bank-issued credit card appeared in Brooklyn in 1946.

42. The card was called the Charg-It card.

43. Purchases could only be made locally and only by customers of the bank.

44. The first credit card that could be used in many different places was the Diners Club card in 1950.

45. Queen Elizabeth II has appeared on more currency than anyone in history.

46. Queen Elizabeth II's portrait has appeared on the currency of 30 different nations.

47. The Massachusetts Bay Colony became the first colony to make coins in 1652.

48. The World Bank was established in 1946 to provide loans for economic development.

49. The Department of the Treasury issued the first paper money in the United States in 1862.

50. America's first paper money came in denominations of 1 cent, 5 cents, 25 cents, and 50 cents.

25 RICHEST PEOPLE IN THE WORLD

Here are the richest people in the world as of March 2020:

1.	Jeff Bezos	$116.9 billion
2.	Bill Gates	$99.9 billion
3.	Bernard Arnault	$91.6 billion
4.	Warren Buffett	$70.5 billion
5.	Larry Ellison	$62.4 billion
6.	Amancio Ortega	$60.9 billion
7.	Michael Bloomberg	$58.7 billion
8.	Mark Zuckerberg	$58.2 billion
9.	Steve Ballmer	$55.5 billion
10.	Françoise Bettencourt Myers	$53.1 billion
11.	Larry Page	$51.6 billion
12.	Carlos Slim Helú	$50.1 billion
13.	Jim Walton	$49.9 billion
14.	Sergey Brin	$49.7 billion
15.	Alice Walton	$49.7 billion
16.	Robson Walton	$49.5 billion
17.	Ma Huateng	$43.2 billion
18.	Julia Koch	$40.3 billion
19.	Charles Koch	$40.3 billion
20.	Mukesh Ambani	$39.9 billion
21.	Jack Ma	$38.9 billion
22.	MacKenzie Scott	$37.3 billion
23.	François Pinault	$35.1 billion
24.	Beate Heister & Karl Albrecht, Jr.	$34.9 billion
25.	Phil Knight	$34.3 billion

60 TERRIFIC FACTS ABOUT TOYS

1. The oldest toys ever found were a set of stone dolls buried with a child in Siberia around 2500 BC.

2. Another ancient toy was a rattle found in Ankara, Turkey. It is 4,000 years old.

3. The yo-yo was invented in ancient China.

4. Yo-yos were originally used as weapons.

5. Legos were invented in 1932.

6. The Legos name comes from the Danish words *leg godt*, which means "play well."

7. Lego mini-figures first appeared in 1978.

8. Since then, more than 4 billion mini-figures have been made.

9. Six standard 8-studded Lego bricks can be combined in more than 915,000,000 ways.

10. Lego makes more than 306 million tiny tires every year.

11. Lego makes more (mini) tires than Goodyear, the leading manufacturer of tires for cars and trucks.

12. The game *Candy Land* was invented to amuse young patients in the polio ward of a hospital.

13. Mr. Potato Head's plastic body wasn't introduced until 1964. Mr. Potato Head was originally just a collection of plastic eyes, noses, and mouths. Kids had to provide their own potato.

14. There were Mr. Potato Head kits for carrots, cucumbers, and peppers, too.

15. Mr. Potato Head became the first toy advertised on TV.

16. Barbie's full name is Barbara Millicent Robinson.

17. Barbie and Ken were named after their inventor's two children.

18. Hasbro created G.I. Joe as the world's first action figure.

19. "G.I." stands for "Government Issue."

20. Hasbro thought that little boys wouldn't play with a doll, but they would play with an action figure.

21. Stretch Armstrong is so stretchy because he's filled with corn syrup.

22. The Super Soaker was invented by a NASA engineer.

23. Tonka is named after Lake Minnetonka in Minnesota.

24. Engineer Richard James invented the Slinky by accident when he watched a spring fall off a shelf and flip over across the floor.

25. In 1991, Little Tykes Cozy Coupe was named the bestselling car in America.

26. Koosh Balls are named for the sound they make when they hit your hand.

27. The Rock 'Em Sock 'Em Robots are named Red Rocker and Blue Bomber.

28. The Hungry Hungry Hippos are named Happy, Henry, Harry, and Homer.

29. Care Bears started as illustrations for greeting cards.

30. The Magic 8-Ball contains a 20-sided die.

31. Sea Monkeys aren't monkeys; they are brine shrimp.

32. The first rag dolls were found in ancient Rome and date from 300 BC.

33. Most seventeenth-century European dolls looked like adults.

34. Childlike dolls did not appear until 1850.

35. "Doll hospitals" specialize in repairing and restoring dolls.

36. *Chutes and Ladders* is based on an ancient Indian game.

37. When *Chutes and Ladders* was first sold in Europe, it was called Snakes and Ladders.

38. *The Game of Life* was invented way back in 1860.

39. The goal of the original *Life* was for players to lead a virtuous life.

40. *Operation* started as a project for a college class in industrial design.

41. The patient's name in *Operation* is Cavity Sam.

42. *Settlers of Catan* has been translated into 30 languages.

43. *Catan* comes in more than 80 official editions and sells nearly 1 million copies a year.

44. Original paper versions of *Battleship* included land areas.

45. A traditional *Connect Four* board has 4,531,985,219,092 possible positions.

46. *Cranium* was the first game sold on Amazon.

47. The name *Jenga* is based on a Swahili word meaning "to build."

48. According to Hasbro, the tallest *Jenga* tower was 40 levels plus 2 pieces on top.

49. Play-Doh was invented to clean wallpaper.

50. Play-Doh wasn't used as a toy until 1954.

51. Play-Doh's unique smell was trademarked in 2017.

52. The first Paddington Bear was made in 1972.

53. Paddington Bear was first introduced in 1952.

54. The teddy bear is named after President Theodore Roosevelt.

55. The longest *Monopoly* game lasted 70 straight days.

56. The prisoner on *Monopoly*'s "Jail" space is named Jake the Jailbird.

57. Hot Wheels were first introduced in 1968.

58. The first Hot Wheels car to be made was a custom Camaro.

59. Hot Wheels introduces 130 new car designs each year.

60. Hot Wheels partners with almost every car maker in the world.

50 TRAVELIN' FACTS ABOUT TRANSPORTATION

13

1. The horse and the donkey were domesticated for transportation around 4000 BC.

2. The horse was domesticated in Mesopotamia.

3. The donkey was domesticated in Egypt.

4. In 1900, Americans owned just 8,000 cars.

5. By 1920, they owned 8 million.

6. By 2000, there were more than 220 million cars in the United States.

7. There are more than 3,980,000 miles of roads in the United States.

8. About one-third of the roads in the United States are unpaved.

9. America has the largest road network in the world.

10. Australia's Ghan is the longest train in the world.

11. The Ghan has 44 cars and 2 locomotives.

12. The Ghan's total length is 3,600 feet (1,097 meters), or more than half a mile (0.8 km).

13. The United States has 200,000 miles (321,869 km) of railroad track.

14. Andrew Jackson was the first sitting president in the United States to ride on a train.

15. He traveled from Baltimore to Ellicott's Mills, Maryland.

16. The most popular car color is white.

17. The first tractor-trailer was invented in 1914 for a customer who wanted to haul a boat.

18. If you lined up every truck in the United States, they would reach the moon.

19. The trucking industry moves about 70 percent of all freight in the United States.

20. Rudolph Diesel created the diesel engine in 1895. His engine could also run on peanut oil.

21. The first car used a lever instead of a steering wheel.

22. The first speeding ticket was issued in 1902.

23. In 2018, Americans took 9.9 billion trips on public transportation.

24. The George Washington Bridge, connecting New York City and New Jersey, is the most traveled bridge in the world.

25. About 100 million vehicles cross the George Washington Bridge each year.

26. One out of every 7 jobs in the United States is related to transportation.

27. The highest mileage on a single car was more than 3 million miles.

28. The car that holds that highest mileage record is a 1966 Volvo.

29. The United States has more than 614,000 bridges.

30. The automobile was invented by Karl Benz in Germany in 1885.

31. The world's first electric traffic signal was installed on the corner of Euclid Avenue and East 105th Street in Cleveland, Ohio, in 1914.

32. The first hot air balloon flight was in France in 1783. Its passengers were a sheep, a duck, and a rooster.

33. The New York City subway has 468 stations, the most of any subway system.

34. The New York City subway also has a record-breaking 24 lines.

35. The Shanghai Metro has the longest subway system, with 341 miles (548 km).

36. The Beijing Subway is the busiest in the world, with 3.4 billion passengers a year.

37. Tokyo subway trains are so crowded that workers called *oshiya* actually shove people onto trains.

38. *Oshiya* means "person who pushes for a living."

39. The tiny Nano sedan was introduced in India in 2008.

40. The Nano has a two-cylinder engine and is just 11 feet (3.4 meters) long and 5 feet (1.5 meters) wide.

41. The Nano does not have power steering, power windows, or air conditioning.

42. The *Trans-Siberian Express* makes the longest regular train trip in the world. It travels between Moscow and Vladivostok, Russia, covering 5,778 miles (9,300 km) and making 91 stops over 9 days.

43. In the United States, interstate highways are marked by blue signs with red tops.

44. US interstate highways that run north-south are odd numbers with one or two digits.

45. US interstate highways that run east-west have even numbers.

46. US highways are marked with black and white signs.

47. North-south US highways also have odd numbers.

48. East-west US highway routes have even numbers.

49. Trains on China's Beijing-Tianjin Intercity Rail line run at a maximum operating speed of 217.5 miles (350 km) per hour.

50. Tests have shown the Beijing-Tianjin trains could run even faster, but the speed is limited for safety reasons.

100 AMAZING FACTS ABOUT NUMBERS

1. There is only one even prime number: the number 2.

2. All other even numbers can be divided by 2.

3. The largest prime number was discovered in 2018.

4. The largest prime number is written as M82589933, which is $2^{82,589,933} - 1$.

5. The word *hundred* comes from the Old Norse *hundrath*, but *hundrath* actually means "120."

6. Zero is the only number that can't be represented in Roman numerals.

7. That's because ancient cultures did not consider zero to be a number.

8. Different cultures discovered zero at different times.

9. Zero was first used by the Sumerians between 4,000 and 5,000 years ago.

10. Sumerians didn't use it to represent nothing, though. Instead, they added it to single numbers to denote tens and hundreds.

11. In the fifth century, an Indian mathematician named Brahmagupta became the first person to use zero as a number.

12. He represented it with a dot, which he wrote under other numbers.

13. The number 4 is the only one spelled with the same number of letters as its value.

14. The number 40 is the only one spelled in alphabetical order.

15. The number 1 is the only number spelled in reverse alphabetical order.

16. The number 6 is the smallest perfect number.

17. That means it is the sum of its integers. 3+2+1=6.

18. The next perfect number is 28.

19. An irrational number is a number that can't be written as a fraction.

20. Pi is an irrational number.

21. Pi never repeats and never ends.

69. Adding up the numbers 1 to 100 gives you the number 5050.

70. Pythagoras, the Greek father of math, used little rocks to represent equations.

71. The word *calculus* is the Greek word for "pebbles."

72. The word *fraction* comes from the Latin "fractio," which means "to break."

73. If you folded a piece of paper in half 103 times, it would be the thickness of the observable universe.

74. The record for folding a piece of paper in half is just 12 times.

75. The numbers on opposite sides of a die always add up to 7.

76. The numbers 1, 2 and 3 all share a vertex on a die.

77. If these three numbers run clockwise around this vertex, then the die is called left-handed.

78. If the three numbers run counter-clockwise round the vertex, then it is right-handed.

79. A three-dimensional parallelogram is called a parallelepiped.

80. A ratio describes the relation between two amounts. It is the number of times one amount is contained in, or contains, the other.

81. A ratio of 1.618 is called the golden ratio.

82. The golden ratio has been used throughout history to design pleasing buildings, artworks, and music.

83. The word *geometry* comes from the Greek words *geo* ("earth") and *metria* ("measure").

84. A Greek mathematician named Euclid is called the father of geometry.

85. Along with arithmetic, geometry was one of the two fields of early mathematics.

86. Ancient Egyptians used geometry as far back as 3000 BC.

87. The equals sign (=) was invented in 1557 by a Welsh mathematician named Robert Recorde.

88. There are 293 ways to make change for $1 using pennies, nickels, dimes, quarters, and half dollars.

89. The number 169 is equal to 13² and its reverse 961 is equal to 31².

90. The Chinese were the first to use negative numbers around 2,200 years ago.

91. The number −40 is the only number equal on both temperature scales.

92. So, −40°C is equal to −40°F.

93. In chess, there are 4,897,256 total possible positions after 5 moves by both players.

94. There is a combination of 26,830 possible Tic-Tac-Toe games.

95. The polar diameter of the Earth is approximately equal to half a billion inches.

96. We use the base 10 or decimal number system.

97. The Mayans counted by 20s, which is called a vigesimal system.

98. The base two, or binary, system only uses the digits 0 and 1.

99. Computers use the binary system to store data.

100. The number 18 is the only one that is twice the sum of its digits. (18: 1 + 8 = 9: 9 × 2 = 18).

70 AWESOME OCEAN AND SEA FACTS

1. The Pacific is the world's largest ocean.

2. The Pacific covers 30 percent of the world's surface.

3. The Pacific is also the deepest ocean.

4. The average depth of the Pacific Ocean is 13,000 feet (4,000 meters).

5. The Pacific Ocean was named by Portuguese explorer Ferdinand Magellan.

6. Magellan called the ocean *mar pacific*, which means "peaceful sea."

7. Roughly 75 percent of the world's active volcanoes are located in the Ring of Fire in the Pacific Ocean.

8. The Ring of Fire has 90 percent of the world's earthquakes.

9. The Pacific is bordered by 55 countries.

10. The Pacific's Marianas Trench is the deepest ocean trench in the world.

11. The Marianas Trench is deeper than Mount Everest is tall.

12. The Pacific contains the second-largest island in the world, New Guinea.

13. There are more than 25,000 islands in the Pacific.

14. Most islands in the Pacific are located south of the Equator.

15. The Pacific has four types of islands.

16. They are continental islands, high islands, coral reefs, and lifted coral platforms.

17. Point Nemo in the Pacific Ocean is called a pole of inaccessibility. It is the farthest location from the ocean to the nearest coastline.

18. Point Nemo got its name from a character in Jules Verne's book *20,000 Leagues Under the Sea*.

19. The world's largest spacecraft cemetery is located near Point Nemo.

20. There are more than 161 pieces of satellites and other spacecraft buried there.

21. Hydrothermal vents at the bottom of the ocean release water that can be as hot as 750°F (400°C).

22. The Atlantic is the second-largest ocean.

23. The Atlantic covers about 41 million square miles (106,190 square km).

24. That's about 20 percent of the Earth's surface.

25. This ocean gets its name from Atlas, a character in Greek mythology who holds up the world.

26. The Atlantic was the first ocean to be crossed by ship.

27. The Atlantic was also the first to be crossed by an airplane.

28. The Mid-Atlantic Ridge is a mountain range underneath the Atlantic.

29. The Mid-Atlantic Ridge is the longest mountain range on the planet.

30. The Mid-Atlantic Ridge can be seen on satellite pictures.

31. The deepest part of the Atlantic Ocean is the Milwaukee Deep, off the coast of Puerto Rico.

32. The Milwaukee Deep is 27,493 feet (8,380 meters) deep.

33. More rivers drain into the Atlantic than any other ocean.

34. There are three types of islands in the Atlantic.

35. They are pure oceanic islands, volcanic islands, and pure continental islands.

36. The Atlantic is the saltiest ocean.

37. Greenland, the largest island in the world, is located in the Atlantic.

38. There is an underwater waterfall between Greenland and Iceland.

39. The waterfall is formed by the temperature difference in the water on either side of the strait.

40. Cold water from the east flows under warmer water from the west, creating a drop of 11,500 feet (3,505 meters).

41. The Indian Ocean covers almost 20 percent of the Earth's surface.

42. The Indian is the third-largest ocean.

43. The Indian's average depth is 12,274 feet (3,741 meters).

44. The Indian is the warmest ocean in the world.

45. Because of its warmth, the Indian Ocean has less sea life than the Atlantic or Pacific Oceans.

46. There is a submerged continent under the Indian Ocean.

47. The submerged continent is called the Kerguelen Plateau.

48. The Southern Ocean is also called the Antarctic Ocean because it surrounds Antarctica.

49. The Southern Ocean is the only ocean that goes all the way around the Earth.

50. Some scientists think the Southern Ocean doesn't really exist.

51. They say this ocean is actually part of the Indian, Pacific, and Atlantic Oceans.

52. The Southern Ocean ranges between 13,000 and 16,000 feet (4,000 and 5,000 meters) deep.

53. During the winter, about half of the Southern Ocean is covered by ice.

54. Many marine animals and birds live in the Southern Ocean.

55. The Arctic Ocean is the world's smallest ocean.

56. The Arctic is also the shallowest.

57. The Arctic Ocean is located around the North Pole.

58. It covers about 5,427,000 square miles (14,056,000 square km).

59. The Arctic's average depth is 3,406 feet (1,038 meters).

60. Its deepest point is Litke Deep, at 17,800 feet (5,450 meters).

61. *Arctic* comes from the Greek word *arktos*, which means "bear."

62. The Great Bear constellation appears just above the North Pole.

63. In 1896, Fridtjof Nansen became the first person to cross the Arctic Ocean by boat.

64. The Arctic can also be crossed by dog sled, as it freezes during the winter.

65. The Pacific is the world's most polluted ocean.

66. There are almost 2 trillion pieces of plastic floating in the Pacific.

67. Much of the plastic is located in several giant garbage patches.

68. Oceans can have lakes and rivers.

69. Seawater creates depressions on the ocean floor. Because the water around these depressions contains more salt than normal seawater, it sinks into the depressions, creating little lakes.

70. Some ocean lakes even have waves.

50 BEAUTIFUL BIRD FACTS

1. There are about 10,000 different species of birds.

2. Scientists believe that birds evolved from dinosaurs.

3. Most hummingbirds weigh less than a nickel.

4. Hummingbirds can fly backward.

5. Ducks that sleep on the edge of a group keep one eye open to watch for danger.

6. Owls swallow small prey whole.

7. After eating, owls throw up pellets filled with their prey's bones and fur.

8. Cardinals often cover themselves with ants.

9. A chemical in the ants keeps away lice and other pests.

10. Flamingos mate for life.

11. A flamingo eats with its head upside-down.

12. Ravens can copy human words and sounds.

13. Parrots can learn to say hundreds of words.

Pigeons are believed to be the first domesticated birds.

Pigeons can be trained to carry messages.

A penguin's black-and-white colors help it hide from predators underwater.

About two-thirds of all bird species are found in tropical rain forests.

The Australian pelican has the longest bill of any bird in the world. It is nearly 2 feet (.5 meters) long.

The sword-billed hummingbird's bill is longer than its body.

Crows make and use tools.

Owls can't swivel their eyes. They move their whole head to see around them.

The kiwi has nostrils at the end of its beak.

The larger the bird, the longer it takes its eggs to hatch.

24. A green woodpecker can eat as many as 2,000 ants per day.

25. The whistling swan has more feathers than any other bird. It has up to 25,000 feathers.

26. Hummingbirds have fewer than 1,000 feathers.

27. A pelican's pouch-like beak can hold up to 2.5 gallons (9.5 liters) of water at a time.

28. A bird's toes automatically clench around a branch when they're sleeping to prevent them from falling off.

29. The pelican's beak shrinks to squeeze out the water before the pelican swallows its food.

30. The heaviest bird of prey is the Andean condor. It can weigh up to 27 pounds (12 kg).

31. Many birds have hollow bones to make them light enough to fly.

32. A bird's feathers weigh more than its skeleton.

33. The shape of a bird's beak can tell you what kind of food it eats.

34. Arctic terns migrate 25,000 miles (40,000 km) between the Arctic to the Antarctic every year.

35. The wandering albatross has the greatest wingspan of any bird.

36. Its wingspan is up to 11.8 feet (3.6 meters) wide.

37. Bar-headed geese fly across the Himalayas, the highest mountains in the world. They fly almost as high as jet planes.

38. The highest-flying bird is the griffon vulture. In 1973, one collided with an airplane more than 6.8 miles (11 km) above Africa.

39. The emperor penguin is the only bird that lays its eggs in the middle of winter.

40. Penguins can jump up to 6 feet (2 meters) in the air.

41. An albatross can soar for up to 6 hours without moving its wings.

42. The kori bustard is the heaviest bird in the air. It weighs about 31 pounds (14 kg).

43. The chicken is the most common species of bird in the world.

44. Since flying is such hard work, kori bustards only fly in emergencies and only over short distances.

45. Gentoo penguins can swim up to 22 miles (36 km) per hour.

46. Parrots are the longest-lived bird species. They often live for 80 to 100 years.

47. A chicken with red earlobes will usually produce brown eggs.

48. A chicken with white earlobes will usually produce white eggs.

49. The hooded pitohui of Papua, New Guinea, is the only poisonous bird in the world.

50. The hooded pitohui's poison is found in its skin and feathers.

50 FACTS ABOUT HEARTS

1. The human heart has four chambers.

2. The top chambers are called atriums. The bottom chambers are called ventricles.

3. The right atrium and right ventricle receive blood from the body and pump it to the lungs.

4. The left atrium receives oxygenated blood from the lungs.

5. The left ventricle pumps blood to other parts of the body.

6. The beating sound of a heart is caused by valves opening and closing.

7. The average adult's heart is the size of a fist.

8. It weighs a little less than 1 pound (.45 kg).

9. A man's heart is a few ounces (grams) heavier than a woman's.

10. The human heart beats about 115,000 times a day.

11. It pumps about 2,000 gallons (7,571 liters) of blood a day.

12. Newborn babies have the fastest heartbeats.

13. An electrical system controls your heartbeat.

14. The heart works twice as hard as the leg muscles of a sprinter.

15. The heart can keep beating even if it's disconnected from the body.

16. Daniel Hale Williams performed the first open-heart surgery in 1893.

17. The youngest person to receive heart surgery was only a minute old.

18. The earliest known case of heart disease was spotted in the remains of a 3,500-year-old Egyptian mummy.

19. A woman's heart beats slightly faster than a man's heart.

20. Laughing is good for your heart.

21. The heart can beat up to 3 billion times during an average lifespan.

22. Your heartbeat can change depending on the type of music you listen to.

23. Every day, your heart creates enough energy to drive a truck for 20 miles (32 km).

24. Your left lung is narrower than your right to make room for your heart.

25. A giraffe's heart is lopsided. The left ventricle is thicker than the right.

26. This is because the left side has to pump blood up the giraffe's long neck.

27. Giraffes have the highest blood pressure of any mammal, measuring 280/180.

28. A wasp called the fairy fly has the smallest heart of any living creature.

29. You need a microscope to see it.

30. Small animals usually have faster heartbeats than large animals.

31. The smallest mammal, the American pygmy shrew, has the fastest heartbeat.

32. A pygmy shrew's heart beats up to 1,200 times per minute.

33. Blue whales have the largest heart of any animal.

34. But a blue whale's heart only beats 6 to 10 times a minute.

35. An octopus has three hearts.

36. A hummingbird's heart rate can be as high as 1,000 beats per minute in some species.

37. Although coronary artery disease is common in people, it is very rare in cats and dogs.

38. Zebrafish can regenerate their hearts.

39. A seal's heart rate can go as low as 10 beats per minute during an extended underwater dive.

40. Mammals have four-chambered hearts.

41. Most reptiles have hearts with only three chambers.

42. Crocodile hearts have four chambers, but they also have an extra flap that can close to keep blood from going to the lungs.

43. After a big meal, a python's heart can double in size to pump extra blood to the stomach.

44. Scientists believe crocodiles can send blood to the stomach to aid digestion.

45. Fish only have a two-chambered heart.

46. A cheetah's heart rate can soar from 120 to 250 beats per minute in just a few seconds.

47. A cow's heart is the size of a human head.

48. Sea stars and jellyfish don't have any hearts at all.

49. Wood frogs freeze solid in the winter, and their hearts stop beating.

50. In the spring, the wood frog thaws out and its heart starts up again.

55 GREAT NATIONAL PARK FACTS

1. The National Park Service (NPS) was created in 1916 by President Woodrow Wilson.

2. The NPS protects 407 sites with 28 different designations.

3. These include 127 historical parks or sites, 78 national monuments, 59 national parks, 25 battlefields or military parks, 19 preserves, 18 recreation areas, 10 seashores, 4 parkways, 4 lakeshores, and 2 reserves.

4. That adds up to more than 84 million acres (34 million hectares) of landscapes and historical sites.

5. Wrangell-St. Elias National Park in Alaska is the largest national park.

6. It covers 13,000 square miles (33,670 square km).

7. Death Valley National Park in California is the largest national park in the lower 48 states.

8. It covers 5,300 square miles (13,727 square km).

9. Hot Springs National Park in Arkansas is the smallest at just 5,500 acres (2,226 hectares).

10. Hot Springs was actually the first piece of land protected by the federal government, before the national park system existed.

11. Yellowstone National Park is the oldest US national park.

12. Yellowstone was founded in 1872.

13. Mackinac National Park in Michigan was established in 1875. It was returned to Michigan in 1896 and is now a state park.

14. Three of the world's highest waterfalls are found in Yosemite National Park.

15. Yosemite's Ribbon Falls is nine times higher than Niagara Falls.

16. Great Smoky Mountains National Park is the most visited national park each year.

17. It welcomes more than 9 million guests per year.

18. Grand Canyon National Park is second-most popular, with more than 4 million visits per year.

19. The tallest point in a national park is Denali in Alaska.

20. Grand Teton National Park and Yellowstone National Park are just 10 miles (16 km) away from each other.

21. California has nine national parks.

22. Alaska is home to eight national parks.

23. Arches National Park has the largest concentration of stone arches in the world.

16.	1931	More than 4 million people are killed in a series of floods along the Yangtze and Huai Rivers in China.
17.	1948	An earthquake in the Soviet Union kills 110,000.
18.	1959	A hurricane kills up to 1,800 people in Mexico.
19.	1960	The powerful Valdivia earthquake hits Chile, killing 5,700 people.
20.	1962	About 4,000 people are killed in avalanches in Huascarán, Peru.
21.	1970	More than 500,000 people are killed when a cyclone hits Bhola in Bangladesh.
22.	1970	The Great Peruvian earthquake and landslide kill up to 70,000, making it Peru's worst disaster.
23.	1975	Typhoon Nina is responsible for 229,000 deaths in China.
24.	1976	Hurricane Liza kills 1,263 people in Mexico.
25.	1976	The Tanghshan earthquake in China killed 655,000.
26.	1980	At least 1,700 die when a heat wave strikes the central and southern parts of the United States.
27.	1982	Hurricane Paul kills more than 1,600 in Mexico, El Salvador, and Guatemala.
28.	1986	A cloud of carbon dioxide erupted from Lake Nyos in Cameroon, suffocating 1,700 people and thousands of cattle.
29.	1989	The Daulatpur-Saturia tornado kills 1,300 people and wipes out entire communities in Bangladesh.
30.	1989	The Kavali cyclone kills 902 people in Thailand.
31.	1990	The Andhra Pradesh cyclone kills 967 people in India.

32.	1997	Up to 500 people die when Hurricane Pauline strikes Mexico.
33.	1998	Hurricane Mitch becomes one of the deadliest hurricanes, killing more than 11,000 people in Central America.
34.	1999	A storm and the resulting floods and landslides killed between 10,000 and 30,000 people in Vargas, Venezuela.
35.	2003	A heat wave kills 70,000 people in Europe.
36.	2004	An earthquake and subsequent tsunami in the Indian Ocean kills 227,898 people in 14 countries.
37.	2005	More than 1,200 are killed when Hurricane Katrina strikes the Gulf Coast of the United States.
38.	2005	The Kashmir earthquake kills at least 79,000 people in India, Pakistan, and Afghanistan.
39.	2008	A blizzard in Afghanistan kills 926 people.
40.	2008	Cyclone Nargis becomes Myanmar's worst natural disaster, killing more than 138,000 people.
41.	2010	About 316,000 are killed in a devastating earthquake in Haiti.
42.	2013	Typhoon Haiyan kills more than 6,300 people in the Philippines.
43.	2015	An earthquake in Nepal kills as many as 9,000 people.
44.	2017	Hurricane Maria kills almost 3,000 in Puerto Rico, the US Virgin Islands, and the Caribbean.
45.	2019	Cyclone Idai kills 1,300 people in Africa.

50 DRY DESERT FACTS

1. A desert receives fewer than 10 inches (25 cm) of precipitation a year.

2. About 20 percent of the Earth's land surface is desert.

3. Europe is the only continent without a large desert.

4. There are four major types of desert.

5. The types of desert are hot and dry, semiarid, coastal, and cold.

6. Antarctica is the world's largest cold desert.

7. The Sahara in Africa is the world's largest hot desert.

8. More than one-sixth of the world's population lives in deserts.

9. Animals, plants, and people have special adaptations for living in the desert.

10. Many desert animals are active only at night when it is cooler.

11. Some desert animals can survive on very little water.

12. Some desert animals get most of the water they need from the food they eat.

13. A cactus has long, deep roots to search out water.

14. Cacti store water inside their stems.

15. A cactus's waxy outer coating keeps water from escaping.

16. Other plants have roots near the surface to capture water before it evaporates.

17. Some parts of the Atacama Desert in Chile have never received any rain.

18. About 46,000 square miles (119,139 square km) of land turn to desert every year due to climate change and practices such as forest clear-cutting.

19. Desertification threatens the livelihoods of more than 1 billion people in 110 countries.

20. The word *desert* comes from a Latin word meaning "abandoned place."

21. Africa's Sahara Desert covers 12 countries.

22. Hot deserts usually feature very high temperatures during the day and very low temperatures at night.

23. Shallow, salty lakes sometimes form in deserts.

24. Deserts often contain large mineral deposits.

25. Deserts can be good places to farm solar energy.

26. Some deserts are so hot that when it rains, the water evaporates before it hits the ground.

27. Desert dust storms can be more than a mile (1.6 km) high and travel over 100 miles (161 km).

28. The giant saguaro cactus can grow 50 feet (15.24 meters) tall.

29. A saguaro can live for 200 years.

30. The elf owl is a little bird that sometimes lives inside a cactus during the day.

31. Dust storms from the Gobi Desert have been known to reach Beijing, China, nearly 1,000 miles (1,609 km) away.

32. The smallest desert in the world is the Carcross Desert in Yukon, Canada.

33. Carcross measures just 1 square mile (2.6 square km).

34. The only places with more diverse ecosystems than deserts are rain forests.

35. The first dinosaur eggs were discovered in the Gobi Desert in 1923.

36. The Gobi Desert covers parts of northwestern China and southern Mongolia. It is the fifth-largest desert in the world.

37. The tall Himalayan Mountains prevent rain from reaching the Gobi.

38. The Gobi Desert is the fastest-growing desert in the world.

39. Most of that expansion is because of cultivation practices and climate change.

40. The Namib Desert in Namibia, Africa, is the oldest desert in the world.

41. Namib is between 55 and 80 million years old.

42. The Sahara is just 2 to 3 million years old.

43. The Namib Desert has the tallest sand dunes in the world.

44. Some of them are up to 984 feet (300 meters) high.

45. Uzbekistan's Aralkum Desert is the world's youngest desert.

46. Aralkum is fewer than 50 years old.

47. Aralkum was created entirely because of disturbances caused by people.

48. The Aralkum Desert is also the most toxic desert in the world because of large amounts of pesticides, fertilizers, chemicals, and polluted runoff from farms and cities.

49. The Sahara Desert is actually shrinking. Climate change is causing the edges of the desert to become greener.

50. The driest desert in the United States is the Mojave.

30

FLYING FACTS ABOUT DRONES

1. The official name for drones is Unmanned Aerial Vehicle, or UAV.

2. They are also known as RPAS, or Remotely Piloted Aircraft Systems.

3. Drones were first developed by the military in the 1990s.

4. Small, lightweight drones can only stay in the air for about 10 minutes.

5. Larger drones can stay up for hours.

6. Police use drones to track criminals.

7. They can also be used to search for missing persons.

8. Drones can deliver food and medicine to people in disaster areas.

9. They can also be used to take amazing photos.

10. Drones must be registered with the Federal Aviation Administration.

11. More than 181,000 Americans have registered their drones.

12. Amazon has tested drones for use delivering packages.

13. Israel was the first country to build drones.

14. The Drone Racing League sets up courses in stadiums and warehouses for people to race their drones.

15. There are drone air shows and light shows.

16. In a 2013 test, Domino's used a drone to deliver a pizza.

17. It is illegal to fly drones near airports or military bases.

18. Drones are also banned in national parks.

19. Drones found the ruins of an ancient Mayan city in Guatemala.

20. There are an estimated 2 million drones in the United States.

21. There are an estimated 7 million drones in the world.

22. The fastest drone is called *Racer X*.

23. In 2017, *Racer X* set a world speed record of 163.5 miles (263 km) per hour.

24. *Racer X*'s propellers spin at 46,000 revolutions per minute.

25. During a test run, *Racer X* caught fire because its motors overheated.

26. In 2010, a French company released the first drone that could be controlled by a smartphone.

27. Drones can be used to create 3D maps.

28. The *Griff 300* drone can lift up to 660 pounds (300 kg).

29. That includes the drone's own weight of 165 pounds (75 kg).

30. Griff Aviation is working on a drone that can lift 1,764 pounds (800 kg).

9

50 EXCELLENT FACTS ABOUT EUROPE

1. The first humans arrived in Europe around 38,000 BC.

2. According to the United Nations, Europe is made up of 44 countries.

3. The largest country in Europe is Russia.

4. The smallest European country is Vatican City.

5. Europe is the second-smallest continent.

6. It covers 3,825,730 square miles (9,908,600 square km).

7. About 740 million people live in Europe.

8. Europeans speak more than 200 different languages.

9. The most common spoken language is English.

10. The highest point in Europe is Mount Elbrus in Russia at 18,514 feet (5,643 meters) above sea level.

11. Its largest lake is Lake Ladoga in Russia, with an area of 6,800 square miles (17,700 square km).

12. The longest river in Europe is Russia's Volga River, which is 2,193 miles (3,530 km) long.

13. There are 10 villages in Denmark, Sweden, and Norway that are spelled with just one letter.

14. The longest place name in Europe is a 57-letter village in Wales.

15. Europe gets its name from Europa, a princess in Greek mythology.

16. There are more bicycles than people in the Netherlands.

17. The oldest European nation is San Marino.

18. It was founded in the year 301.

19. San Marino is located inside the country of Italy.

20. So is Vatican City, home of the Roman Catholic pope.

21. Germany has the most McDonald's in Europe.

22. France has the second-most McDonald's, and the United Kingdom has the third-most.

23. Twelve countries in Europe have monarchies.

24. They are Andorra, Belgium, Denmark, Liechtenstein, Luxembourg, Monaco, the Netherlands, Norway, Spain, Sweden, the United Kingdom, and the Vatican.

25. The Danish monarchy is the oldest royal family in Europe.

26. It was founded in 935.

27. Monaco has the highest life expectancy in Europe and the world.

28. The average lifespan in Monaco is 89 years old.

29. Europeans eat 50 percent of all the world's chocolate.

30. The airport in Brussels, Belgium, sells more chocolate than anywhere else in the world.

31. Belgian chocolate is really (really) good.

32. The Czech Republic has the most castles in the world—932 of them.

33. There are about 7,000 lakes in Switzerland.

34. They are fed by melting snow from the Alps.

35. Vienna, Austria, is home to Schönbrunn Zoo, the oldest zoo in the world.

36. The Schönbrunn Zoo opened in 1752.

37. Germany's Volkswagen is the largest company in Europe.

38. St. Peter's Basilica in Vatican City is the largest church in Europe.

39. St. Peter's is 730 feet (222.5 meters) long, 500 feet (152 meters) wide, and almost 450 feet (137 meters) tall, and can hold up to 60,000 people.

40. Europe's most active volcano is Mount Etna in Sicily.

41. Istanbul, Turkey, is the largest city in Europe.

42. Azerbaijan, Georgia, Kazakhstan, Russia, and Turkey stretch across both Europe and Asia.

43. Christianity is the most popular religion in Europe.

44. About 76 percent of Europeans say they are Christian.

45. The second-most-popular religion is Islam.

46. Paris is the most popular tourist destination in Europe.

47. There are two Europe Days to celebrate European unity.

48. One is May 5 and one is May 9.

49. One-third of the world's wealth is in Europe, making it the richest continent.

50. The Perucica Forest in Bosnia and Herzegovina is the last surviving rain forest in Europe.

50 SUGARY SWEET CANDY FACTS

1. The candy bar was probably invented in England in 1847.

2. More than 400 million M&M's are made every day.

3. About 64 million Tootsie Rolls are made every day.

4. Candy corn was originally called chicken feed.

5. Candy corn was invented in 1898.

6. M&M's are the world's bestselling candy.

7. Snickers is the world's bestselling candy bar.

8. The Snickers bar was named after a horse.

9. The lollipop was also named after a horse, Lolly Pop.

10. Americans eat 2.8 billion pounds (1.3 kg) of chocolate every year.

11. That's 11 pounds (5 kg) per person.

12. Chocolate can be poisonous to dogs.

13. A dentist named William Morrison invented cotton candy.

14. He originally called it fairy floss.

15. White chocolate doesn't contain any cocoa solids, so it's not really chocolate.

16. M&M's are named after Mars and Murrie, the two men who invented the candy.

17. Forrest Mars, Sr., got the idea for M&M's after seeing soldiers eating chocolate covered with a hard shell to keep it from melting.

18. During World War II, M&M's were sold only to the military.

19. The filling between the layers of a Kit Kat bar is made from ground-up Kit Kat bars.

20. President Ronald Reagan was a huge fan of Jelly Belly jelly beans.

21. Junior Mints were named after a 1940s Broadway play titled *Junior Miss*.

22. The candy company Haribo gets its name from the first two letters of its inventor's first and last names and his hometown: **Ha**ns **Ri**egel from **Bo**nn, Germany.

23. Haribo gummy bears were introduced in 1922 and were the first gummy candy ever made.

24. Mike and Ike candy first appeared in 1940.

25. It comes in almost 40 different flavors.

26. The word *candy* comes from an ancient Indian word, *khanda*, which means "piece of sugar."

27. Candy first came to America in the early 1700s from Great Britain and France.

28. Daniel Peter and Henri Nestlé invented milk chocolate in 1875.

29. Tootsie Rolls were once marketed as a health food.

30. Hershey's Kisses and their eye-catching silver wrappers first appeared in 1906.

10 Most Popular and Least Popular Halloween Candies

10 MOST POPULAR

1. Reese's Peanut Butter Cups
2. Snickers
3. Twix
4. Kit Kats
5. M&M's
6. Nerds
7. Butterfinger
8. Sour Patch Kids
9. Skittles
10. Hershey's Bar

10 LEAST POPULAR

1. Candy Corn
2. Circus Peanuts
3. Mary Jane Taffy
4. Wax Coke Bottles
5. Necco Wafers
6. Tootsie Rolls
7. Smarties
8. Licorice
9. Good & Plenty
10. Bit-O-Honey

25

COOL CORAL REEF FACTS

1. Coral reefs have been called "the rain forests of the sea."

2. Coral reefs are made from the hard exoskeletons of corals.

3. They cover just 1 percent of the ocean but contain 25 percent of all marine species.

4. Coral reefs are the largest biological structures on Earth.

5. There are three types of coral reefs.

6. Fringing reefs are the most common. They grow on shore out to the sea.

7. Barrier reefs are separated from the shore by an area of deep water.

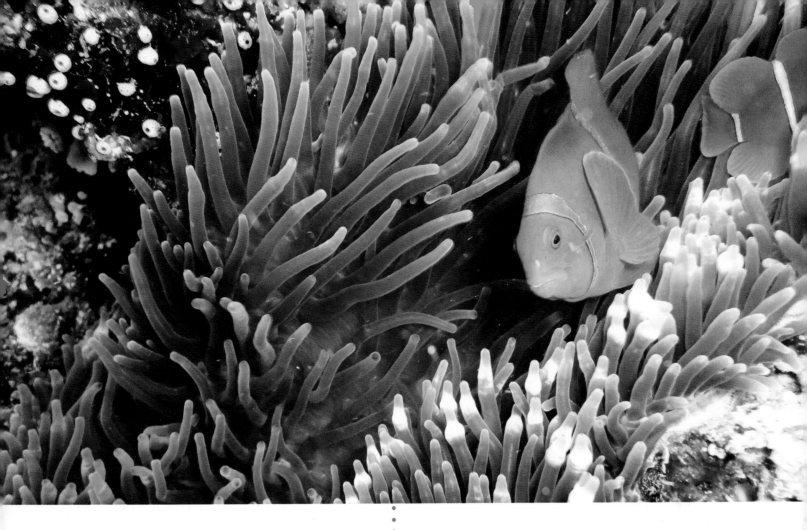

8. Atolls form when a fringing reef grows up from a volcanic island.

9. Atolls are usually circular or oval and have a lagoon in the center.

10. Coral reefs get their bright colors from algae that live inside the coral.

11. About 25 percent of the Earth's coral reefs are badly damaged.

12. Coral reefs can be damaged by pollution, destruction from fishing boats, overfishing, and coral harvesting.

13. Coral reefs only grow about 1 inch (2.5 cm) a year.

14. They come in a variety of shapes, sizes, and colors.

15. Coral reefs can't grow in water deeper than about 150 feet (46 meters). That's because deeper waters are too cold.

16. Most coral reefs grow on the eastern side of land masses, probably because it is warmer on that side.

17. Coral reefs grow best where stronger currents and waves bring more food to the reef.

18. The animals and plants in a coral reef rely on each other to survive.

19. The plants and animals that live in coral reefs are an important source of new medicines.

20. Australia's Great Barrier Reef contains more than 2,900 individual reefs and 1,050 islands.

21. The Mesoamerican Barrier Reef between Cancun to Honduras is the second-largest coral reef system.

22. It covers more than 550 miles (885 km).

23. Coral reefs have been on Earth for at least 230 million years.

24. Coral reefs can protect the shoreline from storm surges and flooding.

25. When coral dies, it turns white.

50
TALL AND STRANGE BUILDING FACTS

1. China is home to 12 of the 25 tallest buildings in the world.

2. Another 19 of them are in Asia.

3. One World Trade Center is the tallest building in the United States.

4. It was built to replace the World Trade Center in New York City.

5. The world's tallest hotel is the Gevora Hotel in Dubai.

6. It measures 1,168 feet (356 meters) tall, just 1 meter taller than the previous record holder.

7. It can be 15 degrees cooler at the top of Burj Khalifa than it is on the bottom.

8. One World Trade Center's 1,776-foot height commemorates the year the United States was born.

9. Tall buildings are constructed to be flexible to withstand changing wind and weather conditions.

10. Saudi Arabia's Makkah Royal Clock Tower boasts the world's largest clock.

11. The Makkah Clock measures 141 feet (43 meters) and can be read from more than 10 miles (16 km) away.

12. Poland's Crooked House is a strange building that looks like it is twisting and melting.

13. Portugal's Stone House is made of two huge rocks linked by concrete.

14. The Inntel Hotel in the Netherlands looks like dozens of traditional houses stacked on top of each other.

15. New York City's 432 Park Avenue is the tallest residential building in the world.

16. India's Lotus Temple is shaped like a lotus flower.

17. The Atomium Building in Belgium is shaped like an iron atom.

18. The Kansas City Library was built to look like a row of books.

19. Ohio's Longaberger Basket Building closed when its namesake company shut down in 2018, but the basket-shaped building may reopen as a hotel.

20. The Cubic Houses in the Netherlands were built on a bridge and look like they are leaning into each other.

21. Prague's Dancing House looks like two towers leaning into each other like dancing partners.

22. The Wonderworks Museum in Tennessee looks like it is upside-down.

23. The Ripley's Museum in Niagara Falls, Canada, looks like it is lying on its side.

24. Bangkok, Thailand's Elephant Building looks like an elephant, down to the tusks and eyes.

25. New Jersey also has an elephant-shaped building, called Lucy the Elephant.

THE 25 TALLEST BUILDINGS IN THE WORLD
As of March 2020:

1.	Burj Khalifa, Dubai	2,717 feet (828 meters)
2.	Shanghai Tower, China	2,073 feet (632 meters)
3.	Makkah Royal Clock Tower, Saudi Arabia	1,972 feet (601 meters)
4.	Ping An Finance Center, China	1,965 feet (599 meters)
5.	Lotte World Tower, South Korea	1,819 feet (554.5 meters)
6.	One World Trade Center, United States	1,776 feet (541.3 meters)
7.	Guangzhou CTF Finance Centre, China	1,739 feet (530 meters)
8.	Tianjin CTF Finance, China	1,739 feet (530 meters)
9.	CITIC Tower, China	1,731 feet (527.7 meters)
10.	Taipei 101	1,667 feet (508 meters)
11.	Shanghai World Financial Center, China	1,614 feet (492 meters)
12.	International Commerce Centre, Hong Kong	1,588 feet (484 meters)
13.	Lakhta Center, Russia	1,516 feet (462 meters)
14.	Vincom Landmark 81, Vietnam	1,513 feet (461.2 meters)
15.	Changsha IFS Tower T1, China	1,483 feet (452.1 meters)
16.	Petronas Twin Tower 1, Kuala Lumpur	1,489 feet (451.9 meters)
17.	Petronas Twin Tower 2, Kuala Lumpur	1,476 feet (450 meters)
18.	Suzhou IFS, China	1,476 feet (450 meters)
19.	Zifeng Tower, China	1,476 feet (450 meters)
20.	The Exchange 106, Kuala Lumpur	1,460 feet (445.1 meters)
21.	Willis Tower, United States	1,451 feet (442.1 meters)
22.	KK100, China	1,449 feet (441.8 meters)
23.	Guangzhou International Finance Center, China	1,439 feet (438.6 meters)
24.	Wuhan Center Tower, China	1,437 feet (438 meters)
25.	432 Park Avenue, United States	1,397 feet (425.5 meters)

25 CREEPY CRYPTIDS

A cryptid is a creature that people claim exists even though there is no proof. Here are some of the creepiest.

1. **Ahools**—These enormous, flesh-eating bats are said to live in rain forests on the island of Java.

2. **Akkorokamui**—This enormous octopus has been spotted off the coast of Japan.

3. **Altamaha-Ha**—This sea monster supposedly lives in a river in Georgia.

4. **Beast of Bodmin Moor**—These giant cats attacked livestock and terrorized the people of Cornwall, England, in 1978, but may have been wild cats who escaped from a private zoo.

5. **Bigfoot**—Also called Sasquatch, these giant, apelike creatures may roam the forests of the American Northwest.

6. **Brosno Dragon**—This monster in Russia's Lake Brosno may actually be a giant fish, a herd of elk swimming in the lake, or even an explosion of underwater volcanic gas.

7. **Champy**—A sea monster in Lake Champlain, between New York and Vermont, this creature has been sighted more than 300 times.

8. **Chupacabra**—A truly horrifying monster reported in Mexico and Central America, this creature supposedly drinks the blood of cattle.

9. **Dobhar-Chú**—A half-dog, half-fish hybrid, this monster has been part of Irish culture for hundreds of years.

10. **Emela-Ntouka**—This horned hippo supposedly lives in Central Africa. Its name means "elephant killer."

11. **Filiko Teras**—Descriptions of this sea monster, seen off the coast of Cyprus, may actually be sightings of giant squid.

12. **Grootslang**—This "great snake" is a legendary monster from South Africa with giant tusks like an elephant on the body of a giant snake.

13. **Jersey Devil**—This horrifying creature has been sighted in the swampy Pine Barrens of New Jersey for centuries.

14. **Kraken**—These legendary sea monsters have been reported in the world's oceans for centuries but are likely to be giant squid.

15. **Loch Ness Monster**—This giant sea serpent has reportedly been swimming in Scotland's Loch Ness for centuries, although no one has ever been able to photograph it.

16. **Mapinguari**—This bear-like, armored monster has been seen in the rain forests near Brazil as recently as 2007.

17. **Mothman**—There were several sightings of this giant, winged monster in the 1960s in West Virginia.

18. **Nahuelito**—This monster lives in Nahuel Huapi Lake in Argentina.

19. **Ogopogo**—A giant sea serpent, the Ogopogo supposedly lives in a lake in British Columbia, Canada.

20. **Olgoi-Khorkhoi**—A grotesque, toxic-slime-covered giant worm that is also called the Mongolian Death Worm and lives under the Gobi Desert.

21. **Momo**—"Momo" is short for Missouri monster. This Bigfoot-like creature was first spotted along the Mississippi River in 1971.

22. **Tatzelwurms**—These lizard-like creatures with long claws and gaping mouths supposedly live in the Alps and have been spotted all over Europe.

23. **Yeren**—A legendary wild man, the Yeren supposedly lives in the mountains of western Hubei, China, and is often called the Chinese Bigfoot.

24. **Yeti**—These giant snow monsters have been reported in the Himalayas for centuries, but scientists believe they only exist in folktales.

25. **Yowie**—These Bigfoot-type monsters were commonly seen in Australia in the 1800s, but today they are thought to be myths.

• • • • • • 13

50 WEIRD AND GROSS HUMAN BODY FACTS

1. The cornea is the only part of the body without a blood supply. It gets its oxygen directly from the air.

2. The human body contains enough fat to make seven bars of soap.

3. Babies have 300 bones, but some fuse together as they grow, so adults only have 206 bones.

4. When you blush, so does the lining inside your stomach.

5. A kind of tumor called a teratoma contains teeth and hair.

6. In cases of extreme starvation, the brain will start to consume itself.

7. The small intestine is about 23 feet long (7 meters).

8. For every organ you have two of, you only need one to survive.

9. If you could stretch out a single body's blood vessels, they would circle the Earth two and a half times.

10. You can't breathe and swallow at the same time.

11. You are taller in the morning than you are at night.

12. Your ears and nose never stop growing.

13. If you could spread out all the wrinkles in your brain, it would be the size of a standard pillowcase.

14. Stomach acid is so strong, it can dissolve metal.

15. Humans shed about 600,000 bits of skin every hour.

16. That works out to more than 8 pounds (3.6 kg) a year.

17. Tongue prints are as unique as fingerprints.

18. A person produces enough saliva in their lifetime to fill two swimming pools.

19. The jaw muscle is the strongest muscle in the body.

20. Blood makes up about 8 percent of a person's body weight.

21. Skin makes up about 15 percent of a person's body weight.

22. If you could spread out your skin, it would cover 20.8 square feet (1.9 square meters).

23. The entire surface of your skin is replaced every month.

24. That means you'll have about 1,000 different skins in your life!

25. The sound made when you crack your knuckles comes from gas bubbles exploding in your joints.

26. Bone marrow is the fastest-growing part of your body.

27. Hair is the second fastest.

28. One out of every 200 people is born with an extra rib.

29. Fingernails grow faster than toenails.

30. Tiny mites live in your eyelashes.

31. Eyelash mites eat skin cells and oils.

32. There are no muscles in your fingers.

33. Fingers move because of muscles in the palm and forearm.

34. The foot is one of the most ticklish parts of the body.

35. The bones in your forearm cross when you twist your wrist.

36. Your body releases about 2 cups of sweat each day.

37. It is almost impossible to keep your eyes open when you sneeze.

38. The lower jawbone is the only bone in the skull that can move.

39. A sneeze can expel material at up to 100 miles (161 km) per hour.

40. More than 1,400 different types of bacteria live in people's belly buttons.

41. Having two different-colored eyes is called heterochromia.

42. There are 10 times more bacteria cells in your body than human cells.

43. There are more lifeforms living on your skin than there are people on Earth.

44. It is impossible to tickle yourself.

45. We swallow around 2.5 pounds (1.14 kg) of mucus every day.

46. Humans actually glow, but the light is too weak to be seen by human eyes.

47. Every human has their own unique smell, except for identical twins, who smell the same.

48. Without saliva, you wouldn't be able to taste your food.

49. Feet have 500,000 sweat glands.

50. Feet can produce more than a pint (0.5 liter) of sweat per day.

40 FANTASTIC LIBRARY FACTS

1. There are almost 117,000 libraries in the United States.

2. Philanthropist Andrew Carnegie donated $55 million between 1886 and 1919 to build 2,509 libraries around the world.

3. Of those libraries, 1,679 of them are in the United States.

4. Before typewriters, librarians had to learn a specific kind of handwriting to fill out catalog cards.

5. This style of writing was called library hand.

6. The Library of Congress is the largest library in the world.

7. It contains more than 170 million items.

8. About half of the Library of Congress's book and serial collections are in languages other than English.

9. The collections contain materials in about 470 languages.

10. Anyone can visit the Library of Congress or do research there, but only members of Congress, the Supreme Court, and other government officials can check out books.

11. The Haskell Free Library and Opera House sits directly on the border between Vermont, United States, and Quebec, Canada.

12. A black line marks the international boundary, but patrons are free to move from one side to the other without a passport.

13. A large number of bats live in the Joanina Library at the University of Coimbra in Portugal. They eat insects that could damage the books.

14. In 2016, patrons at the San Jose Public Library in California owed $6.8 million in overdue fines.

15. In 2016, the granddaughter of a man who had taken out *The Microscope and Its Revelations* from Hereford Cathedral School in the United Kingdom returned the title 120 years after it had been borrowed. The library waived the fines.

16. The New York Public Library includes 87 libraries across New York City.

17. Two stone lions stand outside the main branch of the New York Public Library in New York City.

18. The lions' names are Patience and Fortitude.

19. The main branch includes 125 miles (201 km) of shelves.

20. The NYPL's collection also includes pieces of Percy Bysshe Shelley's skull and locks of hair from several famous writers.

21. The oldest library in the world is the Library of Ashurbanipal in Ninevah, Assyria (now in Iraq). It was founded in the seventh century BC.

22. Its "books" were actually stone tablets.

23. The Great Library of Alexandria in Egypt was the largest and most important library in the ancient world.

24. It was established around 295 BC and contained thousands of papyrus scrolls.

25. All ships visiting Alexandria had to surrender their books to the library of Alexandria to be copied. The original would be kept in the library and the copy given back to the owner.

26. The Osmothèque is a library of smells in Versailles, France. Founded in 1990, the library contains more than 3,200 kinds of perfumes.

27. As of 2017, there were 194,000 librarians, 40,000 library technicians, and 96,000 library assistants working in the United States.

28. Today's libraries loan many different items besides books.

29. Some libraries loan tools, baking supplies, telescopes, taxidermy samples, and more.

30. About 150 libraries in the world loan people who tell their life stories.

31. There are more public libraries than McDonald's in the United States.

32. An abandoned Walmart in McAllen, Texas, was turned into the largest single-floor public library in the United States.

33. The McAllen Library measures 124,500 square feet (11,567 square meters).

34. There were more than 1.35 billion visits to public libraries in the United States in 2016.

35. Almost 98 percent of libraries provide public computers and wifi for patrons to use.

36. People go to the library three times more often than they go to the movies.

37. The Yale University Beinecke Rare Book and Manuscript Library is the largest building in the world for preserving rare books and manuscripts.

38. Beinecke's central shelving area includes glass walls and soft lighting to protect the works from direct light.

39. The Library of Parliament in Ottawa, Canada, is pictured on that nation's ten-dollar bill.

40. Several other world cities, such as Beijing, have library vending machines in public places.

25 MARSUPIAL FACTS

1. Unlike other mammals, baby marsupials are very undeveloped when they are born.

2. The tiny, blind, hairless babies must crawl into a pouch on their mother's stomach.

3. They remain in the pouch for up to 40 days while they grow.

4. Almost all species of marsupials live in Australia.

5. Opossums are the only marsupials that live in North America.

6. When opossum babies get bigger, they hang on to their mother's back for travel.

7. The largest marsupial is the red kangaroo. They can weigh up to 200 pounds (91 kg).

8. The smallest is the long-tailed planigale. This little creature is just about 2 inches (5 cm) long.

9. Tasmanian devils can scare away predators with their powerful sneezes.

10. Numbats use their long tongues to eat up to 20,000 termites per day.

11. Marsupials have very short pregnancies. The shortest is the bandicoot, which is only pregnant for 12 days before giving birth.

12. Newborn dunnarts can breathe through their skin.

13. Koalas sleep up to 20 hours a day.

14. The prehistoric diprotodon was the largest-ever marsupial.

15. The diprotodon's jawbone alone was 1 foot (0.3 meter) long.

16. Its pouch was large enough to carry a human!

17. Marsupials have more teeth than other mammals.

18. Their diet is mostly made up of eucalyptus leaves.

19. Koalas eat up to 2.5 pounds (1.1 kg) of eucalyptus leaves a day.

20. Gliders have folds of skin extending from their wrists to their ankles. They use this like a sail to glide between trees.

21. Gliders also spin their tails around while they glide.

22. The Tasmanian devil is the largest living carnivorous marsupial.

23. South America's monito del monte is called a living fossil because it is the only living member of the order *Microbiotheria*.

24. There are more than 40 species of kangaroos.

25. Kangaroos can hop up to 40 miles (64 km) per hour and leap over 10-foot (3-meter) obstacles.

45

MICROSCOPIC FACTS ABOUT BACTERIA AND GERMS

1. Bacteria are microscopic organisms that live everywhere on our planet.

2. Bacteria are the oldest living things on Earth.

3. They've been on the planet for more than 3.5 billion years.

4. Bacteria survive by eating carbon.

5. Most consume dead organic materials.

6. Bacteria play a big part in decomposition.

7. A bacterium is just one single cell.

8. A bacterium can move about 100 times its body length in one second.

9. Bacteria can survive almost anywhere.

10. They have been found in ice, hot springs, and even radioactive waste.

11. Bacteria in your stomach and intestines help you digest food.

12. You have more bacterial cells in your body than human cells.

13. Foods such as yogurt, cheese, sourdough bread, and kimchee are made with bacteria.

14. There are more bacteria on Earth than any other living thing.

15. If all the bacteria on Earth were lined up, they would reach to the end of the universe.

16. Bacteria weren't discovered until 1674.

17. That's when a scientist named Antonie van Leeuwenhoek spotted them with a new invention called the microscope.

18. Van Leeuwenhoek called the tiny creatures animacules.

19. Antibiotics kill bacteria, but bacteria can adapt quickly to resist the medicine.

20. Some bacteria are shaped like a comma or corkscrew.

21. Bacteria communicate with each other using electrical signals.

22. A colony of billions of bacteria can communicate and work together as one organism.

23. One type of ocean-dwelling bacteria can reproduce just 10 minutes after it is born.

24. Bacteria reproduce by dividing in half.

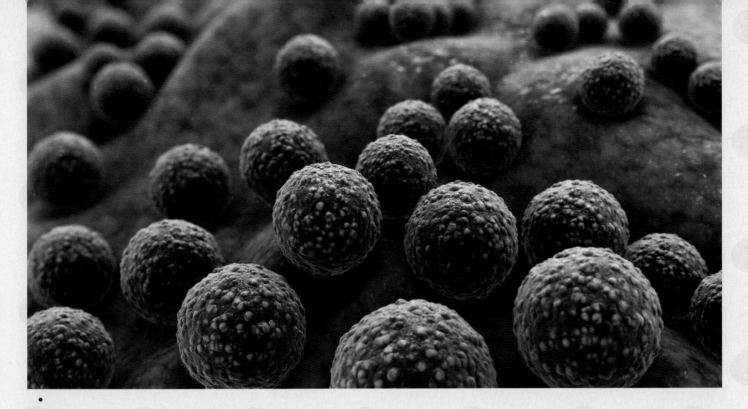

25. Bacteria have odd shapes. They are usually shaped like a sphere, rod, or spiral.

26. Most bacteria haven't been identified yet.

27. Floating bacteria are really good at causing condensation, leading some scientists to propose seeding clouds with bacteria to aid droughts.

28. Bacteria that cause disease are called pathogens.

29. Germs are tiny organisms that cause disease.

30. You can pick up germs by touching objects or by breathing them in.

31. Germs can survive for up to three hours on your hands.

32. One germ can multiply into more than 8 million germs in one day.

33. Almost 80 percent of germs are spread by hands.

34. There are more germs on your phone, keyboard, and cutting board than on a toilet seat.

35. When you flush the toilet, germs can spray up to 6 feet (1.8 meters). Close the lid!

36. More germs are transferred by shaking hands than by kissing.

37. There are four types of germs: bacteria, viruses, fungi, and protozoa.

38. It takes a minimum of 20 seconds washing hands with soap to kill germs.

39. Scientists are working on a type of bacteria that loves to eat oil so it can be used to clean up oil spills.

40. Bacteria in the mouth are what cause bad breath.

41. Bacteria also causes body odor.

42. Without bacteria, Earth would have no soil in which to grow plants.

43. Some bacteria can live without oxygen.

44. Damp hands spread 1,000 times more germs than dry hands.

45. Forty-million-year-old bacteria have been extracted and grown from a fossilized bee.

50 ROCKIN' MUSIC STARS AND STYLES FACTS

1. Bruno Mars appeared as an Elvis impersonator in a movie when he was four years old.

2. Lady Gaga was one of the first music stars to have her own social networking website.

3. Lady Gaga is the godmother of Elton John's son.

4. Justin Bieber was offered a spot on a Canadian minor-league hockey team.

5. Kanye West worked at the Gap before he was famous.

6. Nicki Minaj worked as a waitress at Red Lobster.

7. Pink worked at McDonald's.

8. Beyoncé's favorite number is four.

9. Michael Jackson's *Thriller* is the bestselling album of all time.

10. Jackson premiered his famous moonwalk on a television special in 1983.

11. Bruce Springsteen's *Born in the USA* was the first CD manufactured in the United States.

12. Rihanna's voice can cover three octaves.

13. Rihanna's full name is Robyn Rihanna Fenty.

14. Lady Gaga's real name is Stefani Germanotta.

15. Lady Gaga got her stage name from the Queen song "Radio Gaga."

16. Taylor Swift grew up on a Christmas tree farm in Pennsylvania.

17. Maroon 5's original name was Kara's Flowers.

18. There's a species of fly named after Beyoncé.

19. Beyoncé's name was chosen because the fly has golden hairs.

20. In 2009, Ed Sheeran played 312 concerts in one year in order to break a record.

21. Elvis Presley failed music class in school.

22. None of the Beatles could read or write music.

23. Paul McCartney said the Beatles' songs "just came to them."

24. Metallica is the first and only band to play on all seven continents.

25. They achieved this feat in one calendar year.

Hip-Hop Won't Stop
The Beat/The Rhymes/The Life

Hip-hop is the embodiment of a spirit of creative rebellion, freedom . . . . People keep looking at it and for it for some type of creative utopian vision.

—Fab Five Freddy

In bleak and forgotten urban spaces of the South Bronx, a new cultural, musical, and aesthetic style arose in the early 1970s. Despite some criticism, today this art thrives, a tribute to African American, Latino, and Caribbean youth who refused to let New York City's harsh economic realities stifle their creative energies. Hip-hop combined DJ-ing, MC-ing (which later developed into rapping), graffiti art, and break dancing (or B-boying) to create both a new sound and a new form of cultural expression.

Hip-Hop Terms

MC-ing— In the early days of hip-hop, the MC, or master of ceremonies, was the person talking over the music, inciting the crowd to dance and have fun. This role came from various traditions. MCing then became a way of talking by rhyming the music being spinned by the DJs; eventually it created rap. Today, the rapper is the most important hip-hop performer.

DJ-ing— The task of playing and announcing records has existed for many years. But three decades ago, new techniques and inventiveness in the use of turntables, mixers, and amplifiers created hip-hop. Jamaican-born Clive Campbell—DJ Kool Herc—is widely regarded as the "godfather" of hip-hop culture. Among other techniques, he devised back-and-forth mixing between two identical records to extend the rhythmic instrumental segment, or break, for the benefit of dancers.

B-Boying— This dynamic dance style originated in the South Bronx in the early 1970s in connection with hip-hop music. It is linked to the percussion breaks in records developed by DJs such as Kool Herc in his block parties. Many famous dance crews popularized the form, including Crazy Legs's group, Rock Steady Crew.

Graffiti— This element of hip-hop developed as a cultural expression mostly associated with markings in and on New York City subway cars. Many consider graffiti a new visual, moving art form, with innovations like the "wild style" of writing, a complicated construction of interlocking letters.

26. Michael Jackson once attempted to buy Marvel Comics because he wanted to play Spiderman in a movie.

27. Michael Jackson has 23 Guinness World Records, 13 Grammys, 40 Billboard Awards, and 26 American Music Awards.

28. Prince played 27 instruments on his first album.

29. Madonna is the bestselling female artist of all time.

30. Madonna has sold more than 200 million records.

31. Whitney Houston was a model when she was a teenager.

32. Fergie voiced Charlie Brown's sister, Sally, in a 1984 cartoon.

36. "Rapper's Delight" by the Sugarhill Gang became the first rap song on the Billboard Top 40 chart when released in 1979.

37. That song also created the name "rap" for that style of music.

38. Hip-hop music began in New York City in the mid-1970s when DJs used two turntables to create dance music at parties.

39. "Rapture" by Blondie was the first song with a rap in it to reach #1 on the Billboard chart.

40. More than 100 K-Pop groups debut every year in South Korea, but fewer than 5 percent are successful.

41. G-Dragon is the most popular K-Pop star in South Korea.

42. G-Dragon has more than 15 million Instagram followers.

43. When K-Pop artists release a new song or album, they appear on up to six music shows a week to promote it.

44. Justin Timberlake appeared on the TV show *The Mickey Mouse Club* when he was young.

45. Britney Spears and Christina Aguilera were also members of *The Mickey Mouse Club* cast.

46. Coldplay's Chris Martin has university degrees in Greek and Latin.

47. In 1962, Decca Records refused to sign the Beatles because they believed "guitar groups are on the way out."

48. Jay-Z is the most financially successful hip-hop artist.

49. Jay-Z became a billionaire in 2019.

50. Nicki Minaj is the richest female rapper, with a net worth of about $80

33. Gwen Stefani's "Hollaback Girl" was the first digital song to sell 1 million copies.

34. Gwen wrote the song after Courtney Love bullied her by calling her a cheerleader.

35. "Hollaback Girl" became Stefani's first

50 UNUSUAL FACTS ABOUT ART AND ARTISTS

1. Art used to be an Olympic event.

2. Between 1912 and 1948, medals were given out for sports-inspired painting, sculpture, architecture, literature, and music.

3. Street artist Banksy once hung his own work in London's Tate Museum.

4. Banksy also created a painting that self-destructed after it sold for $1.4 million.

5. No one knows Banksy's real name or what he looks like.

6. Leonardo da Vinci left hundreds of notes and sketches behind when he died.

7. Pierre-Auguste Renoir had such bad arthritis, an assistant had to place his paintbrush in his hand.

8. Roman statues were made with detachable heads.

9. Jackson Pollack used sticks, knives, and trowels to create his abstract painting *Autumn Rhythm (Number 30)*.

10. Pollack laid his canvases on the floor instead of on an easel.

11. He created a style called drip painting, where paint was dripped or splattered on the canvas.

12. Piet Mondrian's *Broadway Boogie Woogie* was based on the grid layout of New York City's streets.

13. There are four different versions of Edvard Munch's *The Scream*.

14. Andy Warhol did a series of 32 paintings of Campbell's soup cans.

15. Each painting showed a different flavor of soup.

16. Vincent Van Gogh painted *Starry Night* while he was in a mental hospital.

17. The couple in Grant Wood's *American Gothic* are father and daughter, not husband and wife.

18. The *American Gothic* painting was meant to express the ideals of rural life.

19. Edward Hopper's *Night Hawks* was meant to show the loneliness of a big city.

20. Salvador Dali's parents told him he was the reincarnation of his dead brother.

21. There is a portrait or silhouette of Dali in every one of his paintings.

22. Henri Matisse's painting *Le Bateau* hung upside-down for 46 days at New York's Museum of Modern Art before anyone noticed.

23. The *Mona Lisa* receives so many love letters, she has her own mailbox at the Louvre in Paris.

24. The *Mona Lisa* was stolen from the Louvre in 1911 but recovered in 1913.

25. The thief wanted to return the painting to its native Italy.

26. Pablo Picasso was considered a suspect in the theft.

27. Pablo Picasso loved animals and had a pet monkey, owl, turtle, goat, and many dogs and cats.

28. Leonardo da Vinci also loved animals and would often buy caged birds to set them free.

29. Da Vinci had no formal education. He created art by observing nature.

30. John James Audubon painted 435 watercolors of birds.

31. Audubon's mission was to paint every species of bird that lived in America.

32. Edgar Degas was so obsessed with ballet, he painted about 1,500 pictures of dancers.

33. Vincent Van Gogh created more than 900 paintings in just 10 years.

34. He only became famous after his death.

35. The world's most expensive painting to sell at auction is Leonardo da Vinci's *Salvator Mundi*. It sold for $450.3 million on November 15, 2017.

36. An art storage company mistook a sculpture by Anish Kapoor for garbage and threw it away.

37. Kapoor received £350,000 (about $430,000 dollars) in damages for the mistake.

38. Kapoor created Vantablack, the blackest black paint in the world.

39. Since Kapoor owns the rights to Vantablack, no one else is allowed to use it.

40. British artist Willard Wigan works between heartbeats so he doesn't destroy the piece he is creating. He uses rice or grains of sand and a surgical blade to create his "micro sculptures."

41. Wigan once accidentally inhaled one of his sculptures.

42. Pablo Picasso could draw before he could walk.

43. Picasso's first word was *lápiz*, or *pencil* in Spanish.

44. When Yves Klein couldn't find exactly the shade of blue he wanted, he invented one, called International Klein Blue.

45. Salvador Dali got the idea for the dripping clocks in *The Persistence of Memory* after watching cheese melt in the sun.

46. The model for Johannes Vermeer's *The Girl with a Pearl Earring* was the painter's daughter.

47. *The Girl with a Pearl Earring* has been called "the Dutch *Mona Lisa*."

48. Picasso's *Guernica* showed the devastation of the city of Guernica after a bombing during the Spanish Civil War.

49. Picasso got the idea for *Guernica* after reading a newspaper article about the destruction.

50. Even though he is one of the most famous painters in history, only 15 of Leonardo da Vinci's paintings exist.

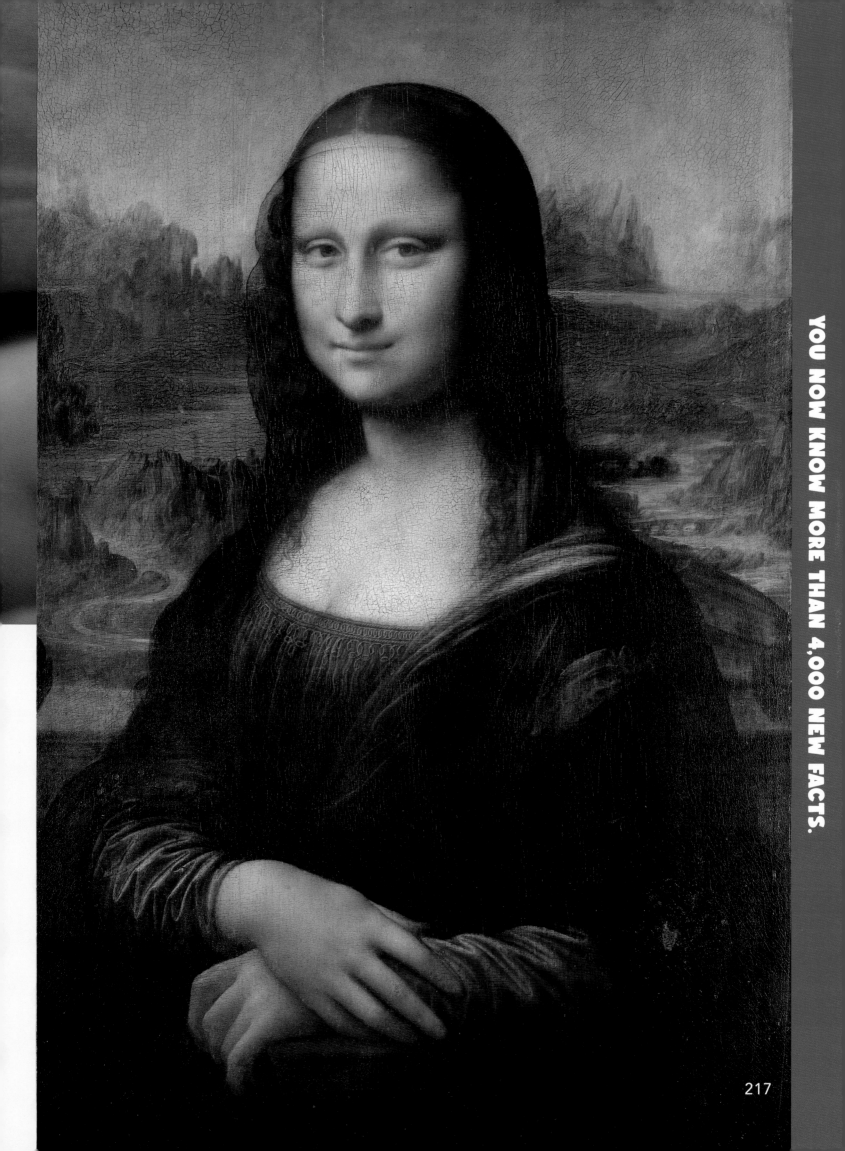

50 FACTS ABOUT WORLD LEADERS

1. In 2010, Dilma Rousseff became the first female president of Brazil.

2. *Forbes* magazine named German chancellor Angela Merkel the most powerful woman in the world in 2019.

3. Andry Rajoelina became the youngest African leader when he was voted president of Madagascar at just 34 years old.

4. Prime minister Mark Rutte of the Netherlands always rides a bicycle to work.

5. Russian leader Vladimir Putin has a black belt in Judo.

6. England's Queen Elizabeth II trained to be an Army truck driver and mechanic during World War II.

7. Barack Obama was the first US president to have a Twitter account.

8. Obama's was the world's most followed Twitter account during his election campaign in 2008.

9. President Xi Jinping of China lived in a cave for seven years after his father was kicked out of the Communist party.

10. Queen Elizabeth II is the only person in the United Kingdom who can drive without a license.

11. Queen Elizabeth II also doesn't have a passport.

12. Angela Merkel is afraid of dogs.

13. Pope Francis worked as a nightclub bouncer when he was young.

14. Pope Francis also swept floors, worked in a chemistry lab, and was a teacher.

15. And the pope likes dancing the tango!

16. Indonesian president Joko Widodo loves heavy metal music.

17. Liberian president George Weah was a famous soccer player who was named FIFA's World Player of the Year in 1995.

18. King Vajiralongkorn of Thailand trained as a fighter pilot and flies his own plane on overseas trips.

19. Angela Merkel grew up in East Germany, where there were often food shortages.

20. To this day, Merkel still hoards food.

21. Canadian prime minister Justin Trudeau enjoys snowboarding and was once a snowboard instructor.

22. Trudeau's father, Pierre Trudeau, was prime minister of Canada during the 1970s.

7

19

23. Before he was king, King Harald V of Norway represented his country in sailing in the 1964, 1968, and 1972 Olympics.

24. King Felipe VI of Spain competed in yachting at the 1992 Olympics in Barcelona.

25. The Dalai Lama likes to repair watches.

26. Israeli prime minister Benjamin Netanyahu spent $2,700 a year on ice cream.

27. Italian prime minister Silvio Berlusconi used to work as a vacuum cleaner salesman.

28. Berlusconi was also a singer on a cruise ship before transitioning into careers in law and business.

29. Finland's Sanna Marin became the world's youngest prime minister when she was elected at age 34 in 2019.

30. North Korea's dictator Kim Jong Un is one of the youngest leaders in the world.

31. Kim Jong Un was around 30 years old when he became Supreme Leader of that nation in 2011, after his father died.

32. However, no one is sure of how old Kim John Un really is.

33. Kim Jong Un went to school in Switzerland.

34. Queen Elizabeth II became Great Britain's longest-reigning monarch in 2015, having served 63 years on the throne.

35. She became the first British monarch to celebrate a Sapphire Jubilee, or 65 years on the throne, in 2017.

36. In 2016, Queen Elizabeth II became the longest-reigning monarch in the world.

37. The previous record holder was Thailand's King Bhumibol Adulyadej.

38. Nelson Mandela was the first black president of South Africa.

39. Before he became president, he spent 27 years in jail for fighting against the nation's system of apartheid.

40. In 2009, the United Nations proclaimed Mandela's birthday (July 18) to be Nelson Mandela International Day.

41. Nelson Mandela International Day asks people to spend 67 minutes doing something good for others to represent the 67 years Mandela spent working for racial equality.

42. In 2014, *Fortune* magazine named Pope Francis as the greatest leader in the world.

43. Angela Merkel and the Dalai Lama were also in the list's top ten.

44. Mohandas "Mahatma" Gandhi's nonviolent protests helped win India's independence from Great Britain and also inspired civil-rights leaders such as Martin Luther King, Jr.

45. Indira Gandhi (no relation to Mahatma Gandhi) was the first (and so far the only) female prime minister of India.

46. Indira's father, Jawaharlal, was India's first prime minister.

47. Indira Gandhi was assassinated in 1984.

48. Indira's son, Rajiv, took over as prime minister after his mother's death.

49. He was the youngest Indian prime minister.

50. Rajiv was assassinated in 1991.

50 FACTS ABOUT NORTH AMERICA

1. North America covers 9.5 million square miles (24.6 million square km).

2. It is the third-largest continent.

3. North America includes Canada, the United States, Mexico, Greenland, and numerous smaller countries in Central America and the Caribbean Sea.

4. North America is home to 23 countries and 9 dependencies (nations controlled by other countries).

5. Its total population is about 565 million people.

6. North America is home to 965 species of mammals.

7. The largest is the bison, which weighs more than 2,000 pounds (907 kg).

8. Mexico City is the continent's largest city.

9. New York City and Los Angeles are numbers two and three.

10. Canada is North America's largest country.

11. It covers almost half of the continent.

12. The United States is second-largest, but it has the largest population.

7

13. The smallest country is the Caribbean island of St. Kitts and Nevis, with about 54,000 people.

14. Montserrat, a British dependency, has fewer than 6,000 residents.

15. Most Canadians live within 125 miles (200 km) of the United States.

16. Denali, in Alaska, is North America's highest point at 20,237 feet (6,168 meters).

17. Denali is also called Mount McKinley.

18. North America's lowest point is Badwater Basin in Death Valley, California.

19. Badwater Basin is 282 feet (86 meters) below sea level.

20. Arizona's Grand Canyon is the world's largest canyon.

21. North America has been home to more than 1,200 indigenous cultures.

22. People have lived in North America for at least 15,000 years.

23. North American cities have hosted the Olympics 12 times as of 2020.

24. The continent is named after Italian explorer Amerigo Vespucci.

25. Lake Superior, between the United States and Canada, is the largest freshwater lake in the world.

26. Canada has 6 time zones.

27. The United States also has 6 time zones.

28. North America contains every natural biome, from rain forests to deserts and more.

29. The earliest record of people in North America was found near what is today Clovis, New Mexico. The Clovis culture dates back about 13,000 years.

30. More dinosaur fossils have been discovered in North America than any other continent.

31. Corn is the most commonly grown crop in North America.

32. North America grows half of the world's corn supply.

33. English, French, and Spanish are the most common languages spoken in North America.

34. However, more than 350 languages are spoken in the United States.

35. The United States does not have an official language.

36. North America is bordered by three oceans: the Atlantic, Pacific, and Arctic.

37. Mexico is the most earthquake-prone country on the continent.

38. Russia sold Alaska to the United States for about two cents per acre.

39. Kansas produces enough wheat in one year to feed everyone in the world for two weeks.

40. The first printing press in North America was used in Mexico City in 1539.

41. There are no landlocked countries in North America.

42. The most popular tourist attractions in North America are New York City, Las Vegas, California, Disney World, and the Caribbean islands.

43. Canada and the United States have the longest land border in the world.

44. The border is 5,525 miles (8,891 km) long.

45. It stretches across 13 US states and 8 Canadian provinces.

46. The Ambassador Bridge between Detroit, Michigan, United States, and Windsor, Ontario, Canada, is the busiest international border crossing in North America.

47. Every 6 years, a 20-foot (6-meter) strip around the US-Canada border is clear-cut by the International Boundary Commission, which calls it "a visible line between friendly neighbors."

48. The strip extends from the Atlantic Ocean to the Pacific Ocean and contains 8,000 monuments and reference points and 1,000 survey control stations.

49. The Rocky Mountains are among the longest mountain ranges in the world.

50. Mount Elbert in Colorado is the Rockies' highest peak at 14,439 feet (4,400 meters).

40 FANTASTIC FOOTBALL FACTS

1. So many football players joined the military during World War II that the Philadelphia Eagles and the Pittsburgh Steelers formed a combined team for the 1943 season.

2. The 1943 combined team was called the Steagles.

3. Football players smear black grease under their eyes to reduce sun glare.

4. Footballs are nicknamed pigskins because they used to be made from inflated pigs' bladders.

5. Today, footballs are made from rubber and cowhide.

6. The average amount an NFL player earns during his career is about $4 million.

7. Peyton Manning earned about $249 million during his NFL career.

8. On November 6, 1869, New Jersey's Princeton University and Rutgers University played the first college football game.

9. The Intercollegiate Football Association was created in 1873.

10. This new association introduced many rules, including the 11-man team and the use of "downs" to move the ball.

11. The American Professional Football League formed in 1920. Two years later, it changed its name to the National Football League.

12. Another league, the American Football League, formed in 1929.

13. Both leagues played separately until 1970, when they combined into the National Football League.

14. The NFL has two conferences based on the original leagues.

15. Unlike some other pro sports, football does not have a minor-league system.

16. Most NFL players are drafted out of college.

17. The first NFL draft was held in 1936.

18. The idea came from Philadelphia Eagles owner Bert Bell, who was tired of owning a losing team and seeing the top teams get the best players.

19. In 1985, TV viewers saw Washington quarterback Joe Theismann suffer a career-ending broken leg when he was tackled by Giants linebacker Lawrence Taylor.

20. Thirty-three years later to the day, TV viewers got to watch Washington quarterback Alex Smith break his ankle after being sacked.

21. Recent medical research suggests that some former football players have serious and even permanent brain damage from injuries suffered while playing.

22. College football did not require helmets until 1939.

23. The NFL didn't require them until 1943.

24. The Football Hall of Fame opened in Canton, Ohio, in 1963.

25. Hall of Fame inductees are announced the night before the Super Bowl.

26. Wilson has made all the footballs used in the NFL since 1941.

27. The company makes 4,000 balls a day.

28. The NFL plays almost every regular season game on a Monday, Thursday, or Sunday.

29. Ernie Nevers scored 40 points in a 1929 NFL game. He scored 6 touchdowns and 4 extra points.

30. Only 500 people watched the first televised football game in 1939.

31. In the past, touchdowns were only worth 4 points. Field goals were worth 5 points.

32. The huddle was first used in 1890 when deaf quarterback Paul Hubbard thought the other team was stealing his hand signals, so he had his players stand around him in a circle.

33. College footballs have white stripes painted on either end. The stripes make it easier to see the ball in the air.

34. Matt Prater scored the longest field goal with a 64-yard kick in 2013.

35. Only 20 field goals of 60 yards or more have been made in NFL regular-season games.

36. The last scoreless NFL game was in 1943, when the Detroit Lions and the New York Giants ended with a 0-0 tie.

37. The Miami Dolphins are the only NFL team to have an undefeated season. They won every game in 1972.

38. They also won that season's Super Bowl.

39. Deion Sanders played both professional football and baseball. He is the only player to score a home run and a touchdown in the same week.

40. Sanders is also the only person to play in both the World Series and the Super Bowl.

50 PERILOUS POISON AND VENOM FACTS

1. A poison is any substance that disrupts the body's function.

2. Venom is a poison injected into the body by a bite or sting.

3. Octopuses use their tough beak and tongue to drill a hole through the prey's shell or exoskeleton. They then insert their venomous saliva into the prey's soft interior to kill it.

4. Bill Haast was called the Snake Man. He was bitten by poisonous snakes at least 173 times.

5. Haast injected himself with snake venom every day for a span of 60 years.

6. Haast saved countless lives by donating his antibody-rich blood.

7. The Brazilian wandering spider is the most venomous spider on Earth.

8. Scientists use many poisons in medical treatment.

9. The venom of the copperhead snake contains a protein that stops cancer cells from spreading.

10. The Gila monster is the only poisonous lizard in the United States.

11. A chemical in the Gila monster's poison can be used to lower blood sugar.

12. A Boomslang snake's venom can cause its victim to bleed through tissues in the body.

13. Box jellyfish's venom is so powerful, human victims have been known to go into shock and drown or die of heart failure before they even reach shore after being bitten.

14. The slow loris is the world's only known venomous primate.

15. The loris sucks venom from a patch in its elbow before biting its victim.

16. The blue-ringed octopus has some of the deadliest venom in the world.

17. We do not currently have an antidote to the blue-ringed octopus's venom.

18. The venom of some giant hornets is strong enough to melt human flesh.

19. Wasp venom contains a chemical that alerts other wasps to locate and sting the victim, too.

20. The tentacles of Australia's Irukandji jellyfish can shoot stingers containing a powerful venom.

21. The decapitated head of a snake can still deliver a venomous bite hours after death.

22. The Australian stonefish is the most venomous fish in the world. Spines on its back inject a deadly venom into a person's foot if they step on it.

23. The smoke from burning poison ivy can cause a rash to form inside a person's lungs.

24. Cashew shells are poisonous to the touch.

25. Pistachios and mangoes are in the same family as poison ivy and poison sumac.

26. The most poisonous animal in America is the rough-skinned newt.

27. This newt's skin contains a poison 10,000 times deadlier than cyanide.

28. The pufferfish contains such toxic venom that, if it is prepared wrong, it will kill the person eating it.

29. Japanese chefs receive special training to prepare pufferfish for sushi.

30. The toxin on the skin of poison dart frogs comes from the beetles they eat.

31. Greeks tipped arrows and spears with poisons and tainted waters with toxic plants.

32. Roman soldiers would throw fragile clay pots filled with venomous snakes or scorpions at their enemies.

33. A platypus has spurs filled with venom above their webbed feet.

34. The flowering "suicide tree" produces a poison in its kernels that has killed hundreds of people.

35. Poisons can enter the body through inhalation, injection, ingestion, or absorption.

36. Botulinum is the deadliest substance known.

37. Botulinum is produced by bacteria.

38. In the 1800s, a poison called mercuric nitrate was used to remove fur from animal skins.

39. The mercuric nitrate caused many hat-makers to behave strangely and led to the phrase *mad as a hatter*.

40. Mercury wasn't banned for hat-making in the United States until 1941.

41. About 8 million people are poisoned in the United States every year.

42. Almost all of those poisonings are accidental.

43. About 60 percent of poisoning victims are children under the age of 6.

44. Many common household cleaning supplies contain poison.

45. There are two poisonous spiders in the United States: the black widow and the brown recluse.

46. Some household plants can make pets sick if they eat them.

47. President Abraham Lincoln's mother died after she drank milk from cows that had eaten a poisonous plant.

48. A dead puss moth caterpillar can still inject venom from hairs on its body.

49. Many mushrooms are poisonous and can kill a person if eaten.

50. Doctors used to advise snakebite victims to have someone suck the poison out of a bite, but that doesn't work.

30
FUN ROLLER COASTER AND AMUSEMENT PARK FACTS

1. The first roller coasters were wood covered in ice and called ice slides.

2. They first appeared in seventeeth-century Russia.

3. Later, wheels and grooved tracks were added to make the cars go faster.

4. Asia has more roller coasters than any other continent.

5. The first roller coaster in the United States opened at New York's Coney Island in 1884.

6. The Coney Island roller coaster was called the switchback railway. It traveled about 6 miles (9.6 km) an hour and cost a nickel to ride.

7. Roller coaster loops are not actually circles.

8. In 1884, Phillip Hinkle invented the chain that pulls roller-coaster cars up that big first hill.

9. Before Hinkle's invention, people had to climb stairs to get onto a roller coaster at the top of the hill.

10. The first hill on a roller coaster is the steepest because that's where all the energy is stored up to power the coaster on the rest of the ride.

11. Ron Toomer, who pioneered steel roller coasters and suspended tracks, suffers from such bad motion sickness that he is unable to ride his own creations.

12. Formula Rossa in United Arab Emirates is the fastest roller coaster in the world, with a top speed of 149 miles (240 km) per hour.

13. Formula Rossa's riders are required to wear safety goggles.

14. The Smiler at Alton Towers in England holds the record for most loops with 14.

15. Kingda Ka, a coaster in New Jersey, is the world's tallest at 456 feet (139 meters).

16. Kingda Ka also has the longest drop at 418 feet (127 meters).

17. The world's oldest operating roller coaster is Leap-the-Dips in Pennsylvania. It opened in 1902.

18. An engineer named George Washington Ferris invented the Ferris wheel as a ride for the 1893 Columbian Exposition in Chicago.

19. Austria's Wiener Reisenrad is the oldest Ferris wheel still in operation today. It was built in 1897.

20. The original pirate ship ride, called the Ocean Wave, was created in Tulsa, Oklahoma, sometime in the 1890s.

21. The first known carousel ride in United States operated in 1799 in Salem, Massachusetts, and was called a "wooden horse circus ride."

22. The world's largest indoor carousel is at the House on the Rock, Wisconsin.

23. It has 269 carousel animals, 182 chandeliers, and over 20,000 lights.

24. There are three general types of animals for carousels, depending on their stance.

25. Standing figures have at least three of their feet on the ground.

26. Prancers have two front feet in the air and two on the ground.

27. Jumpers have all four feet in the air, as if they are running.

28. Jumpers are also the horses that move up and down.

29. The first patent for bumper cars was filed in 1920.

30. The original bumper cars were quite dangerous and often fell apart during the ride.

30 ENERGETIC EXERCISE FACTS

1. Exercise increases the production of cells responsible for memory and learning.

2. Exercise also improves brain performance.

3. Listening to music while exercising can improve your performance by 15 percent.

4. Running at a 10-minute mile pace burns 104.3 calories per mile.

5. A pound of muscle burns three times more calories than a pound of fat.

6. Exercise boosts the immune system, so you get sick less often.

7. Exercise improves self-confidence.

8. Exercise can help you sleep better.

9. People who don't exercise regularly can lose up to 80 percent of their muscle strength by age 65.

10. Regular exercise lowers blood pressure and cholesterol levels.

11. Your metabolism stays elevated after you're done exercising, which helps you burn more calories.

12. The average person walks about 7,500 steps per day.

13. You use 200 muscles to take one step forward.

14. When you run, the pressure on your feet is about 3 to 4 times your body weight.

15. Dehydration reduces exercise performance.

16. Your breathing speeds up when you exercise to send more oxygen into your blood.

17. People who cross-train are less prone to injury than people who just do one type of exercise.

18. The knee is the most likely muscle to be injured while exercising.

19. Walking at a fast pace burns almost as many calories as running.

20. Swimming is great exercise because it includes both cardio and strength training.

21. Regular weight training increases the number of calories burned during regular activities.

22. Exercise strengthens the muscles of your heart and cardiovascular system.

23. The most popular exercise in the United States is walking.

24. About 70 percent of people say walking is their main form of exercise.

25. Women have greater muscle endurance than men.

26. If you can't carry on a conversation while exercising, you might be overdoing it.

27. Kids and teens should get at least 60 minutes of physical activity per day.

28. Almost 50 percent of young people are not vigorously active on a daily basis.

29. Exercise builds strong muscles and healthy bones.

30. For every pound of muscle gained, the body burns 50 extra calories per day.

50 DEADLY ANIMAL FACTS

1. If the vicious bite of the Komodo dragon doesn't kill its prey, the nasty bacteria in its mouth will. Bites often become infected and kill the injured animal.

2. The saltwater crocodile holds the record for the strongest bite. It can bite down with a force of 3,700 pounds (1,678 kg) per square inch.

3. Hippos kill about 500 people per year in Africa by turning over boats or drowning or crushing their victims.

4. Hippos are the world's deadliest large land mammal.

5. The snake known as the black mamba's bite has been called the "kiss of death."

6. This snake's bite has enough venom to kill 10 people.

7. A school of piranha can strip a cow down to its skeleton in minutes with their very sharp teeth.

8. A large swarm of Asian giant hornets can easily kill a person.

9. A poison dart frog's bright colors are meant to scare away predators. Good thing, because these frogs are coated with deadly poison.

10. Africa's Cape buffalo have been known to attack moving cars and keep charging even if they're injured.

11. These buffalo have killed more people than any other creature in Africa.

12. They have been nicknamed "Black Death."

13. A pufferfish has enough venom to kill 30 humans.

14. The mosquito is the deadliest insect on the planet.

15. Mosquitoes have spread diseases that have killed millions of people.

16. The tsetse fly is another deadly insect, estimated to kill 10,000 people a year through disease.

17. Tigers attack more people than any other large cat.

18. Nepal's Champawat Tiger holds the Guinness World Record for the most human fatalities by a single tiger.

19. This tiger killed 436 people before it was killed in 1907.

20. Lions can eat up to 75 pounds (34 kg) of meat at a time.

21. Lions may rest for a week between kills.

22. More than 25 million people died of bubonic plague between 1348 and 1353. The disease was spread by rats and fleas.

23. The Asian sun bear has the largest teeth in proportion to its body.

24. The Asian sun bear is the smallest bear, but it is one of the most dangerous animals in the jungle.

25. The bull shark has the strongest bite of any shark.

26. Boars have been known to circle humans and attack from behind. Their long, sharp tusks can inflict deadly wounds.

27. Africa's deathstalker is responsible for three-quarters of all scorpion-related deaths in the world.

28. A biologist trying to breed bees that produced more honey accidentally released Africanized killer bees into the world. These aggressive bees have killed about 1,000 people since their release.

29. Killer whales hunt in packs like wolves and can easily take down birds, sea turtles, and seals.

30. The cassowary is a flightless bird that can run up to 30 miles (48 km) an hour and attack with long, razor-sharp claws.

31. The pretty cone snail can inject a deadly venom that can kill a person in minutes.

32. Dogs kill about 25,000 people a year, mostly from contracting rabies.

33. Roughly 36 percent of the world's rabies deaths occur in India, which has a large number of stray dogs.

34. Surprise! The deadliest animal in North America is the deer.

35. Deer are responsible for more than 100 deaths in car accidents every year.

36. Moose are another animal that can easily kill drivers and passengers if hit by their car.

37. Great white sharks have killed more than 220 people since 1907.

38. Australia has more deadly snakes than any other country in the world.

39. The inland taipan is Australia's—and the world's—most venomous snake.

40. Fortunately, they rarely attack humans, but their venom can quickly kill other animals.

41. Elephants have been known to attack and destroy entire villages.

42. Polar bears are the largest carnivore in the world and have no natural predators.

43. A wolverine can easily take down elk and caribou and will not back down from a fight with a bear or cougar either.

44. A wolverine's bone-crushing jaws are filled with long, sharp teeth, and their back teeth can rotate 90 degrees.

45. Freshwater snails carry parasitic worms that kill tens of thousands of people a year.

46. Estuarine crocodiles are considered the most likely to feed on people.

47. A pack of hyenas can kill and eat an entire zebra in half an hour.

48. Kissing bugs got their name because they bite people on the lips. They spread a deadly illness called Chagas disease.

49. Chagas disease spread by kissing bugs kills up to 10,000 people a year.

50. The kissing bug is also known as the assassin bug, which is probably a better name for it.

25 HISTORY MYSTERIES

1. **The Bermuda Triangle:** Why have so many ships and planes disappeared in a triangle-shaped area in the Atlantic Ocean? Theories include aliens, UFOs, sea monsters, and a portal to another world. Or the answer could be huge waves that submerge ships and aircraft.

2. **The Voynich Manuscript:** This fifteenth-century manuscript is written in a mysterious code that no one has ever been able to break.

3. **Stonehenge:** Who built this collection of upright standing stones, and why? Theories abound, but there is no real answer as to how prehistoric people could have moved such heavy stones over long distances.

4. **Jack the Ripper:** The identity of the person who gruesomely killed five women in London in 1888 has been debated for more than a century. There are many suspects and theories, but the crimes will likely never be solved.

5. **William Shakespeare:** Did a simple, not-well-educated man really write so many plays and poems that changed English literature? Scholars have been debating the identity of the author for centuries and have suggested many noblemen or other writers as the "real" author.

6. **The Shroud of Turin:** Long claimed to be Jesus's burial shroud, this mysterious piece of cloth has mystified scientists for a long time. It might be a fake or it might be real. We may never know.

40 TERRIFIC TREASURE FACTS

1. For centuries, people have been searching for a pirate's treasure supposedly buried on Oak Island off the coast of Nova Scotia.

2. Even President Franklin D. Roosevelt joined a group of Oak Island treasure hunters before he was elected.

3. In 1840, a group of workmen dug up a box of Viking treasures from a riverbank in England.

4. Their find included more than 8,600 items.

5. Scuba divers exploring an area off the coast of Israel discovered a priceless treasure of more than 2,000 gold coins minted between the tenth and twelfth centuries.

6. London's British Museum has several collections of ancient treasure, including Roman coins and Viking hoards.

7. More than 20,000 gold ornaments were recovered from burial mounds in Tillya Tepe, Afghanistan.

8. The discovery, called the Bactrian Treasure, is more than 2,000 years old and includes items from China, India, and Greece.

9. The ancient Copper Scroll lists 60 locations in the Middle East where untold amounts of gold, silver, and other treasures are buried.

10. In 2015, explorers claim to have found the treasure of legendary pirate Captain Kidd off the coast of Madagascar.

6

11. Treasure hunters often find ancient shipwrecks filled with treasure.

12. The *San Miguel* was a Spanish ship carrying large amounts of precious metals and stones that sank in a storm off Cuba in 1715 and has never been found.

13. Some think the *San Miguel* is one of the richest treasure ships ever to have been lost.

14. The Scepter of Dagobert was part of France's crown jewels. It was made of solid gold but disappeared in 1795, never to be seen again.

15. The huge Florentine Diamond was last seen after World War I ended in 1918, when it was taken into exile by Austria's royal family.

16. In 1816, Thomas Beale and a few companions hid a treasure of gold and silver in the Rocky Mountains, then wrote a coded letter describing where it could be found. Beale disappeared, and no one was ever able to decode the letter.

17. On his deathbed, Jacob "The Dutchman" Waltz described a huge gold mine in Arizona's Superstition Mountains, but no one has ever been able to find it.

18. Historians and treasure hunters still wonder what happened to millions of dollars in gold owned by the Confederacy and which vanished after the Civil War.

19. The Russian royal family had a collection of eggs made of gold and precious stones created by the famous jeweler Fabergé. After the Russian Revolution in 1917, seven of the eggs disappeared and have yet to be found.

20. Gangster Dutch Schultz supposedly left a treasure buried in New York's Catskill Mountains before his death in 1935, but no one has ever been able to find it.

21. Dr. E. Lee Spence may be the youngest treasure hunter. He found his first shipwreck when he was just 12 years old.

22. Dr. Spence has recovered more than $100 million in treasure.

23. Mel Fisher spent 16 years searching for the *Nuestra Señora de Atocha*, which sank off the coast of Florida in 1622.

24. The shipwreck was finally found in 1985 by Fisher's son, and over $400 million in treasure was recovered and shared by the Fisher family and others.

25. Fisher's find led Congress to pass a law to prevent people from pillaging and profiting from shipwrecks.

26. Treasure hunters often face danger and even death from smugglers, drug dealers, and pirates.

27. Phillip Masters spent years researching the pirate Blackbeard and his treasure ship, *Queen Anne's Revenge*.

28. In 1996, Masters and a group of archaeologists found the wreck of *Queen Anne's Revenge* off the coast of North Carolina.

29. It was one of the most complete shipwrecks ever found.

30. Vero Beach, Florida, is home to many shipwrecks. Treasure hunters have found gold coins there in water less than 6 feet deep.

31. In 1925, Colonel Perry Fawcett and his team vanished in the Amazonian rain forest while searching for the legendary El Dorado, or City of Gold.

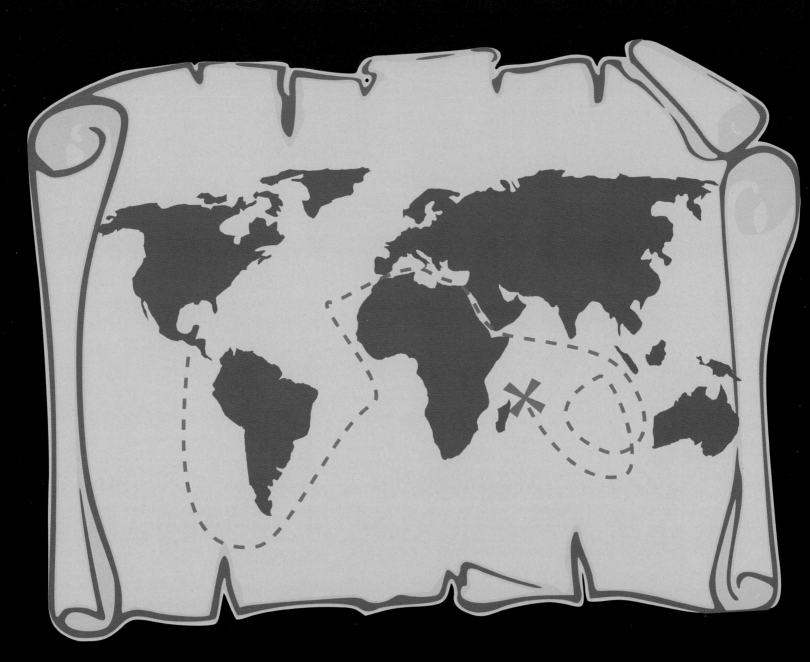

32. Robert McKinnon has found several Revolutionary War–era ships off the coast of Cape Breton Island in Canada.

33. McKinnon's finds include American gold coins and china and silverware taken from the White House when it was raided by British and Canadian soldiers during the War of 1812.

34. The United States, Great Britain, and Canada are still fighting over that treasure.

35. In 1911, Hiram Bingham II discovered the lost city of Machu Picchu in Peru despite having no formal training as an archaeologist.

36. In 2014, the FBI raided the home of noted treasure hunter Donald Miller.

37. During that raid, they found thousands of artifacts including Aztec figurines, Chinese jade, and an Egyptian sarcophagus that Miller had stolen from tombs around the world.

38. Most of Miller's treasures were returned to the countries they came from.

39. Brenton Easter is a Homeland Security agent who hunts down smugglers and has recovered more than 2,500 stolen artifacts worth at least $250 million.

40. Easter likes to dress up as Indiana Jones on Halloween.

50
FACTS ABOUT US STATES

1. **Alabama:** The first state to declare Christmas a legal holiday.

2. **Alaska:** Has more glaciers than any other state.

3. **Arizona:** Has the most telescopes in the world.

4. **Arkansas:** Home of the only active diamond mine in the United States.

5. **California:** The only state to host both the summer and winter Olympics.

6. **Colorado:** No US president or vice president has ever been born here.

7. **Connecticut:** The first American cookbook was published here in 1776.

8. **Delaware:** The first log cabins in North America were built here.

9. **Florida:** The flattest state.

10. **Georgia:** The Girl Scouts were founded here in 1912.

11. **Hawaii:** The only state that has its own time zone.

12. **Idaho:** Has the only state seal designed by a woman.

13. **Illinois:** Home to the world's largest bottle of ketchup.

14. **Indiana:** Produces 20 percent of the nation's popcorn.

15. **Iowa:** Pigs outnumber people 7 to 1.

16. **Kansas:** Helium was discovered here.

17. **Kentucky:** The underground vaults at Fort Knox hold more than half of all the nation's gold.

18. **Louisiana:** Milk is the official state beverage.

19. **Maine:** The state flower, the pinecone, is not a flower.

20. **Maryland:** The Ouija board was invented here.

21. **Massachusetts:** Both basketball and volleyball were invented here.

22. **Michigan:** Battle Creek, Michigan, produces most of the nation's cereal.

23. **Minnesota:** Home to the largest mall in the United States.

24. **Mississippi:** Has more churches per capita than any other state.

25. **Missouri:** Four of the largest earthquakes in American history occurred here between 1811 and 1812.

26. **Montana:** One-third of the land is owned by the federal government (most of that in national parks).

27. **Nebraska:** About 80 percent of the world's sandhill crane population lands on the Platte River during the cranes' annual spring migration.

28. **Nevada:** The driest state.

29. **New Hampshire:** The state's license plates, which include the statement "*Live Free Or Die,*" are made by prison inmates.

30. **New Jersey:** Has more horses per square mile than any other state.

31. **New Mexico:** Has the highest state capital, Santa Fe, which sits at 7,200 feet (2,194 meters) above sea level.

32. **New York:** The first state to require license plates on cars.

33. **North Carolina:** Home of the Biltmore Estate, the largest privately owned home in the country.

34. **North Dakota:** Contains the geographic center of North America.

35. **Ohio:** Has the only state flag that isn't a rectangle.

36. **Oklahoma:** The official state meal includes fried okra, squash, cornbread, barbecue pork, biscuits, sausage and gravy, grits, corn, strawberries, chicken-fried steak, pecan pie, and black-eyed peas.

37. **Oregon:** Has a 2-foot (0.19-meter)-square park for leprechauns.

38. **Pennsylvania:** Its name is spelled with just one "n" on the Liberty Bell and in the Constitution.

39. **Rhode Island:** The smallest state has the longest official name (State of Rhode Island).

40. **South Carolina:** The state's Morgan Island is home to more than 4,000 monkeys used for medical research.

41. **South Dakota:** Has the geographic center of the United States.

42. **Tennessee:** The first miniature golf course was built here.

43. **Texas:** It's legal to hunt Bigfoot here.

44. **Utah:** The Cleveland-Lloyd Dinosaur Quarry has the highest concentration of Jurassic-era remains ever found with more than 12,000 dinosaur bones and one egg.

45. **Vermont:** Billboards are banned in this state.

46. **Virginia:** Eight presidents and six first ladies were born here.

47. **Washington:** The Boeing assembly factory is the world's largest building by volume, covering 98.3 acres (40 hectares).

48. **West Virginia:** Has the most mountains.

49. **Wisconsin:** The QWERTY keyboard was invented here.

50. **Wyoming:** The first state to have a female governor.

50 CREEPY-CRAWLY FACTS ABOUT INSECTS AND SPIDERS

1. Scientists estimate there are 6 to 10 million different species of insects.

2. There are about 91,000 different kinds (species) of insects in the United States.

3. All insects have three body parts, two antennae, and six legs.

4. Spiders have two body parts and eight legs.

5. All bugs are insects, but not all insects are bugs.

6. Bugs have a straw-shaped mouth used to suck juices from plants or blood from animals.

7. All insects and spiders are cold-blooded.

8. Many adult insects die in winter but lay eggs that survive to emerge in the spring.

9. Other insects hibernate or migrate to warmer places.

10. Some insects can walk on water.

11. Only male crickets chirp.

12. Fireflies use their lights to find mates.

13. Some cicadas make sounds that register up to 120 decibels. That's loud!

14. A ladybug can eat up to 5,000 insects in its lifetime.

15. Fruit flies were the first insect sent into space.

16. Fruit flies are often used in genetic experiments.

17. An assassin bug piles its ant victims onto its body to scare away predators.

18. Butterflies taste with their feet.

19. Ants can lift and carry up to 50 times their own weight.

20. About one-third of all insect species are carnivorous.

21. Instead of lungs, an insect breathes through a network of tiny tubes called tracheae, found along its abdomen.

22. Insects evolved from crustaceans.

23. Insects were the first animals to fly, about 400 million years ago.

24. The oldest insect fossil is estimated to be between 396 and 407 million years old.

25. There are more than 380,000 species of beetles.

26. That makes beetles the most biodiverse group of creatures known on Earth.

27. There are about 1.4 billion insects for every person on Earth.

28. The total weight of all the insects on Earth is about 70 times the weight of all people.

29. Dragonflies have been on Earth for 300 million years.

30. The Australian tiger beetle is the world's fastest running insect. It can run as fast as 5.6 miles (9 km) per hour while chasing its prey.

31. The fastest flying insect is the horsefly. This insect has been recorded at speeds up to 90 miles (145 km) per hour.

32. Hercules beetles can lift 850 times their own weight.

33. Locusts can eat their own weight in food in a day.

34. The praying mantis can turn its head to look over its shoulder.

35. A wingless midge called *Belgica Antarctica* is the only insect native to Antarctica.

36. Scarab beetles were important religious symbols in ancient Egypt.

37. There are about 40,000 species of spider.

38. All spiders spin silk.

39. One spider can produce up to seven different types of silk.

40. Some types are used to spin webs. Others are used to catch insects.

41. Female spiders can lay up to 3,000 eggs at a time.

42. Jumping spiders can jump up to 50 times the length of their bodies.

43. Most spiders have eight eyes.

44. Spiders are nearsighted.

45. The ogre-faced spider uses its web like a net to scoop up prey.

46. The bolas spider swings a long line of silk with a sticky end to catch its prey.

47. Diving bell spiders live underwater.

48. Diving bell spiders create air bubbles so they can breathe underwater.

49. Spider silk is one of the strongest natural materials on Earth.

50. Spiders don't have muscles. They use internal fluids to move their legs.

40 HOCKEY FACTS

1. No one knows who invented hockey or when.

2. Legend has it that frozen cow poop was used for pucks in the early days of hockey.

3. Hockey pucks are frozen before a game to prevent them from bouncing.

4. The Pittsburgh Penguins used to have a live penguin as their mascot.

5. The penguin's name was Slapshot Pete.

6. Every member of the team that wins the Stanley Cup gets the cup for one day to do whatever he likes with it.

7. Many players have eaten food out of the Cup, including cereal, meatballs, and ice cream.

8. Hockey legend Mario Lemieux scored five goals five different ways during a game in 1988.

9. He scored a goal at even strength, got one on the power play, another shorthanded, another on a penalty shot, and a final one into an empty net with one second left in the game.

10. Lemieux is the only NHL player to ever score "five goals, five ways" in one game.

11. If all the team's goalies are injured during a game, the rules say a fan can take their place on the ice.

12. The first organized indoor hockey game was played on March 3, 1875, in Montreal.

13. Most of the players were students at McGill University.

14. The National Hockey League (NHL) was founded in 1917.

15. A hockey puck measures 3 inches (7.6 cm) in diameter.

16. Bobby Hull recorded the fastest slapshot on record, at 118 miles (190 km) per hour.

17. The shortest NHL player was Roy Worters, who was just 5 feet, 3 inches (1.6 meters) tall.

18. The tallest was Zdeno Chara at 6 feet, 9 inches (2 meters) tall.

19. Goalies often have artists design and paint their masks.

20. The Montreal Canadiens have won 24 Stanley Cups, by far the most of any team.

21. Wayne Gretzky holds 61 NHL records.

22. Dave Ritchie of the Montreal Wanderers scored the first official NHL goal in 1917.

23. The Stanley Cup is named after a former Canadian Governor General, Lord Stanley of Preston, who donated the trophy in 1893.

24. The original Cup was only 7 inches (17.8 cm) high.

25. Today's Cup is 3 feet (1 meter) high.

26. Each winning team and its players and staff have their names engraved on the Stanley Cup. The Cup includes many spelling errors.

27. Henri Richard's name is on the Stanley Cup the most times with 11.

28. It's a tradition for fans to throw octopuses onto the ice during Detroit Red Wings games.

29. In 1974, Andy Brown was the last goaltender to play a game without a mask.

30. Goaltender Manon Rhéaume was the first and (so far) only female hockey player to play in the NHL. She played an exhibition game for the Tampa Bay Lightning in 1992.

31. Rhéaume later played for several teams in the International Hockey League.

32. Rhéaume's brother, Pascal, also played in the NHL.

33. The biggest hockey prank happened in 1974 when the general manager of the Buffalo Sabres "drafted" a player from Japan who never existed.

34. Darryl Sittler of the Toronto Maple Leafs scored a record 10 points in a single game in 1976.

35. Phil Esposito was the first player to score more than 100 points in a season.

36. Esposito scored 126 points in 1969.

37. Before 1914, referees placed the puck on the ice between both centers' sticks. This resulted in lots of injuries to the refs!

38. In 1914, the rule was changed so that referees could drop the puck on the ice instead.

39. The Anaheim Ducks used to be called the Mighty Ducks, after the team in the same-named Disney movie.

40. At the time, Disney owned the team.

· · 23

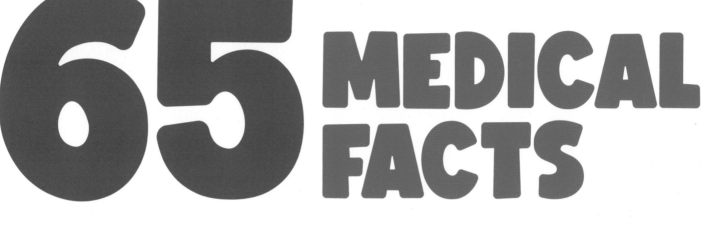

65 MEDICAL FACTS

1. Children of identical twins are genetically half-siblings, not cousins.

2. Full siblings share 50 percent of their DNA, and half-siblings share 25 percent.

3. Cousins only share 12.5 percent of their DNA.

4. Humans share more than 98 percent of their DNA with chimpanzees.

5. Humans also share 70 percent of their DNA with slugs.

6. Crying really can make you feel better. The tears you shed when you cry contain stress hormones.

7. Your brain replaces itself every 2 months.

8. Your liver replaces itself every 6 weeks.

9. Your skin regenerates every 35 days.

10. Your stomach lining replaces itself every 3 to 4 days.

11. Humans have 46 chromosomes.

12. Most people have 24 ribs; some are born with 25.

13. Most people with an extra rib are men.

14. The female egg is the largest cell in the human body.

15. The average person has about 100,000 hairs on their head.

16. Beards are the fastest-growing hair on the human body.

17. When you look at an object, the image of it appears upside-down on your retina.

18. Your brain automatically corrects the image, so you see it right-side-up.

19. The soles of your feet contain more sweat glands than any other part of your body.

20. They also contain more pressure-sensitive nerve endings.

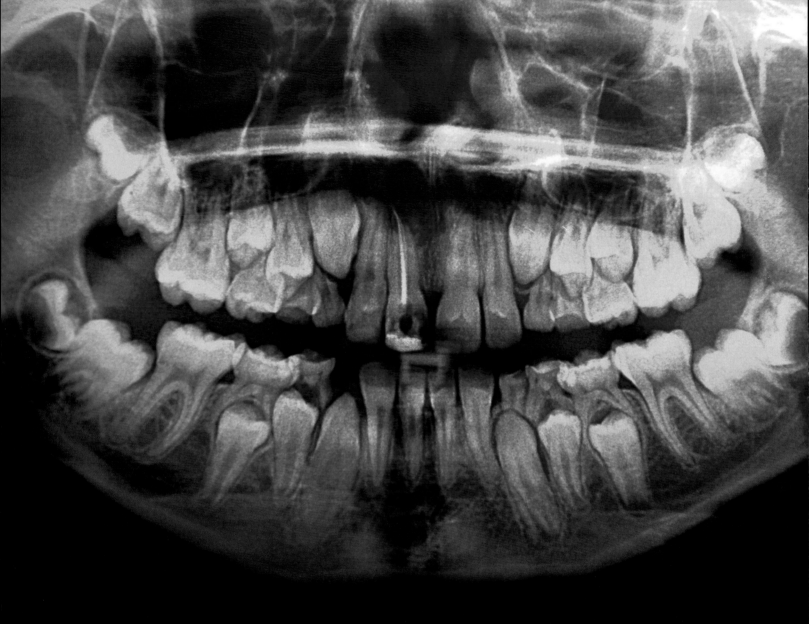

21. Kidneys filter your blood up to 300 times per day.

22. During the first 6 weeks, there is no difference between male and female embryos.

23. Fetuses kick when they hear loud music.

24. Human fingers stretch and bend about 25 million times in a normal lifetime.

25. The average red blood cell lives for 120 days.

26. There are roughly 2.5 trillion red blood cells in your body at any moment.

27. About 2.5 million new red blood cells are produced every second by your bone marrow.

28. More than 25 million new cells of all kinds are produced by your body every second.

29. Our eyes can distinguish up to 10 million colors.

30. The nose can warm cold air and cool hot air as we breathe.

31. One square inch (6.45 square cm) of your hand contains 9 feet (2.7 meters) of blood vessels, 600 pain sensors, 9,000 nerve endings, 36 heat sensors, and 75 pressure sensors.

32. Our bodies contain copper, zinc, cobalt, calcium, manganese, phosphates, nickel, and silicon.

33. The enamel on teeth is the hardest substance in the human body.

34. Scientists believe the purpose of our eyebrows is to keep sweat out of our eyes.

35. Eyelashes keep dust and dirt out of our eyes.

36. The average person breathes in 45 pounds (20.4 kg) of dust in their lifetime.

37. After the age of 30, most people begin to shrink because of bone loss.

38. Most people have lost 50 percent of their taste buds by the time they are 60 years old.

39. Humans have fewer muscles in their body than caterpillars do.

40. Of course, a human's muscles are a lot bigger than a caterpillar's!

41. If you could save all the times your eyes blink in one lifetime and use them all at once, you would see blackness for 1.2 years.

42. Babies dream before they are born.

43. The average human head weighs about 10 pounds (4.5 kg).

44. The average human brain weighs about 3 pounds (1.4 kg).

45. The biggest muscle in your body is your gluteus maximus, or your butt.

46. Each of those two muscles weighs about 2 pounds (0.9 kg).

47. The stapedius in the middle ear is the tiniest muscle in the body.

48. It is just one-fifth of an inch (0.5 cm) long.

49. A human has 22 muscles on each side of their face.

50. That's more than any other animal.

51. Some surgeons operate on babies before they are born.

52. For most of history, anesthesia was not used during surgery.

53. Without anesthesia, operations were performed as quickly as possible.

54. Some surgeons could perform an amputation in less than 30 seconds.

55. Not everyone thought anesthesia was a good idea.

56. Doctors still aren't sure exactly how anesthesia works.

57. There are 14 recognized surgical specialties.

58. They are vascular, gynecologic/obstetric, maxillofacial, ophthalmic, cardiothoracic, colorectal, general, oncologic, neurologic, orthopedic, otorhinolaryngologic, pediatric, plastic surgery, and urologic.

59. During the nineteenth century, as many as 1 in 4 people died as a result of surgery.

60. Most of those deaths came from infections.

61. Leeches are sometimes used after surgery to suck out excess blood.

62. Doctors can also use maggots to remove dead flesh without harming healthy tissue.

63. People used to get rid of lice by pouring gasoline over their hair.

64. Some seizure disorders are treated by removing half of the patient's brain.

65. A doctor in Antarctica once performed a successful appendectomy—on himself!

46 AMAZING ISLAND FACTS

1. Islands are areas of land that are not connected to a continent and are surrounded by water. Small islands are sometimes called cays, keys, or islets.

2. A group of islands is often called an archipelago.

3. There are two main types of islands.

4. Continental islands are part of a continental shelf.

5. Oceanic islands don't sit on a continental shelf.

6. Many oceanic islands are formed by undersea volcanoes.

7. Greenland is the world's largest island that is not a continent.

8. Even though Greenland is huge, hardly anyone lives there because most of the island is covered with ice.

9. Islands in rivers are sometimes called aits or eyots.

10. About 80 percent of animals and plants on Madagascar, off the coast of Africa, aren't found anywhere else on Earth.

11. Java is the world's most populated island.

12. About 130 million people live on Java.

13. Puncak Jaya on the island of New Guinea is the highest mountain on an island.

14. It is 16,024 feet (4,884 meters) tall.

15. Some islands are made by people.

16. A desert island isn't a desert. It is deserted, with no people on it.

17. Around 1 in 6 people on Earth live on an island.

18. Two of New York City's five boroughs are islands: Manhattan and Staten Island.

19. Bishop Rock, off the coast of Great Britain, is the smallest island with a building on it.

20. Bishop Rock's only building is a lighthouse.

21. Tristan da Cunha is the world's most remote inhabited island chain.

22. Tristan da Cunha is 1,750 miles (2,816 km) from South Africa and 2,000 miles (3,219 km) from South America.

23. Only about 265 people live on Tristan da Cunha.

24. Anybody can live and work on the Norwegian archipelago of Svalbard no matter what country they are citizens of.

25. New York State's Thousand Islands include an island called Just Enough Room.

26. There is "just enough room" there for a tree and a house.

27. Treasure Island is an island located within Lake Mindemoya. That lake is located on Manitoulin Island, which is located within Lake Huron.

28. So Treasure Island is the world's largest island in a lake on an island in a lake.

29. Catalina Island, off the coast of Los Angeles, has a population of non-native buffalo that were brought over for a silent film and abandoned about 100 years ago.

30. The population of buffalo has increased to about 150 today.

31. Devon Island in the Canadian Arctic is the world's largest uninhabited island.

32. NASA uses it to simulate conditions on Mars.

33. The only residents of Pig Beach in the Bahamas are swimming pigs.

34. One-third of the plant life on the island of Socotra, near Yemen, is found nowhere else on the planet.

35. Socotra has been described as the most alien-looking place on Earth.

36. The island of Molokai in Hawaii was once a leper colony.

37. Venice Island was built on a foundation of tree trunks. About 1,200 years later, those same trunks still support almost all of central Venice.

38. Ilha da Queimada Grande has so many poisonous snakes that the Brazilian Navy has quarantined it.

39. A biologist once said that when on Ilha da Queimada Grande, you are never more than 3 feet (1 meter) from death.

40. An isolated tribe still inhabits the North Sentinel Island in the Indian Ocean, living as simple hunter-gatherers.

41. The islanders have attacked outsiders trying to get on the island.

42. In 1982, Great Britain and Argentina went to war for 10 weeks over the Falkland Islands.

43. The world's smallest island nation is Nauru in the Pacific Ocean with an area of 8.5 square miles (22 square km) and a population of fewer than 10,000 people.

44. The 1856 Guano Islands Act gave Americans the right to mine bird dung on any uninhabited island.

45. The Canary Islands are named after dogs not canaries.

46. *Insulae Canariae* is Latin for "the islands of dogs."

75 REPTILE AND AMPHIBIAN FACTS

1. Crocodiles are related to dinosaurs.

2. Some turtles can live more than 100 years.

3. Reptiles are covered in scales or have a hard shell.

4. Lizard and snake species make up the largest number of reptiles.

5. Evidence of the first reptiles dates back to about 320 million years ago.

6. There are four kinds of reptiles.

7. They are turtles and tortoises, snakes and lizards, crocodilians, and tuataras.

8. Crocodilians include crocodiles, alligators, caimans, and gharials.

9. Tuataras only live on a few islands in New Zealand.

10. Some reptiles shed their skin.

11. Turtles and iguanas are the only reptiles that are herbivores.

12. All other reptiles eat other animals.

13. Most reptiles have a three-chambered heart.

14. Crocodilians have a four-chambered heart.

15. Amphibians have a two-chambered heart.

16. Scientists think reptiles are an evolutionary stage between fish and amphibians and birds and mammals.

17. Reptiles were the first land creatures to lay hard-shelled eggs.

18. Crocodilians and some turtles lay a large number of eggs and bury them.

19. The temperature outside the eggs determines whether the babies will be male or female.

20. Usually, crocodilian eggs in very cold or very hot temperatures will hatch males.

21. Crocodilian eggs in medium temperatures will hatch females.

22. For turtles, cooler eggs hatch males and warmer eggs hatch females.

23. Only boas and pythons give birth to live young.

24. Young reptiles can survive on their own right after they are born.

25. Some species of crocodiles swallow rocks so they can sink deeper under the water.

26. Alligators and crocodiles can move very quickly when they are attacking prey.

27. Snakes move by flexing muscles in their bodies.

28. Many snakes are constrictors.

29. Constrictors squeeze their prey so it can't breathe and then swallow the prey whole.

30. If a snake eats a large meal, it can go weeks before it has to eat again.

31. The largest turtle is the leatherback turtle.

32. It can weigh up to 1,800 pounds (816 kg).

33. The leatherback turtle's shell can be 8 feet (2.4 meters) long.

34. The smallest reptile is the mini chameleon from Madagascar.

35. This miniature reptile is only 1 inch (2.5 cm) long.

36. The smallest snake is the thread snake at just 4 inches (10 cm) long.

37. A spiny-tailed iguana can run up to 20 miles (32 km) per hour.

38. The black mamba is the fastest snake.

39. They can move up to 12.5 miles (20 km) per hour.

40. Frogs can breathe through their lungs and also through their skin.

41. Some snakes have more than 300 pairs of ribs.

42. A turtle's shell is made of about 60 connected bones.

43. Turtles have no ears, but they have excellent eyesight and sense of smell.

44. Turtles can also feel vibrations from loud noises.

45. Snakes and lizards smell with their tongues.

46. Snakes have very poor hearing.

47. Because snakes only have an inner ear, they can only detect vibrations through their jaws.

48. Reptiles have a specialized chemically sensitive organ called the Jacobson's organ that can convert tastes into smells.

49. Snakes also have a special organ that senses heat.

50. Some snakes have these heat-seeking organs around their mouths.

51. Pit vipers have them on either side of their heads.

52. These organs can detect a temperature change as little as 2/1000 of a degree.

53. This helps the snake detect and strike at prey even in complete darkness.

54. Some species of lizards and iguanas have a third eye.

55. This eye is located on top of the head and can only sense light and dark.

56. Turtles can "feel" with their shells.

57. Some turtles hibernate underwater.

58. They "breathe" by absorbing air through thin skin around their butts.

59. American alligators make such loud roars when they are looking for mates that they can be heard from miles away.

60. Snakes and crocodilians are constantly losing and replacing teeth.

61. Many times, these lost teeth are expelled through their droppings.

62. Snakes and crocodilians have "back-up" teeth that drop into place after a tooth has been lost.

63. Frogs swallow their food whole.

64. Amphibians live the first part of their lives in the water.

65. Their bodies change through metamorphosis so they can live on land.

66. There are three types of amphibians: frogs and toads, newts and salamanders, and caecilians.

67. Caecilians don't have legs and look a lot like snakes.

68. Most amphibians live in or near water.

69. Amphibian larvae eat plants, but adults are carnivores.

70. Frogs cannot live in salt water.

71. The word *amphibian* comes from the Greek *amphibious*, which means "two lives."

72. A small cave salamander called the olm is the world's longest-lived amphibian.

73. It can live for more than 100 years.

74. Most amphibians only live for a year or two.

75. Amphibians have excellent eyesight and can see in color.

50 SUPER SHARK FACTS

1. There are more than 500 species of sharks.

2. Scientists classify 143 of them as endangered.

3. Sharks can have up to 15 rows of teeth.

4. They lose and replace up to 50,000 teeth in their lifetime.

5. There are trillions of shark teeth on the ocean floor.

6. The dwarf lantern shark is about the size of your hand.

7. The largest is the whale shark, measuring about 40 feet (12 meters) long.

8. Sharks have been around for 400 million years.

9. Goblin sharks have been called "living fossils" because they are older than dinosaurs.

10. Goblin sharks are bright pink.

11. Sharks have a sixth sense.

12. They can sense electrical discharges from other animals in the water.

13. A shark's body is made of cartilage, not bone.

14. Female sharks are almost always larger than male sharks.

15. Some shark embryos kill other embryos before they are born.

16. Not all sharks live in the ocean.

17. Bull sharks live in tropical rivers and lakes.

18. River sharks live in rivers in Australia, New Guinea, and South Asia.

19. The spiny dogfish shark's pregnancy lasts for two years.

20. Some sharks give birth to more than 100 babies in one litter.

21. A prehistoric shark called *Carcharodon megalodon* was 55 feet (16.8 meters) long and weighed as much 25 tons.

22. It was the largest predator that ever lived.

23. Sharks have an excellent sense of smell.

24. They also have powerful hearing.

25. A shark can hear a sound up to 3,000 feet (914 meters) away.

26. Sharks can move both the upper and lower jaws.

27. A whale shark's skin is 6 inches (15 cm) thick.

28. Tiger sharks will eat just about anything.

29. Scientists have found license plates from almost every US state, video cameras, dog leashes, a bag of money, and many other odd things inside tiger sharks' stomachs.

30. Baby sharks are born with all their teeth.

31. Sharks have active and restful periods, but they do not sleep like other animals do.

32. Sharks need to keep moving so water flows over their gills.

33. Sharks have no vocal cords and do not make sounds.

34. Sharks live in all the world's oceans.

35. More than half a shark's weight is muscle.

36. That makes them heavier than water, so they have to keep swimming or they will sink.

37. A shark has a canal filled with fluid called a lateral line inside its body.

38. The lateral line helps the shark sense movement in the water.

39. Great white sharks are dark on top and white on the bottom.

40. This coloring helps camouflage them against the bright sky and the dark sea.

41. Great white, tiger, and bull sharks are the most dangerous to people.

42. Sharks attack 50 to 80 people a year.

43. Most shark attacks happen in Florida, California, Australia, and South Africa.

44. Mako sharks leap out of the water to catch their prey.

45. Lantern sharks glow in the dark.

46. When it is threatened, a swell shark doubles in size by swallowing water.

47. Then it barks and burps out the water to return to normal size.

48. Carpet sharks can change their skin color to camouflage themselves.

49. Hammerhead sharks can use their strange-shaped head to pin stingrays to the ocean floor.

50. They also have 360-degree vision, which means they can see in a complete circle.

50 FACTS ABOUT SOUTH AMERICA

1. South America is the fourth-largest continent in size.

2. It covers 6,890,000 square miles (17,845,000 square km).

3. South America is home to 387,489,196 people, making it the fifth-largest continent in population.

4. South America borders the Pacific Ocean, the Atlantic Ocean, and the Caribbean Sea.

5. The highest point in South America is Cerro Aconcagua in the Andes Mountains in the country of Argentina.

6. The highest waterfall in the world is Salto del Angel (Angel Falls) in Venezuela.

7. It is 3,212 feet (979 meters) high.

8. South America includes 12 countries and 3 dependent territories.

9. South America's countries include Argentina, Bolivia, Brazil, Chile, Colombia, Ecuador, Guyana, Paraguay, Peru, Suriname, Uruguay, and Venezuela.

10. Its dependent territories are the Falkland Islands (controlled by Great Britain), French Guiana (controlled by France), and South Georgia and the South Sandwich Islands (Great Britain).

11. Argentina's name for the Falkland Islands is the Malvinas.

12. Brazil is the largest South American country in both size and population.

13. Suriname is the smallest country.

14. Fewer than 500,000 people live in Suriname.

15. Almost 95 percent of Suriname is covered by rain forests.

16. Paraguay and Bolivia are the only South American countries that are landlocked.

17. Bolivia and Peru share Lake Titicaca, the largest lake on the continent.

18. Like North America, South America was named after Italian explorer Amerigo Vespucci.

19. The Andes are the longest mountain range in the world.

20. Five of the top 50 largest cities in the world are located in South America.

21. They are Sao Paulo (Brazil), Lima (Peru), Bogota (Colombia), Rio de Janeiro (Brazil), and Santiago (Chile).

22. The Amazon rain forest has the greatest biodiversity in the world.

23. Simon Bolivar is one of the greatest military and diplomatic figures in South American history.

24. Bolivar led five countries—Colombia, Venezuela, Ecuador, Peru, and Bolivia—to independence from the colonial powers.

25. Some indigenous tribes in the Amazon rain forest have had no contact with modern civilization.

26. South Americans speak more than 300 languages.

27. The most common are English, Spanish, and Portuguese.

28. South America was claimed and settled by Spain, except for Brazil, which was claimed by Portugal.

29. About 90 percent of South Americans are Christian, and 80 percent are Roman Catholic.

30. South America's resources include large deposits of gold, silver, iron, and petroleum.

31. Three of the world's greatest empires were in South America.

32. Those empires were the Inca, the Maya, and the Aztecs.

33. Argentina is named for the Latin word for silver.

34. The popular dances samba and tango started in South America.

35. Bolivia's Salar de Uyuni are the largest salt flats in the world. They cover more than 3,861 square miles (10,000 square km).

36. Part of *The Last Jedi* was filmed at Salar de Uyuni.

37. South America is shaped like a triangle.

38. Its shape means it has the least amount of coastline of any continent.

39. Brazil produces one-third of the world's coffee.

40. About 90 percent of South America is located in the Southern Hemisphere.

41. Venezuela, Guyana, Suriname, and French Guiana are located in the Northern Hemisphere.

42. So are the northern parts of Ecuador, Colombia, and Brazil.

43. South America is home to many endangered mammals, including the jaguar, the giant otter, and the Amazonian manatee.

44. Venezuela was named after the Italian city of Venice.

45. Ecuador is home to more than 1,000 species of orchids.

46. Quechua is the most common indigenous language in South America.

47. Quechua has 46 dialects and is spoken by 8 million people across Peru, Bolivia, Colombia, Ecuador, Chile, and Argentina.

48. The capybara, the largest rodent on Earth, lives in South America.

49. The world's largest flying bird, the condor, is native to Chile, Ecuador, and Peru.

50. Peru's biggest tourist attraction, the Inca citadel Machu Picchu, was built in the fifteenth century.

••••••• **50**

50
DEADLY FACTS ABOUT
WARS AND BATTLES

10 HISTORICAL FACTS ABOUT WARS AND BATTLES

1. The last veteran of World War I died in 2011.

2. World War II had the highest death toll of any war. More than 56.4 million people were killed.

3. Poland lost 17 percent of its population during World War II.

4. In the Paraguayan war of 1864–70 against Brazil, Argentina, and Uruguay, Paraguay's population was cut almost in half.

5. Fewer than 30,000 survivors in Paraguay were adult males.

6. The Battle of Antietam is called "the bloodiest day in US history."

7. The United States has fought 13 wars between 1775 and 2020.

8. The Spanish–American War had the fewest US battle deaths with 385.

9. More than 16 million US soldiers served in World War II.

10. Russia had the largest number of World War II casualties with about 21 million.

TOP 10 DEADLIEST BATTLES IN HISTORY
Note: Casualties include both soldier and civilian deaths and injuries.

1.	Mongol Sacking of Baghdad	1258	2 million casualties
2.	Brusilov Offensive	1916	1.6 million casualties
3.	Battle of the Dnieper	1945	1.58 million casualties
4.	German Spring Offensive	1918	1.55 million casualties
5.	Operation Barbarossa	1941	1.4 million casualties
6.	Taking of Berlin	1945	1.3 million casualties
7.	Operation Ichi-Go	1944	1.3 million casualties
8.	Battle of Stalingrad	1942–43	1.25 million casualties
9.	Battle of the Somme	1916	1.12 million casualties
10.	Siege of Leningrad	1941–44	1.12 million casualties

10 BATTLES THAT CHANGED HUMAN HISTORY

	NAME OF BATTLE	YEAR	WHY IT WAS IMPORTANT
1.	Battle of Yorktown	1781	Ended the American Revolution and won American independence.
2.	Battle of Hastings	1066	Introduced a new order to Great Britain.
3.	Battle of Stalingrad	1942–43	The beginning of the end for Germany during WWII.
4.	Battle of Leipzig	1813	The first time European nations united against a common enemy.
5.	Battle of Antietam	1862	Stopped the Confederate invasion of the North.
6.	Battle of Cajamarca	1532	Opened the way for Spain to colonize much of South America.
7.	Atomic Bombing of Japan	1945	First use of nuclear weapons in battle; ended WWII.
8.	Battle of Huai-Hai	1948	Placed China in the hands of the Communist government.
9.	Battle of Waterloo	1815	Ended French domination of Europe.
10.	Battle of Vienna	1529	The beginning of the end of the Ottoman Empire.

TOP 10 BLOODIEST CAMPAIGNS IN US MILITARY HISTORY

1.	Meuse-Argonne Offensive	WWI, 1918	26,277 dead
2.	Battle of the Bulge	WWII, 1944–45	19,200 dead
3.	Battle for France	WWII, 1944	17,844 dead
4.	Invasion of Normandy	WWII, 1944	16,293 dead
5.	March Through Western Germany	WWII, 1945	15,000+ dead
6.	Battle of Okinawa	WWII, 1945	12,500+ dead
7.	Huertgen Forest	WWII, 1944	12,000+ dead
8.	Luzon	WWII, 1945	10,380 dead
9.	Gothic Line	WWII, 1944–45	8,486 dead
10.	Operation Dragoon	WWII, 1944	7,301 dead

TOP 10 BLOODIEST BATTLES IN THE US CIVIL WAR

	NAME OF BATTLE	YEAR	CASUALTIES (DEAD AND INJURED)
1.	Gettysburg	1863	23,049 Union/25,000 Confederate
2.	Spotsylvania Courthouse	1864	18,399 Union/12,687 Confederate
3.	Chickamauga	1863	16,170 Union/18,454 Confederate
4.	Battle of the Wilderness	1864	17,666 Union/11,033 Confederate
5.	Antietam	1862	12,410 Union/10,316 Confederate
6.	Shiloh	1862	13,047 Union/10,699 Confederate
7.	Chancellorsville	1863	17,287 Union/13,303 Confederate
8.	Second Battle of Bull Run	1862	14,462 Union/11,739 Confederate
9.	Stone's River	1863	12,906 Union/11,739 Confederate
10.	Fredericksburg	1862	12,653 Union/4,201 Confederate

40 EXCELLENT EXPLORER FACTS

1. The Vikings and Norse explorer Leif Erikson were probably the first Europeans to reach America.

2. In 1960, archaeologists discovered a Norse settlement at L'anse aux Meadows, Newfoundland, Canada, dating back to 1,000 AD.

3. Erikson was carrying on a family tradition. His father, Erik the Red, was the first to land on Greenland, and his great-great-great-grand uncle, Naddodd, discovered Iceland.

4. Between 1405 and 1433, Chinese explorer Zheng He led seven expeditions, establishing trade routes as far away as western Africa.

5. The first explorers to circumnavigate Africa were the Phoenicians, way back in the sixth century BC.

6. Hecataeus, a Greek explorer from the sixth century BC believed the earth was a perfect circle and that a ring of ocean surrounded all land.

EUROPE

OCEAN

Scythia

Caspian Sea

Celts

Adria

Issedones

Thrace

Media

Tartessus

Athens

Syracuse

Miletus

India

Carthage

Assyria

ASIA

Memphis

Babylon

Susa

Persia

Egypt

LIBYA

Thebes

Arabia

7. Dutch explorer Abel Tasman was the first European to spot New Zealand and Tasmania in 1642. However, he completely missed Australia until a second expedition two years later.

8. Amerigo Vespucci got his start selling pickles to Christopher Columbus for two of his voyages.

9. Vespucci was the first to say that the Americas were separate continents and not part of Asia.

10. Vespucci also estimated the circumference of the globe within 50 miles (80 km).

11. Great Britain's James Cook was one of the most successful explorers of the eighteenth century.

12. Cook visited Newfoundland, circumnavigated New Zealand, and was the first European to set foot on both Hawaii and Australia.

13. New York City's Explorers Club houses mementos and artifacts from some of the most famous expeditions in history.

14. One object, Flag 161, has traveled to the summit of Mount Everest and bottom of the Marianas Trench.

15. Most people have never heard of Alexander von Humboldt. However, he has mountains in North America, South America, New Zealand, and Antarctica; species of penguin, squid, and skunk; several universities; and even a sea on the Moon named after him.

16. The years 1400 to 1700 were called "the golden age of exploration."

17. Golden-Age explorers came from England, France, Spain, Portugal, Holland, and Italy.

18. Many explorations were financed by kings and queens in order for them to claim new land.

19. Explorers are usually motivated by one or more of these five reasons.

20. The reasons are: claiming new land, discovering new trade routes, scientific discovery, finding treasure, and the challenge.

21. While exploring South Dakota in 1822, Hugh Glass was left for dead after being mauled by a grizzly bear. Glass set his broken leg then crawled 200 miles to the nearest settlement, living off berries and roots along the way.

22. Explorer David Douglas died during an exploration in Hawaii when he fell into an animal trap and was crushed by a bull that had fallen into the same trap.

23. Marco Polo traveled from Italy to Asia between 1271 and 1295, spending 17 of those years in China.

24. Polo wrote a bestselling book called *The Adventures of Marco Polo*.

25. Many people did not believe the stories in Polo's book and called it *Il Milione*, or *The Million Lies*.

26. On his deathbed, Polo said, "I have not told half of what I saw."

27. Juan Ponce de Leon explored the southern part of North America, searching for the mythical Fountain of Youth.

28. Thomas Jefferson asked Meriwether Lewis and William Clark to explore the vast lands the United States gained in the Louisiana Purchase.

29. Lewis and Clark and their Corps of Discovery traveled all the way from St. Louis to the Pacific Ocean and back between 1804 and 1806, covering more than 7,000 miles (11,265 km).

30. Only one man in the Corps of Discovery died during the journey; cause of death was a burst appendix.

Top 10 Famous Explorers

1. **Leif Erikson** (970–1020)—amazing Viking explorer

2. **Marco Polo** (1254–1324)—Italian who explored Central Asia and China

3. **Christopher Columbus** (1451–1506)—opened the New World to European civilization

4. **Bartolomeu Dias** (1451–1500)—the first European to sail around the southern tip of Africa

5. **Amerigo Vespucci** (1454–1512)—explored the New World and named North America, South America, and Venezuela

6. **Juan Ponce de Leon** (1474–1521)—led first European expedition to Florida

7. **Ferdinand Magellan** (1480–1521)—first explorer to circumnavigate the globe

8. **Hernando De Soto** (1497–1542)—believed to be the first European to cross the Mississippi River

9. **Sir Francis Drake** (1540–1596)—famous English captain who led the second circumnavigation of the globe

10. **Samuel de Champlain** (1574–1635)—founded New France and Quebec City

25 STRANGEST PLACES IN THE WORLD

1. **Lake Natron, Tanzania:** This lake contains a huge amount of sodium bicarbonate, turning any animals that die in the lake into weird statues.

2. **Dead Vlei, Namibia:** This dried-out oasis is filled with skeletal camel thorn trees, some scorched black from the sun.

3. **Eternal Flame Falls, New York, USA:** A natural gas vent behind a waterfall creates a flame burning underneath the falls.

4. **Silfra Rift, Iceland:** This underwater crack separates two continents and two tectonic plates.

5. **Caño Cristales, Colombia:** Plants in this river turn the water different colors. Also called the Rainbow River or the River of Five Colors.

6. **Sea of Stars, Maldives:** Bioluminescent sea plankton give the water an eerie glow at night.

7. Crooked Forest, Poland: A mysterious grove of crooked trees in an otherwise normal forest, the Crooked Forest is definitely a strange place.

8. Giant Crystal Cave, Mexico: This underground mine is filled with huge mineral pillars that have been growing for more than 500,000 years.

9. Vinicunca Rainbow Mountain, Peru: No one knows why these mountains are covered in lines of bright colors, but the result is very beautiful.

10. The Wave, Arizona, USA: This ancient rock formation is a beautiful and strange swirl of colors and lines.

11. Mount Kelimutu, Indonesia: A volcanic eruption created three lakes, and each one is a different color.

12. Al Naslaa Rock Formation, Saudi Arabia: These two huge rocks are separated by a perfectly straight, thin line, creating a very weird appearance.

13. Mendenhall Ice Caves, Alaska, USA: For some unknown reason, the ice crystals inside this cave are all different shades of blue.

14. Fingal's Cave, Scotland: Most caves are round, right? Not this cave, which is square and symmetrical.

15. Oneuli Beach, Hawaii, USA: This beach looks weird because it is covered with black sand as a result of volcanic eruptions.

16. The Doorway Railway, Vietnam: You must jump quickly out of the way to avoid the speeding trains that travel down this very narrow city street.

17. Mount Roraima, Venezuela: This flat-topped mountain is said to be one of the most mysterious places on Earth and is filled with unusual plants and animals.

18. Danakil Depression, Ethiopia: These pools aren't filled with water—they are filled with acid and surrounded by brittle crusts of salt and sulfur.

19. The Giant's Causeway, Ireland: An ancient volcanic eruption created dozens of huge pillars leading out into the sea.

20. Lencois Maranhenses National Park, Brazil: This area is filled with small pools of bright blue water surrounded by white sand dunes.

21. Red Beach, China: This beach turns bright red in the fall because of a plant that covers almost all of the beach.

22. Seven Giants, Russia: Somehow, frost and snow created seven tall, oddly shaped rock formations in the Ural Mountains.

23. Cat Island, Japan: Cat lovers should definitely visit this island, which is home to thousands of cats and only 100 humans.

24. Sailing Stones, California: What causes huge stones to slide across the desert on their own? No one is sure, which makes this area of Death Valley a very weird place.

25. Spotted Lake (Kliluk), Canada: The most mineralized place in the world, this lake is covered by 365 separate pools.

50 FACTS THAT ARE JUST PLAIN WEIRD

1. Lots of dead blackbirds fell from the sky on New Year's Eve 2011 in Arkansas.

2. In 2012, it happened again.

3. In 1942, a lake full of skeletons was found in India. Scientists think the bodies were people who died in a freak hailstorm more than 1,000 years ago.

4. There is a Museum of the Weird in Austin, Texas.

5. Its collection includes shrunken heads.

6. Astrologer John Hazelrigg predicted that the men elected US presidents in 1920, 1940, and 1960 would all die in office. He was right.

7. Spiders have clear blood.

8. Vampire flying frog tadpoles have fangs.

9. They use them to eat their mother's unfertilized eggs after the tadpoles hatch.

10. The Darvaza Gas Crater in Turkmenistan has been burning since 1971.

11. A coal seam fire underneath Centralia, Pennsylvania, has been burning since 1962.

12. Graves fell into the fire, and the whole town had to be evacuated.

13. Five residents refused to leave Centralia and still live there.

14. "Ring Around the Rosy" is a nursery rhyme that describes symptoms of the plague.

15. Foods can contain small amounts of rodent droppings and insect parts and still be sold in stores.

16. A moonbow is a rainbow that happens at night.

17. Moonbows usually happen around waterfalls or mist during full moons.

18. Gelatin is made from cow and horse hooves.

19. A man sculpted a statue of himself using his own teeth, hair, and nails.

20. The *Titanic* sank on its first voyage in April 1912. In 1898, a book was published that described the sinking of an ocean liner called the Titan on its first voyage in the month of April.

21. Charles Osborne had the hiccups for 68 years, a Guinness World Record.

22. Most homes in France have pink toilet paper.

23. Eight of the 10 largest statues in the world are of Buddha.

24. Tigers have striped skin, not just striped fur.

25. Each tiger's stripe pattern is unique.

26. Bananas are the most popular item sold in Walmart.

27. Dogs are banned in Antarctica so they don't spread diseases to seals.

28. Hart Island is the final burial place to over 1 million of New York City's unclaimed bodies.

29. It is thought to be the largest government-sponsored mass grave on Earth.

30. February used to be the last month of the year, which is why it has the shortest number of days.

31. Dead people can get goosebumps.

32. Shoe shops used x-ray machines to measure shoe sizes in the 1940s before the risks of x-rays were fully understood.

33. Squirrels are behind most power outages in the United States.

34. The monarch owns all the swans in England.

35. Every July, the swans on the River Thames are counted in a practice called "swan upping."

36. Long ago, spider webs were used as bandages.

37. They really worked!

38. In 2006, someone tried to sell New Zealand on eBay.

39. A woman who lost her wedding ring in 1995 found it in 2012 in a carrot in her garden.

40. The electric chair was invented by a dentist as a painless way to execute criminals.

41. The inventor of the Pringles can asked to be buried in one.

42. When he died, his children bought a can of Pringles at a drug store to fulfill his wishes.

43. Most people in Iceland believe in fairies.

44. The world's quietest place is a soundproof chamber in Minnesota.

45. People can't stand to be in the chamber for more than 45 minutes.

46. People with omphalophobia are afraid of belly buttons.

47. Scotland's national animal is a unicorn.

48. A glass ball can bounce higher than a rubber ball.

49. France executed the last person by guillotine in 1977.

50. It's impossible to hum while holding your nose.

YOU NOW KNOW 5,001 NEW FACTS.

index